ZIONISM AND THE BLACK CHURCH

Why Standing with Israel Will Be a Defining Issue for Christians of Color in the 21st Century

By
Dumisani Washington

UMNDENI
PRESS

Umndeni Press 2021

Published by
Umndeni Press
Charlotte, North Carolina
© 2021 by Dumisani Washington. All rights reserved.

Originally published by Institute for Black Solidarity with Israel (IBSI), 2014

ISBN (978-0-578-24569-0)

To the remnant

ACKNOWLEDGMENTS

I wish to thank my wife of 32 years, mother of our six children, for her unwavering support since we were teenagers. I also wish to thank the Congregation of Zion in Stockton, California. Finally, special thanks to Melva L. Henderson, Wendy Cruz, Leah Washington, Gerri Pinkston, and Yasha Washington for your tireless help in making this second edition a reality.

INTRODUCTION

There is one universal Church. The Body of Christ is not Black or White. It is one Body. This book is not an effort to further divide Christians by race or ethnicity. The term *Black Church* in the title does not refer exclusively to a specific group of Christians, be they Baptist, Church of God in Christ, African Methodist Episcopal (AME), Hebrew Roots, Messianic any other denomination. From the birth of the Church at Pentecost in First Century Jerusalem, there have been multiethnic congregations. *Black Church* symbolizes Black Christians or other Christians of color, whatever their theological leaning may be. Also, Christian Zionism is a discussion that is paramount for all Christians regardless of ethnicity and for our Jewish brothers and sisters who may want to know more.

Zionism and the Black Church attempts to speak to the cause of Israel and the Jewish people to a community purposefully targeted with an anti-Zionist message. Once the lowest caste of any people in the Western world, chattel slavery, Black Americans generally have a sought-after perspective on issues of humanity. This is especially true of the Black Church. The Black, legendary struggle for justice has historically given the Black Church an air of validity and authority. Though a smaller portion of the U.S. population, Black people have influenced everything from music and art to theology, politics, education, and, of course, civil rights.

I started the Institute for Black Solidarity with Israel (IBSI) in July 2013, responding to what I can only explain as a divine call. In September 2014, I became the Diversity Outreach Coordinator for the now nearly ten million member Christians United for Israel (CUFI). My son, Joshua, currently serves as IBSI's Director. By profession, I am a musician, a piano performance graduate of the San Francisco Conservatory of Music. I am a pastor, a husband of 32 years, and a father of six extraordinary children, just like their mother. I am also a Christian Zionist, meaning I believe the Jews are God's chosen people, and the land of Israel belongs to them. But, Israel's right to live in peace goes well-beyond scriptural interpretation. When I advocate for the Jewish State outside of religious circles, I rarely quote the Bible. However, this book is a combination of history, politics, and preaching. There will be scriptures quoted in both English and Hebrew.

I was born Dennis Ray Washington on February 17, 1967, in Little Rock, Arkansas, the segregated South. I am the youngest of seven children. We moved to California when I was about one, so I have no early memories of Arkansas. I legally changed my first name to Dumisani in the early 1990s to embrace my African heritage. Dumisani means *praise* from the Zulu phrase *dumisani u Yehovah* (praise the Lord). My dear friend and *sister* Nomathemba Sithole, a South African national of the Zulu tribe, helped me choose my new name. Nomathemba is affectionately known to our family as *Malume* - Aunty.

My parents, David and Lillian Washington, were both from the Little Rock area born in the early 1940s and were part of a vibrant Black community. My mother was a seamstress from a young age. My father's father was a sharecropper, so my father grew up on a large farm complete with cows, chickens, pigs, horses, cats, and dogs. They grew all sorts of crops, including cotton. My father did not graduate from high school in large part because he had to run the entire farm by himself when both his brother and father fell ill.

My mother often spoke about Little Rock and the life of the community she loved. We were active members of King Solomon Baptist Church, where Reverend Thomas was the pastor. As my mother told me, I loved music so much as a baby that I would rock and sway as the choir sang. Unfortunately for Reverend Thomas, I was not fond of preaching. I would cry at the top of my lungs whenever he took the podium. My mother had to take me out of the sanctuary virtually every week after the music ended. Perhaps I just wanted the music to continue. Either way, Mama said I gave our pastor a complex. She was not joking.

INTRODUCTION

My father was a gifted singer, a leader of the men's chorus, and served on the deacon board. My mother was a deaconess and worked with the youth ministry, among many other things. She graduated from the only high school for Black children in Arkansas, Scipio Africanus Jones High School in Little Rock. S. A. Jones High School was the pride of Arkansas. Like many Black schools during segregation, there was a deep sense of connectedness among the teachers, administrators, and students. Throughout the history of Black people in America, education was the primary means of freedom and upward mobility. Black students from S. A. Jones graduated and went on to become doctors, lawyers, politicians, athletes, clergy . . . anything they aspired to be. My uncle, Dr. Levi Adams class of '51, had a long and illustrious career with the medical school administration at Brown University in Rhode Island. There is an award at Brown that bears my uncle's name.[1] [2]

Though I never directly experienced it, hearing my parents describe life in North Little Rock gave me a great sense of pride as well. I learned of the *Little Rock Nine*[3] from my parents, who knew the families involved. I learned of the internal debate over integration. Many Black people knew that it would mean the end of their beloved S. A. Jones and other Black institutions in Little Rock. S. A. Jones closed in 1970 because of integration. The teachers and administrators were released and not allowed to work in the now "integrated" schools. For this reason and many others, my mother explained to me at a very young age; she was vehemently against forced integration.

My parents did not teach us hatred and contempt for White people. They taught us what racism was so that we would be prepared to face it. They taught us not to ascribe virtue or wickedness to someone simply based on their ethnicity. One's character was who one was, not one's race. They also taught us to speak our minds and not be afraid of anyone's disapproval, a lesson they demonstrated as much

---

[1] The Levi C. Adams Citation honors a senior undergraduate for distinction in service in a religious organization, project or initiative at Brown University. The honor was inaugurated in 2001, 7 years following Adams' retirement.

[2] See also the Levi C. Adams Medical Scholarship introduced in 2018, which offers financial support to African American physicians working to earn M.D.s at Brown's Warren Alpert Medical School.

[3] Group of nine African Americans who enrolled at and participated in the desegregation of Central High School in Little Rock, Arkansas in 1957. See "Little Rock Nine," by Encyclopedia of Arkansas (2010) for more information.

as they articulated. It was always in their blood. One of the most vivid stories my father told me was when he was about ten years old. The White landowner had come to the farm to check on my grandfather's work. As my father and grandfather were busy in the field, the landowner pulled up in his pickup truck and began berating my grandfather. My grandfather stood silently, avoiding eye contact as the man disrespected him in front of his young son. After a few moments, my father had all he could take. He abruptly climbed up the driver's side door of the pickup, got directly in the White man's face, and said, "Hey, mister! I don't like the way you talkin' to my daddy!" At ten years old, my father did not fully understand that what he had just done could have gotten both he and his father killed. My grandfather gently removed my father from the man's truck, saying, "Junior, get down."

No more than ten at the time, I asked, "What did the man do, Daddy?"

"Nothing," my father replied. "He was stunned. He just looked at my father, then looked at me, then looked back at my father, and drove away."

I read the Bible as a child and was intrigued by all things Israelite. Though I loved reading the gospels and "walking with Jesus" through the scriptures, I was even more drawn to the Old Testament. I knew the stories of David and Goliath, the Patriarchs, and the Exodus by heart. As a young adult, I wanted to learn more about the Hebrew roots of my faith and met Jewish musicians who introduced me to the feasts (Passover, Tabernacles, etc.). They shared songs and prayers in Hebrew that began to transform my worship and my songwriting. Around the mid-1990s, I began researching the Israelite Diaspora, as I was captivated by news of Beta Israel, the Jews of Ethiopia. I began to follow current events regarding Israel and Africa and learned about the absorption process of the Ethiopian Jews. All of these seemingly disparate strands of my life would become woven together years later.

My good friend Victor Styrsky was the Eastern Region Coordinator for Christians United for Israel (CUFI). Like me, Victor is a musician and leads a band called Wild Branches. Based on Romans 11 (wild branches grafted into Israel), Wild Branches sings a unique style of the *Songs of Zion* and the Jewish people. They provided music for CUFI's Night to Honor Israel and Victor invited me to play the keyboard. At the CUFI events, I began learning more

INTRODUCTION

about modern-day Israel, the people, the culture, its global charitable work, its breakthroughs in innovation and technology, and Israel's defense and military concerns. I also began to learn of the Palestinian refugee crisis and the nature of the Arab-Israeli conflict.

Black American history was something I first learned in my home as a child at the dining room table, in my mother's sewing room, and kitchen. As a young adult, I learned of the Black African fight against apartheid from Malume (Nomathemba), who lived it. Knowing the atrocities of apartheid, laid bear the false claims of Israeli apartheid. When I understood how the historic Black struggle for justice was used by Israel's enemies to demonize her, I was personally offended. I discovered Black Americans in the 1970s who were also offended at the falsehood that *Zionism is Racism* and voiced their loud and eloquent opposition. Knowing this gave me great comfort.

The first time I spoke publicly on the subject of Israel was at a Sacramento City Council meeting in 2012. The leaders were considering a measure to become a sister city with Ashkelon, Israel, and there was an open hearing. In a packed room divided along ideological lines, I experienced my first virulently hostile, anti-Israel crowd. I heard the false accusations of Israeli apartheid, Jim Crow racism and segregation, the genocide of the Arab Palestinians—the attacks were relentless and baseless. When it was my turn to take the podium, I refuted the claims of Israel's racism and discrimination. I explained that while no nation is perfect, Israel was nothing like what my parents experienced in Little Rock, or Malume experienced in Durban. Israel is a free, pluralistic society forced to defend herself against an untold number of enemies bent on her annihilation. Comparing the Jewish State to what my family endured was beyond egregious, and I let everyone in the chamber know I was there to defend my legacy. I quickly learned that people who opposed Israel did not respond well to Black people defending Israel. It was interesting hearing the racist comments directed at me by people who were there to "combat" racism. The combination of shamelessly abusing my people's heritage *and* lying about Israel, Africa's most significant regional partner, lit a fire in me that has not dimmed.

In the many Israel events where I've spoken since 2012, I've heard even more outlandish terms like a *sort of apartheid* and a *type of Jim Crow*, even a *symbolic genocide*. There is no *sort of* apartheid. There is no *type of* Jim Crow. And genocide

vi

is *real* killing, not *symbolic*. I also quickly learned that when it came to slandering the Jewish State, no people's history or legacy was off-limits. Anyone's story, no matter how sacred or painful, would be exploited to attack the Jews and their homeland. Today, there is virtually no topic concerning Israel, which will not be controversial. There is just too much disinformation and anti-Israel propaganda to even expect anything less.

Unbeknownst to me at the time, my advocacy for the State of Israel had officially begun. After my first trip to Israel during Hanukkah of 2012, I returned and started the Institute for Black Solidarity with Israel (IBSI). During my first speaking tour in which I met diverse anti-Zionists, I would often reflect on the words of my friend, Yaffa Tegegne. Yaffa is an Ethiopian Jew and daughter of the late Baruch Tegegne, a pioneer in the movement that saw the Jews of Ethiopia finally return to Israel. As a Black Jew and vocal Zionist during her college years in Canada, Yaffa's antagonists did not understand her.

> I studied politics at Concordia University ... probably one of the biggest Arab student populations in North America. In 2002-2003 [Israeli Prime Minister] Netanyahu was supposed to come and there was a riot, and we had a huge solidarity for Palestinian rights movement, and there were terrible incidents. I used to literally argue on campus all the time, and I think I was the only Ethiopian Jew and the only Ethiopian they had ever met, and it was very difficult for them. They didn't know how to deal with it, because it went fundamentally against their entire notion. Like, "here's a contemporary story of why we still need Israel. It's not just the Holocaust. This [Jewish persecution] has been continuously happening in recent times." So they would have a really hard time dealing with me because I didn't fit the mold of what their argument was.[4]

My experience in Sacramento that night was similar to what Yaffa described. For many anti-Zionists, a Black person standing with Israel is offensive. They are unaware of or don't care about the long tradition of Black-Jewish cooperation in this nation. As it has not been as visible over the past fifty years, I could not say I blamed them. During the void of Black vocal support for Israel and the Jewish people, many falsehoods and deceptions have been put in place. It has become quite common to meet Black people, especially on college campuses, who have a

---

[4] Y. Tegegne during an interview with Institute for Black Solidarity with Israel (IBSI) (2013).

INTRODUCTION

negative view of Israel, if not Jews in general. As Jamie Kirchick noted in his 2018 Commentary article *The Rise of Black Anti-Semitism*:

> Attitudinal surveys conducted by the ADL [Anti-Defamation League] consistently show that African Americans harbor "anti-Semitic proclivities" at a rate significantly higher than the general population (23 percent and 14 percent respectively in 2016).[5]

Much of this is the effect of the anti-Israel miseducation directed towards the Black community. In 1992, that same ADL survey found antisemitism in the Black community as high as 37%.[6]

In the 1960s, Dr. King completely understood the factors that were adversely affecting the Black-Jewish relationship and the antisemitic feeling fomenting in some circles. He offered a partial explanation in *Where Do We Go From Here: Chaos or Community*.

> Negroes nurture a persistent myth that the Jews of America attained social mobility and status solely because they had money. It is unwise to ignore the error for many reasons. In a negative sense it encourages anti-Semitism and overestimates money as a value. In a positive sense the full truth reveals a useful lesson. Jews progressed because they possessed a tradition of education combined with social and political action.[7]

Some of Dr. King's most impassioned pleas for Black-Jewish continued cooperation came towards the end of his life. This was also when Israel's enemies were attempting to drive a wedge between Blacks and Jews, between Israel and the African nations.

Mark Twain once said, "history doesn't repeat itself, but it does rhyme." I believe we live in a time similar to the transitional period of the late 60s and 70s. Christians are called to stand with and be a blessing to Israel and the Jewish

---

[5] From "The Rise of Black Anti-Semitism," by J. Kirchick, 2018, *Commentary Magazine*.

[6] From "Black-Jewish relations: ADL survey finds anti-Semitism high in black community," by Jewish Virtual Library, 1998, *Jewish Virtual Library*.

[7] From "Where Are We Going?" by M. L. King, Jr., 2010, *Where Do We Go From Here: Chaos or Community?*, p. 163. Copyright 1968 by Martin Luther King, Jr. Copyright.

viii

people. Black Americans have a long history of shared struggle with the Jewish people. What's more, the issue of Black civil rights took center stage once again with the 2020 police killings of George Floyd, Breonna Taylor, Ahmad Arbery, and others. Israel's enemies are using those tragedies and other challenges within the Black community to manipulate people into blaming and hating Israel and the Jews. The exploitation is worse now than it was since its beginning in the 1960s. Black Christians will be pivotal in this renewed fight for the direction of our community, the Church in general, and our country.

I am humbled to do the work of strengthening the Black-Jewish, Africa-Israel alliance. Not only that, I am extremely optimistic about the future. As Dr. King said, "We've got some difficult days ahead,"[8] but we will reach the Promised Land. Church, we will see God move on behalf of those who stand with His *firstborn*—the Jewish people.

I pray that the reader of this book will receive the true message of Zionism and solidarity with Israel. I also pray that fellow pastors and ministry leaders will exhort their people to walk in the blessing and not the curse.

> Genesis 12.3
> *And I will bless those who bless you, and the one who curses you I will curse, and all the families of the earth shall be blessed in you.*
>
> ג וַאֲבָרֲכָה מְבָרְכֶיךָ וּמְקַלֶּלְךָ אָאֹר וְנִבְרְכוּ בְךָ כֹּל מִשְׁפְּחֹת הָאֲדָמָה׃
> (The Complete Jewish Bible with Rashi Commentary, Genesis 12.3)

---

[8] See "I've been to the mountaintop," by M. L. King, 1968.

TABLE OF CONTENTS

CHAPTER 1
THE AFRICAN BIBLICAL TIE TO ISRAEL   1

CHAPTER 2
THE JEWISH DIASPORA AND
PROPHETIC RETURN TO ISRAEL   25

CHAPTER 3
ZIONISM AND THE HISTORIC
BLACK STRUGGLE FOR FREEDOM   50

CHAPTER 4
THE PRO-ISRAEL LEGACY OF THE
REVEREND DR. MARTIN LUTHER KING, JR.   77

CHAPTER 5
ANTI-ZIONISM: HATRED FOR ISRAEL   103

CHAPTER 6
WHAT WE MUST DO NOW   163

BIBLIOGRAPHY   184

CHAPTER 1
THE AFRICAN BIBLICAL TIE TO ISRAEL

Exodus 2.5-6

5 *Pharaoh's daughter went down to bathe, to the Nile, and her maidens were walking along the Nile, and she saw the basket in the midst of the marsh, and she sent her maidservant, and she took it.*

6 *She opened [it], and she saw him the child, and behold, he was a weeping lad, and she had compassion on him, and she said, "This is [one] of the children of the Hebrews."*

ה וַתֵּרֶד בַּת־פַּרְעֹה לִרְחֹץ עַל־הַיְאֹר וְנַעֲרֹתֶיהָ הֹלְכֹת עַל־יַד הַיְאֹר וַתֵּרֶא אֶת־הַתֵּבָה בְּתוֹךְ הַסּוּף וַתִּשְׁלַח אֶת־אֲמָתָהּ וַתִּקָּחֶהָ:
ו וַתִּפְתַּח וַתִּרְאֵהוּ אֶת־הַיֶּלֶד וְהִנֵּה־נַעַר בֹּכֶה וַתַּחְמֹל עָלָיו וַתֹּאמֶר מִיַּלְדֵי הָעִבְרִים זֶה:

(The Complete Jewish Bible with Rashi Commentary, Exodus 2.5-6)

Genesis chapter 10 is known as the *Table of Nations*, where the Bible tells us how the three sons of Noah repopulated the earth after the Flood. Few passages of scripture are more controversial than Genesis 10 as it has caused endless debates regarding ethnicity and race. However, to understand the African connection to Israel, we must start at the beginning. This is not an attempt to solve any deep anthropological mysteries, but rather point to the line connecting Israel and the continent of Africa, to clarify words as well as their meaning.

We begin with the word *Africa*, which has no biblical origin but today is used to denote an immense land and category of people. The origin of the name Africa has been in dispute for centuries. In the article, *Idea of Africa - Origins of the Name Africa*, the Science Encyclopedia states:

> At least seven origins have been suggested: (1) it is a Roman name for what the Greeks called "Libya," itself perhaps a Latinization of the name of the Berber tribe Aourigha (perhaps pronounced "Afarika"); (2) it is derived from two Phoenician terms either referring to corn or fruit (pharika), meaning land of corn or fruit; (3) it comes from a Phoenician root faraqa, meaning separation or diaspora; a similar root is apparently found in some African languages such as Bambara; (4) it is drawn from the Latin adjective aprica (sunny) or the Greek aprike (free from cold); (5) it might even stem from Sanskrit and Hindi in which the root Apara or Africa denotes that which, in geographical terms, comes "after"—to the west—in which case Africa is the western continent; (6) it is the name of a Yemenite chief named Africus who invaded North Africa in the second millennium B.C.E. and founded a town called Afrikyah; or (7) it springs from "Afer" who was a grandson of Abraham and a companion of Hercules (Ki-Zerbo; Spivak).[1]

In the Bible, the African nations of Egypt and Ethiopia (Cush) were sometimes referred to as dual kingdoms and were also called the *Land of Ham*.

> Psalm 68.31 (verse 32 in Jewish *Tanakh* or Christian Old Testament)
> *Gifts will be brought from Egypt; Cush will cause his hands to run to God.*
>
> לב יֶאֱתָיוּ חַשְׁמַנִּים מִנִּי מִצְרָיִם כּוּשׁ תָּרִיץ יָדָיו לֵאלֹהִים:
> (The Complete Jewish Bible with Rashi Commentary, Psalm 68.31)

Psalm 105.23
Israel came to Egypt, and Jacob sojourned in the land of Ham.

כג וַיָּבֹא יִשְׂרָאֵל מִצְרָיִם וְיַעֲקֹב גָּר בְּאֶרֶץ־חָם:
(The Complete Jewish Bible with Rashi Commentary, Psalm 105.23)

---

[1] From "Origins of the name Africa," by Science Encyclopedia, n.d., in Idea of Africa.

Isaiah 20.5
And they shall be broken and ashamed because of Cush, their expectation, and because of Egypt, their boasting.

ה וְחַתּוּ וָבֹשׁוּ מִכּוּשׁ מַבָּטָם וּמִן־מִצְרַיִם תִּפְאַרְתָּם:
(The Complete Jewish Bible with Rashi Commentary, Isaiah 20.5)

As is the case with language, the word Africa morphed and was eventually used to refer to the entire continent. The Bible names lands after their human progenitors. What is known today as Africa and parts of the Middle East were originally territories named after Noah's grandsons, the sons of Ham.

Genesis 10.1
And these are the generations of the sons of Noah: Shem, Ham, and Japheth, and sons were born to them after the Flood.

א וְאֵלֶּה תּוֹלְדֹת בְּנֵי־נֹחַ שֵׁם חָם וָיָפֶת וַיִּוָּלְדוּ לָהֶם בָּנִים אַחַר הַמַּבּוּל:
(The Complete Jewish Bible with Rashi Commentary, Genesis 10.1)

We learn that Japheth, the youngest of Noah's three sons, is the father of those who settled on the coastal lands of the Mediterranean spreading north into Europe and parts of Asia. We also learn that Shem, from whom we get the term Shemite or Semite, is the father of many tribes in the Afro-Asiatic region, including Eber, from whom we get the word *Ivrit* or Hebrew.

Genesis 10.22
The sons of Shem were Elam and Asshur and Arpachshad and Lud and Aram.

כב בְּנֵי שֵׁם עֵילָם וְאַשּׁוּר וְאַרְפַּכְשַׁד וְלוּד וַאֲרָם:
(The Complete Jewish Bible with Rashi Commentary, Genesis 10.22)

Genesis 10.24
And Arpachshad begot Shelah, and Shelah begot Eber.

כד וְאַרְפַּכְשַׁד יָלַד אֶת־שָׁלַח וְשֶׁלַח יָלַד אֶת־עֵבֶר:
(The Complete Jewish Bible with Rashi Commentary, Genesis 10.24)

In Genesis 11.10–26, we learn that six generations separate Eber from Abram, whose name God changed to Abraham, the chief patriarch of the children of Israel. The line of succession from Abraham to Israel is as follows: Abraham and his wife Sarah had a son named Isaac. Isaac and his wife Rebekah had a son named Jacob. God changed Jacob's name to Israel (Genesis 32). Jacob fathered twelve sons with his two wives, Leah and Rachel, and their maidservants. Those sons became the heads of the twelve tribes of the Israelite nation. The Israelites have many titles including, *children of Israel, children of Jacob, children of Abraham, Jewish people,* and *Jews,* from the word Judah. The term Israeli is a general word used for a citizen of the modern Jewish State, whether they are ethnically Jewish or not.

Though Abraham established no organized religion, Abraham is known as the father of the world's three largest and most influential religious faiths: Judaism, Christianity, and Islam.

> Genesis 10.6
> *And the sons of Ham were Cush and Mizraim and Put and Canaan.*
>
> ו וּבְנֵי חָם כּוּשׁ וּמִצְרַיִם וּפוּט וּכְנָעַן:
> (The Complete Jewish Bible with Rashi Commentary, Genesis 10.6)

It is interesting to note that, of Noah's three sons, it is only Ham that receives the group designation *Land of Ham* in the Bible. There does not seem to be a similar title, *Land of Shem* or *Land of Japeth*. According to scripture, the descendants of all three sons populated the entire earth, and as such, covered vast regions of the globe. Yet, Land of Ham seems to have a dual meaning of both land (Egypt, Ethiopia) and people (referred to as *Africans* today).

As Genesis chapter 10 unfolds, we learn that the descendants of each of the four sons of Ham settle the regions of Ethiopia (Cush or Kush), Egypt (Mizraim), Libya (Put or Phut), and Canaan. The descendants of these four sons of Ham inhabited virtually all of the continent we call Africa and portions of present-day Saudi Arabia. So the biblical land of Ham can, in one sense, refer to Africa and parts of Southwest Asia (Middle East). However, based on Western teaching,

Noah's descendants (Table of Nations)

NOAH

Japheth
Gomer, Magog, Madai, Javan, Tubal, Meshech, Tiras

Sons of Gomer
Ashkenaz, Riphath, Togarmah

Sons of Javan
Elishah, Tarshish, Kittim, Dodanim

biblestudy.org

Shem
Elam, Asshur, Arphaxad, Lud, Aram

Son of Arphaxad
Salah

Son of Salah
Eber

Sons of Eber
Peleg, Joktan

Sons of Joktan
Almodad, Sheleph, Hazarmaveth, Jerah, Hadoram, Uzal, Diklah, Obal, Abimael, Sheba, Ophir, Havilah, Jobab

Sons of Aram
Uz, Hul, Gether, Mash

Ham
Cush, Mizraim, Phut, Canaan

Sons of Cush
Seba, Havilah, Sabtah, Raamah, Sabtecha, Nimrod

Sons of Raamah
Sheba, Dedan

Sons of Mizraim
Ludim, Anamim, Lehabim, Naphtuhim, Pathrusim, Casluhim, Caphtorim

Sons of Canaan
Sidon, Heth, Jebusite, Amorite, Girgashite, Hivite, Arkite, Sinite, Arvadite, Zemarite, Hamathite

---

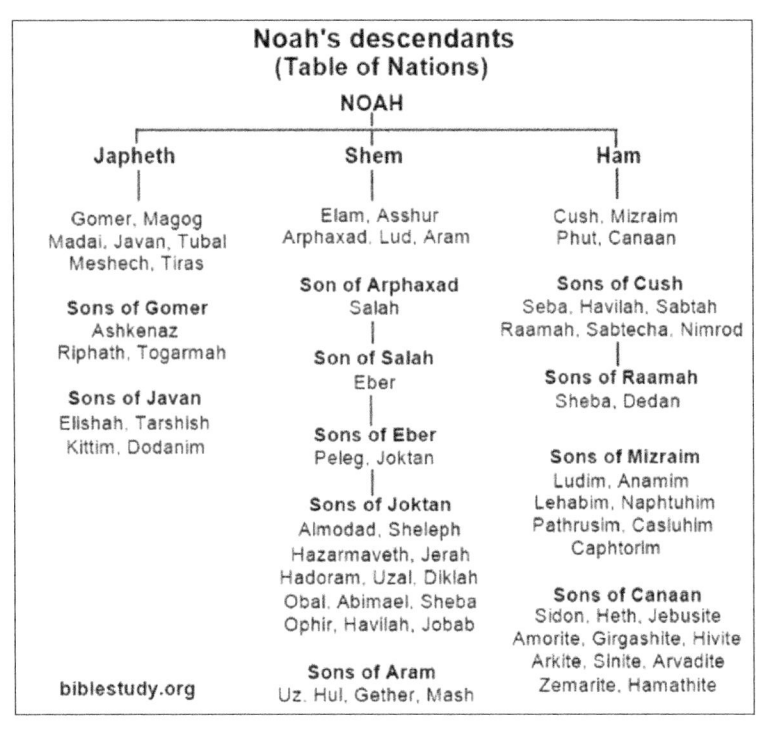

both biblical and secular, Hamite is generally used to describe sub-Saharan Africans. While referring to sub-Saharan Africans as Hamites is not entirely inaccurate, it is somewhat misleading for three fundamental reasons:

1. Ham had four sons representing four distinct branches of the Hamitic tree stretching throughout Africa (including east, west, and north) and the Middle East.
2. Throughout biblical history, Hamites and Semites intermingled. For example, Ishmael is the son of Abram—a Semite, and Hagar—a Hamite (Egyptian).
3. The misapplication or manipulation of race/ethnicity, or modern notions of race and anti-Black bias read into the scriptures.

It is difficult to overstate the issue of race/color in American or Western society. If the reader of this book is not from the United States or is unaware of our history with Black versus White relationships, they may not fully appreciate the complexity of this topic. In 1883, Frederick Douglass, a former slave and abolitionist described the "color line," a term used to reference racial segregation in the United States after the abolition of slavery. The color line still haunts us in various forms today as racial strife persists, especially when used by those in power to divide. To remain focused and on topic, we will concern ourselves with race and the Church. To that end, we must address the centuries-old false teaching of the *Curse of Ham*. It is arguably the faux proof text of biblically-based racism and the biblical justification for hatred and discrimination against black Africans.

THE CURSE OF HAM

In Genesis chapter nine, the Bible tells of Noah becoming drunk, and his son, Ham, saw his father naked in his tent and left without covering his body. Noah's other sons, Shem and Japheth, entered their father's tent, walking backward so as not to see his nakedness, and covered him. After he awoke, Noah uttered these words:

> Genesis 9.25–26
> *26 ". . . Cursed be Canaan; he shall be a slave among slaves to his brethren." 25 And he said, "Blessed be the Lord, the God of Shem, and may Canaan be a slave to them.*
>
> כה וַיֹּאמֶר אָרוּר כְּנָעַן עֶבֶד עֲבָדִים יִהְיֶה לְאֶחָיו:
> כו וַיֹּאמֶר בָּרוּךְ יְהֹוָה אֱלֹהֵי שֵׁם וִיהִי כְנַעַן עֶבֶד לָמוֹ:
> (The Complete Jewish Bible with Rashi Commentary, Genesis 9.25-26)

As previously mentioned, this story is often referred to as the Curse of Ham. For generations, this text was used to justify, even celebrate the enslavement and subjugation of African people. The curse was defined as *black skin* and was a sign of perpetual servitude. Of the many things incorrect about this teaching, two are most glaring:

1. Nowhere in Genesis nine is hue or skin color mentioned.
2. Ham was not cursed. His son, Canaan, was.

> Most people believe Ham was cursed and, therefore, so were all black people of African/Hamitic descent. However, careful study of the Scriptures reveals that the curse was placed upon Canaan (Gen 9.25),

a son of Ham. However, Ham's other sons, Mizraim, Phut, and Cush . . . were not cursed. This particular curse justified Abraham's inheritance of the land of Canaan as his blessing because Shem and his descendants (Gen 9.26) received the blessing of his father Noah due to his strong desire to be in his father's image and his love for God.[2]

In his book Africa and the Bible, Edwin M. Yamauchi also affirms that Ham was not cursed and dispels that somehow Hamitic blackness is undesirable.

Rabbinic literature in general, following the Bible, holds that Canaan, not Ham, is cursed. According to [Ephraim] Isaac [a scholar from Ethiopia], for the Rabbi's, "Canaan's dark complexion, which was not unlike that of the Israelites, was said to be ugly; Cush's blackness, on the other hand, which was deep and distinguished, had no such stigma attached to it." This was the view also of the main medieval commentators, such as Rashi (d. 1105), Abraham Ibn Ezra (d. 1167), Rambam (d. 1274), and Sforno (d. 1550).[3]

Why did God punish Ham's son for his father's offense? That is a mystery we will not attempt to unravel in this book. Our goal is simply to set the record straight. God never cursed Ham or the African people. He showed neither disdain for people of dark skin nor preference for people with light skin. As the scriptures teach, "God is not a respecter of persons." Further, the physical sign of God's curse on Canaan was not black skin. We do not know exactly what hue Canaan was before or after the curse, and the Bible does not mention a visible sign, unlike the mark God put on Cain after he killed his brother, Abel (Gen 4.15).

Again, the term Hamite generically referring to Africans is not wholly accurate because Ham had four sons. Here the purveyors of racist biblical teaching are hard-pressed to explain how Ham was indeed cursed with black skin but was also the father of the Egyptians (Mizraim), whom they often claim were White, not Black. In his foreword to Diop's *Civilization or Barbarism: An Authentic*

---

[2] From "The Curse of Canaan", 1993, *The Original African Heritage Study Bible: James Version*, (p. 15). In C. H. Felder & J. W. Peebles. Copyright 1993 by The James C. Winston Publishing Company.

[3] From "The Curse of Ham," by E. M. Yamauchi, 2004, *Africa and the Bible*, p. 25. Copyright 2004 by Edwin M. Yamauchi.

Anthropology, Dr. John Henrik Clarke addresses the Western race-bias that has obscured the identity of the children of Mizraim.

> If Egypt is a dilemma in Western historiography, it is a created dilemma. The Western historians, in most cases, have rested the foundation of what is called "Western Civilization" on the false assumption, or claim, that the Egyptians were white people. To do this they had to ignore great masterpieces of Egyptian history written by other white historians who did not support this point of view, such as Gerald Massey's great classic, *Ancient Egypt, The Light of the World* (1907), and his subsequent works, *The Book of the Beginnings and The Natural Genesis*. Other neglected works by white writers are *Politics, Intercourse, and Trade of the Carthaginians and Ethiopians* by A. H. L. Heeren (1833) and *The Ruins of Empires* by Count C. F. Volney (1787).[4]

The people of Canaan and Phut are also from the line of Ham. Dark or light, all of the tribes would be considered *people of color* today, all originating from Africa and the Middle East.

Hamites, or the sons of Ham, have come to mean African, but the term is rarely used to describe the people of ancient Libya, Canaan, or Egypt. Today, the entire area of North Africa (Libya, Egypt, Morocco, Tunisia, and Algeria) is Arabic. Though these nations are a part of the African continent, they were conquered and resettled after the death of the Arab Islamic prophet, Muhammad.

> When Muhammad, the Prophet of Islam, died in 632 the new religion had already gathered a number of impressive victories on the battlefield. The armies of Islam quickly and easily conquered the Arabian peninsula before moving on to take the homelands of their various neighbours. Marching out of Arabia in 639 they entered non-Arab Egypt; 43 years later they reached the shores of the Atlantic; and in 711 they invaded Spain. In just 70 years they had subdued the whole of North Africa, instituting a new order. This conquest, from the Nile to the Atlantic,

---

[4] From "Foreword" by C. A. Diop, 1991, *Civilization or Barbarism: An Authentic Anthropology*. p. xix. Copyright 1991 by Lawrence Hill Books.

was more complete than anything achieved by previous invaders and the changes it wrought proved permanent.[5]

Generally, the Arab people who now inhabit North Africa do not consider themselves *African* in the genealogical sense. In biblical times, Arabs were located in the region of present-day Saudi Arabia. Again, this area in antiquity was part of the Cushite/Ethiopian territory—*the horn of Africa*.

Third, the children of Ham and Shem, like all tribes, experienced some intermingling. Within the narrative of the Israelite people (descendants of Shem), we often read of Hamites being included, further complicating who indeed is a biological son or daughter of Abraham.

Though it is speculated that Moses ultimately had two wives, at least one was a Cushite (Ethiopian).

> Numbers 12.1
> *Miriam and Aaron spoke against Moses regarding the Cushite woman he had married, for he had married a Cushite woman.*

א וַתְּדַבֵּר מִרְיָם וְאַהֲרֹן בְּמֹשֶׁה עַל־אֹדוֹת הָאִשָּׁה הַכֻּשִׁית אֲשֶׁר לָקָח כִּי־אִשָּׁה כֻשִׁית לָקָח:

(The Complete Jewish Bible with Rashi Commentary, Numbers 12.1)

Rahab, the Canaanite of Jericho from the line of Ham, married an Israelite man, and became part of the genealogical line of King David, the Messianic line of Jesus.

> Joshua 6.25
> *But Rahab the harlot, and her father's household, and all that she had, Joshua saved alive; and she dwelt in the midst of Israel to this day; because she hid the messengers, whom Joshua sent to spy out Jericho.*

כה וְאֶת־רָחָב הַזּוֹנָה וְאֶת־בֵּית אָבִיהָ וְאֶת־כָּל־אֲשֶׁר־לָהּ הֶחֱיָה יְהוֹשֻׁעַ וַתֵּשֶׁב

---

[5] From "Arab Invasions: The First Islamic Empire," by E. Gearon, 2011, *History Today*, 61(6).

THE AFRICAN BIBLICAL TIE TO ISRAEL

בְּקֶרֶב יִשְׂרָאֵל עַד הַיּוֹם הַזֶּה כִּי הֶחְבִּיאָה אֶת־הַמַּלְאָכִים אֲשֶׁר־שָׁלַח יְהוֹשֻׁעַ לְרַגֵּל אֶת־יְרִיחוֹ:

(The Complete Jewish Bible with Rashi Commentary, Joshua 6.25)

Matthew 1.1–6a
1 The book of the genealogy of Jesus Christ, the son of David, the son of Abraham. 2 Abraham was the father of Isaac, and Isaac the father of Jacob, and Jacob the father of Judah and his brothers, 3 and Judah the father of Perez and Zerah by Tamar, and Perez the father of Hezron, and Hezron the father of Ram 4 and Ram the father of Amminadab, and Amminadab the father of Nahshon, and Nahshon the father of Salmon, 5 and Salmon the father of Boaz by Rahab, and Boaz the father of Obed by Ruth, and Obed the father of Jesse, 6 and Jesse the father of David the king.
(English Standard Version, Matthew 1.1-6a)

Both Hamites and Semites, the "mixed multitude," left Egypt during the Exodus of the children of Israel.

Exodus 12.37–38
37 The children of Israel journeyed from Rameses to Succoth, about six hundred thousand on foot, the men, besides the young children. 38 And also, a great mixed multitude went up with them, and flocks and cattle, very much livestock.

לז וַיִּסְעוּ בְנֵי־יִשְׂרָאֵל מֵרַעְמְסֵס סֻכֹּתָה כְּשֵׁשׁ־מֵאוֹת אֶלֶף רַגְלִי הַגְּבָרִים לְבַד מִטָּף:
לח וְגַם־עֵרֶב רַב עָלָה אִתָּם וְצֹאן וּבָקָר מִקְנֶה כָּבֵד מְאֹד:

(The Complete Jewish Bible with Rashi Commentary, Exodus 12.37-38)

In the book of Nehemiah, we learn that all of the people who returned to Israel after 70 years of exile were not Israelite, inferring interbreeding with their Babylonian (Hamite) and Persian captors.

Nehemiah 7.63–64
63 And of the priests: the children of Hobaiah, the children of Hakkoz, the children of Barzillai, who took [a wife] from the daughters of Barzillai the Gileadite and was called by their name. 64 These who traced their genealogy

sought their records, but they were not found, and they were disqualified from the priesthood.

סג וּמִן־הַכֹּהֲנִים בְּנֵי חֲבַיָּה בְּנֵי הַקּוֹץ בְּנֵי בַרְזִלַּי אֲשֶׁר לָקַח מִבְּנוֹת בַּרְזִלַּי הַגִּלְעָדִי אִשָּׁה וַיִּקָּרֵא עַל־שְׁמָם:
סה וַיֹּאמֶר הַתִּרְשָׁתָא לָהֶם אֲשֶׁר לֹא־יֹאכְלוּ מִקֹּדֶשׁ הַקֳּדָשִׁים עַד עֲמֹד הַכֹּהֵן לְאוּרִים וְתֻמִּים:

(The Complete Jewish Bible with Rashi Commentary, Nehemiah 7.63-64)

We reiterate that *Hamite* and *Semite* do not denote Black versus White or Black versus non-Black. We are very narrowly focusing on tribal affiliation or genealogy. The descendants of Ham, son of Noah, were the people who settled in what is called Africa and parts of the Middle East. The descendants of Shem, son of Noah and brother of Ham, were people who settled in much of the Middle East, including Arabs. Both groups share common physical features, though the people of Cush and Mizraim were known for their darker complexion. We will say more about the descendants of Japheth, Noah's third son, in the next chapter.

As we stated, the initial challenge to understanding Africa's place in scripture is language. One will not find the word *Africa* in virtually any Bible translation. However, few nations appear more frequently in the Bible than Egypt (Mizraim) and Ethiopia (Cush). Also, no other nation is more prominent in the story of Israel's beginning than Egypt. It is important to note that the regions of Egypt and Ethiopia are much different than the borders of those countries today. Some historians believe biblical Egypt and Ethiopia were much larger than the modern states. Ancient Cush could well have included modern-day Yemen, Somalia, Sudan, Kenya, Zimbabwe, and a large portion of what is known today as sub-Saharan Africa. Again, other possible evidence of the larger size of biblical Egypt and Ethiopia is that they are often referred to as dual kingdoms (Isaiah 20, Psalm 105). Today, the African continent is made up of 54 states and provinces. Much of that land division occurred during the relatively recent European colonial era (late 19th century to mid-20th century). By 1900, a handful of European nations controlled 90% of Africa's lands after the signing of the "Treaty of Berlin." It is crucial to know the biblical names and geography of African lands.

For now, we return to the African lands most often mentioned in the Bible: Egypt and Ethiopia—the land of Ham. Their significance cannot be overstated as the

people and their nations are mentioned prominently in all three sections of the Hebrew Bible (Tanakh), what Christians call the "Old Testament."
It was to Egypt that Abraham and Sarah (then Abram and Sarai) sojourned because of a famine (Genesis 12). Generations later, Abraham's great-grandson, Joseph, would be sold into slavery by his brothers and taken into Egypt (Genesis 37). It was in Egypt that Joseph rose from slave to prime minister, second in command only to Pharaoh. Joseph's brothers and his father, Jacob, were reunited in Egypt, and their descendants remained for 430 years (Genesis 46). It was Moses, the deliverer, who led the children of Israel out from bondage, infanticide, and the oppression of Pharaoh, who "knew not Joseph" (Exodus 1-12).

Underscoring the lack of physical distinction between the two, Jethro's daughters mistook Moses, a Semite, for an Egyptian, a Hamite (Exodus 2). It was to Egypt that the Israelites were accustomed to fleeing when they felt threatened (Isaiah 31). It is from Egypt and Ethiopia that Psalm 68 declares dignitaries will come to Zion or Jerusalem. In the New Testament, it was to Egypt that Joseph was instructed by an angel to take Mary and the child Jesus until Herod died (Matthew 2). Similarly to Moses, the Apostle Paul, a Semite, was thought to be an Egyptian, a Hamite (Acts 21.37-39). These are but a few references that illustrate the long and complicated relationship that Israel had (and still has) with the land and people of Mizraim, son of Ham.

If Mizraim/Egypt has a close relationship with Israel in the Bible, then Cush/Ethiopia's is even more significant. Again, Moses' wife, Zipporah, was a Cushite or Ethiopian (Numbers 12). Moses and Zipporah had at least two children together, and these sons may very well represent the very first "Ethiopian Israelites."

> Exodus 18.1–5
> *1 Now Moses' father in law, Jethro, the chieftain of Midian, heard all that God had done for Moses and for Israel, His people that the Lord had taken Israel out of Egypt.*
> *2 So Moses' father in law, Jethro, took Zipporah, Moses' wife, after she had been sent away,*
> *3 and her two sons, one of whom was named Gershom, because he [Moses] said, "I was a stranger in a foreign land,"*
> *4 and one who was named Eliezer, because [Moses said,] "The God of my father came to my aid and rescued me from Pharaoh's sword."*

5 Now Moses' father in law, Jethro, and his [Moses'] sons and his wife came to Moses, to the desert where he was encamped, to the mountain of God.

א וַיִּשְׁמַ֞ע יִתְר֨וֹ כֹהֵ֤ן מִדְיָן֙ חֹתֵ֣ן מֹשֶׁ֔ה אֵת֩ כָּל־אֲשֶׁ֨ר עָשָׂ֤ה אֱלֹהִים֙ לְמֹשֶׁ֔ה וּלְיִשְׂרָאֵ֖ל עַמּ֑וֹ כִּֽי־הוֹצִ֧יא יְהֹוָ֛ה אֶת־יִשְׂרָאֵ֖ל מִמִּצְרָֽיִם׃
ב וַיִּקַּ֗ח יִתְרוֹ֙ חֹתֵ֣ן מֹשֶׁ֔ה אֶת־צִפֹּרָ֖ה אֵ֣שֶׁת מֹשֶׁ֑ה אַחַ֖ר שִׁלּוּחֶֽיהָ׃
ג וְאֵ֖ת שְׁנֵ֣י בָנֶ֑יהָ אֲשֶׁ֨ר שֵׁ֤ם הָֽאֶחָד֙ גֵּֽרְשֹׁ֔ם כִּ֣י אָמַ֔ר גֵּ֣ר הָיִ֔יתִי בְּאֶ֖רֶץ נָכְרִיָּֽה׃
ד וְשֵׁ֥ם הָאֶחָ֖ד אֱלִיעֶ֑זֶר כִּֽי־אֱלֹהֵ֤י אָבִי֙ בְּעֶזְרִ֔י וַיַּצִּלֵ֖נִי מֵחֶ֥רֶב פַּרְעֹֽה׃
ה וַיָּבֹ֞א יִתְר֨וֹ חֹתֵ֥ן מֹשֶׁ֛ה וּבָנָ֥יו וְאִשְׁתּ֖וֹ אֶל־מֹשֶׁ֑ה אֶל־הַמִּדְבָּ֗ר אֲשֶׁר־ה֛וּא חֹנֶ֥ה שָׁ֖ם הַ֥ר הָאֱלֹהִֽים׃

(The Complete Jewish Bible with Rashi Commentary, Exodus 18.1-5)

The Queen of Sheba traveled to Jerusalem to visit King Solomon in 1 Kings 10. In the Ethiopian historical record called the *Kebra Negast* (Glory of the Kings), this queen was Makeda, who reigned in Aksum. It was this very Queen and this same journey that Jesus referenced in one of his sermons (Luke 11). Zerah, the Ethiopian ruler, commanded one million men in his army—the largest in scripture (2 Chronicles 14). It was an Ethiopian soldier who delivered the news of David's son, Absalom, being killed (2 Samuel 18). It was an Ethiopian eunuch who showed kindness to the prophet Jeremiah when no one else would (Jeremiah 38). The Ethiopian finance minister of Queen Candace was joined in his chariot by the apostle Phillip while on his way back to Cush/Ethiopia from worshipping in Jerusalem (Acts 8). Bible scholars and students for ages have imagined what "gift" Ethiopia will bring to Israel.

Isaiah 18.7

At that time, there shall be brought a gift to the Lord of Hosts, a people pulled and torn, and from an awesome people from its beginning and onward, a nation punished in kind and trampled, whose land the rivers have plundered, to the place of the name of the Lord of Hosts, Mount Zion.

ז בָּעֵת֩ הַהִ֨יא יֽוּבַל־שַׁ֜י לַיהֹוָ֣ה צְבָא֗וֹת עַ֚ם מְמֻשָּׁ֣ךְ וּמוֹרָ֔ט וּמֵעַ֥ם נוֹרָ֖א מִן־ה֣וּא וָהָ֑לְאָה גּ֣וֹי ׀ קַו־קָ֣ו וּמְבוּסָ֗ה אֲשֶׁ֨ר בָּזְא֤וּ נְהָרִים֙ אַרְצ֔וֹ אֶל־מְק֛וֹם שֵׁם־יְהֹוָ֥ה צְבָא֖וֹת הַר־צִיּֽוֹן׃

(The Complete Jewish Bible with Rashi Commentary, Isaiah 18.7)

Finally, it is from beyond the rivers of Cush/Ethiopia that God will call his scattered children—His "dispersed," from which we get the word *diaspora*.

Zephaniah 3.9–10

9 For then I will convert the peoples to a pure language that all of them call in the name of the Lord, to worship Him of one accord.
10 From the other side of the rivers of Cush, My supplicants, the community of My scattered ones-they shall bring Me an offering.

ט כִּי־אָז אֶהְפֹּךְ אֶל־עַמִּים שָׂפָה בְרוּרָה לִקְרֹא כֻלָּם בְּשֵׁם יְהֹוָה לְעָבְדוֹ שְׁכֶם אֶחָד:
י מֵעֵבֶר לְנַהֲרֵי־כוּשׁ עֲתָרַי בַּת־פּוּצַי יוֹבִלוּן מִנְחָתִי:

(The Complete Jewish Bible with Rashi Commentary, Zephaniah 3.9-10)

This prophecy in Zephaniah reveals Ethiopia as the principal location of the African Israelite Diaspora and bastion of the Jewish faith. Israelites, many from the priestly tribe of Levi, who migrated to Ethiopia during the First Temple period, remained for over two millennia. In his book written in 1968, *Ethiopia and the Bible*, Dr. Edward Ullendorf shares the experience of a colleague:

> Outside the bustling modern towns of Ethiopia remains a haven of peace where priests are dancing before the ark and the courtesies of the ancient Orient continue to live. The scene of David and all the house of Israel playing before the Lord on harps and lyres, drums and sistra, dancing with all their might, and bringing up the ark with shouting and the sound of the trumpet is a spectacle that is eminently alive in Ethiopia and can be seen . . . on many occasions.[6]

Though it is true that by 1900 ninety percent of Africa's lands were controlled by European colonial powers, it is also true that Ethiopia represents a portion of the ten percent which remained independent. Despite centuries of Arab Islamic and European imperial attempts to conquer Ethiopia, Ethiopia never ultimately fell (Italy invaded Ethiopia briefly in the 1930s but soon withdrew). The Nuba mountains surrounding Ethiopia also preserved one of the most ancient Israelite communities in the world—the Ethiopian Jews, or as they preferred to be called in Ethiopia, Beta Israel (House of Israel).

---

[6] From "Introduction," by E. Ullendorf, 1968, *Ethiopia and the Bible: The Schweich Lectures (1967)*, pp. 2-3. Copyright 1968 by The British Academy.

Africa's connection to Israel stretches throughout the vast regions of the continent. Evidence of everything from subtle Hebraisms to knowledge of Israelite history was present in southern and western Africa long before the arrival of Europeans. We are not referring to remnants or echoes of Judaism exported throughout the Motherland by non-Africans, but ethnic Jewish communities in the southern, central, and western regions of Africa; the Igbo, the Lemba as well as Beta Israel; the Jews of African descent. (We will discuss the Jews of the African Diaspora in chapter two.)

THE UNIVERSALITY OF MOSES

The single most identifiable story of the Israelites of the Bible is the Exodus from Egypt. The most identifiable character of the Exodus is Moses the Lawgiver, God's prophet to Pharaoh, and deliverer of God's people. Just as Jesus is the preeminent figure of the New Testament, so Moses is the figure associated with the Torah. As the events of the Exodus all took place in the land of Ham, Africans, particularly Egyptians and Ethiopians, would have had ancient knowledge of Moses and the Israelites.

Of Africa's historic and intimate awareness of Moses, Harlem Renaissance author Zora Neale Hurston said:

> There are other concepts of Moses abroad in the world. Asia and all the Near East are sown with legends of this character. They are so numerous and so varied that some students have come to doubt if the Moses of the Christian concept is real. Then Africa has her mouth on Moses. All across the continent there are legends of the greatness of Moses.[7]

One reason for Moses' renown is God's promise to make him a deity to Pharaoh.

> Exodus 7.1
> *The Lord said to Moses, "See! I have made you a lord over Pharaoh, and Aaron, your brother, will be your speaker.*

---

[7] From "Author's Introduction," by Z. N. Hurston, 1991, *Moses, Man of the Mountain*, p. xxiii. Copyright 1990 by Henry Louis Gates, Jr.

א וַיֹּאמֶר יְהֹוָה אֶל־מֹשֶׁה רְאֵה נְתַתִּיךָ אֱלֹהִים לְפַרְעֹה וְאַהֲרֹן אָחִיךָ יִהְיֶה נְבִיאֶךָ:

(The Complete Jewish Bible with Rashi Commentary, Exodus 7.1)

Again, Zora Neale Hurston:

> Wherever the children of Africa have been scattered by slavery, there is the acceptance of Moses as the fountain of mystic powers. This is not confined to Negroes. In America there are countless people of other races depending on mystic symbols and seals and syllables said to have been used by Moses to work his wonders ... Nobody can tell how many tales and legends of Moses are alive in the world nor how far they have travelled, so many have collected around his name.[8]

In his book, *The Rescue of Jerusalem: The Alliance Between Hebrews and Africans in 701 BC*, author Henry T. Aubin explains that Africa and Israel had close ties that included military cooperation—the original Africa-Israel coalition. In the following quote, Aubin uses the ancient Egyptian name *Khor* to denote Israel, the Palestinian Territories, Jordan, Lebanon, and Syria.

> Contrary to popular understanding, sub-Saharan soldiers were no strangers to that part of the world. Records indicate their involvement in Khor for at least 1,500 years prior to Sennacherib's invasion. Indeed, some six centuries before that conflict, Kushite soldiers serving under the ultimate authority of Egypt were actually posted in Jerusalem as defenders of that town. Prior to 701 [BC], the most recent involvement of black Africans in Khor would have probably been [circa] 712, when some served as mercenaries in the Asdodite rebellion against Assyria.[9]

NEGRO SPIRITUALS

Pan-African history is immensely varied and spans several millennia. It is the story of religion and culture; of kingdoms and empires; of wars and tragedies;

---

[8] From "Author's Introduction," by Z. N. Hurston, 1991, *Moses, Man of the Mountain*, p. xxiv. Copyright 1990 by Henry Louis Gates, Jr.

[9] From "The Kushites' Self-Interest," by H. T. Aubin, 2002, *The Rescue of Jerusalem*, p. 77. Copyright 2002 by Henry T. Aubin.

of colonization and slavery; of life, death, and rebirth. The Trans-Atlantic Slave Trade is among the most defining events of modern African history. From the 16th to the 19th century, some 12 million souls were taken from the *Land of Ham* and brought on ships like chattel to the New World. Of the many parallels between the African and Israelite people is the story of forced bondage by an all-powerful oppressor. The children of Jacob remained in Egypt 430 years before God finally sent Moses to lead them to the Promised Land. Likewise, African slaves in America toiled for centuries before Emancipation. The most famous abolitionist and Underground Railroad Conductor was Harriet Tubman, known to many as *Moses*.

As the children of Israel served the Pharaohs (and later the Babylonians), they remembered their God in stories and songs. They encouraged themselves with hopes of a greater future amid a mournful present reality.

Psalm 137.1–6
1 By the rivers of Babylon, there we sat, we also wept when we remembered Zion.
2 On willows in its midst we hung our harps.
3 For there our captors asked us for words of song and our tormentors [asked of us] mirth, "Sing for us of the song of Zion."
4 "How shall we sing the song of the Lord on foreign soil?"
5 If I forget you, O Jerusalem, may my right hand forget [its skill].
6 May my tongue cling to my palate, if I do not remember you, if I do not bring up Jerusalem at the beginning of my joy.

א עַל־נַהֲרוֹת ׀ בָּבֶל שָׁם יָשַׁבְנוּ גַּם־בָּכִינוּ בְּזָכְרֵנוּ אֶת־צִיּוֹן׃
ב עַל־עֲרָבִים בְּתוֹכָהּ תָּלִינוּ כִּנֹּרוֹתֵינוּ׃
ג כִּי שָׁם שְׁאֵלוּנוּ שׁוֹבֵינוּ דִּבְרֵי־שִׁיר וְתוֹלָלֵינוּ שִׂמְחָה שִׁירוּ לָנוּ מִשִּׁיר צִיּוֹן׃
ד אֵיךְ נָשִׁיר אֶת־שִׁיר־יְהֹוָה עַל אַדְמַת נֵכָר׃
ה אִם־אֶשְׁכָּחֵךְ יְרוּשָׁלָ͏ִם תִּשְׁכַּח יְמִינִי׃
ו תִּדְבַּק לְשׁוֹנִי ׀ לְחִכִּי אִם־לֹא אֶזְכְּרֵכִי אִם־לֹא אַעֲלֶה אֶת־יְרוּשָׁלַ͏ִם עַל רֹאשׁ שִׂמְחָתִי׃

(The Complete Jewish Bible with Rashi Commentary, Psalm 137.1-6)

Likewise, the African slaves sang, told stories and dreamt of freedom. It was those heart-gripping, soul-stirring songs that were Black people's greatest gift to

THE AFRICAN BIBLICAL TIE TO ISRAEL

Western music and the foundation of *virtually* every form of America's music, from folk to gospel to jazz to rock—the Negro Spiritual.

One of the mainstays which fostered mental stamina for the...Egyptian/ Ethiopian descendants that crossed the Middle Passage was the ability to feel the Spirit of God through emotions, songs, and dances. For this cause the captains of slave ships would allow the Africans to dance on the deck of the ship as a means of physical exercise.

This practice of singing and dancing among the Africans was allowed as they endured the four hundred years in . . . captivity. The African captives began to sing about the "Deliverer" whom they once knew in their native folktales, like Moses, the deliverer who had once brought them from the land of captivity in Egypt. "Go Down, Moses" became a popular slave song even among white slaveholders. The slave songs . . . were drawn from the rich memory brought with them from the land across the waters. They had a rich repertoire of biblical stories.[10]

The African slaves' "rich repertoire of biblical stories" were very commonly, though not exclusively, based on the Old Testament (Jewish Bible). The persons enshrined in song ranged from Moses to David to Elijah. This reveals that it was not only the biblical motifs of bondage and freedom that found their expression in African slave songs, but continual praise of the God of Israel who moved on behalf of His people. It also reveals that, long before European slave traders learned to penetrate Africa's interior, the descendants of Ham knew full-well who the God of Abraham was. And, as evidenced in the spirituals, they worshiped and revered Him.

Go Down, Moses
When Israel was in Egypt's land
Let my people go
Oppressed so hard they could not stand
Let my people go

---

[10] From "The Africology of Music," in C. H. Felder (Ed.), 1993, *The Original African Heritage Study Bible*, p. 1842. Copyright 1993 by The James C. Winston Publishing Company.

18

(Chorus)
Go down (go down)
Moses (go down Moses)
Way down in Egypt's land
Tell old, Pharaoh
Let my people go!

Verse 2
Thus saith the Lord, bold Moses said
Let my people go
If not, I'll smite your first born dead
Let my people go

Verse 3
No more shall they in bondage toil
Let my people go
Let them come out with Egypt's spoil
Let my people go

Roll Jordan, Roll
(Chorus)
Roll, roll Jordan, roll
I want to go to heaven when I die
To hear Jordan roll (roll, roll, roll)
Roll, roll Jordan, roll
I want to go to heaven when I die
To hear Jordan roll (roll, roll, roll)

Now brother, you ought to been there
Yes, my Lord
A sitting in the Jordan kingdom
To hear Jordan

Joshua Fit the Battle of Jericho

(Chorus)
Joshua fit the battle of Jericho
Jericho Jericho
Joshua fit the battle of Jericho
And the walls come tumbling down

Good morning sister Mary
Good morning brother John
Well I wanna stop and talk with you
Wanna tell you how I come along

I know you've heard about Joshua
He was the son of Nun
He never stopped his work until
Until the work was done

You may talk about your men of Gideon
You may brag about your men of Saul
There's none like good old Joshua
At the battle of Jericho

Up to the walls of Jericho
He marched with spear in hand
Go blow them ram horns, Joshua cried
'Cause the battle is in my hands

They tell me, great God that Joshua's spear
Was well nigh twelve feet long
And upon his hip was a double edged sword
And his mouth was a gospel horn

Yet bold and brave he stood
Salvation in his hand
Go blow them ram horns Joshua cried
'Cause the devil can't do you no harm

Up to the walls of Jericho
He marched with spear in hand
Go blow them ram horns, Joshua cried
'Cause the battle is in my hands

Then the lamb ram sheep horns began to blow
The trumpets began to sound
Old Joshua shouted glory
And the walls came tumblin' down

Swing Low, Sweet Chariot
(Chorus)
Swing low, sweet chariot,
Comin' for to carry me home;
Swing low, sweet chariot,
Comin' for to carry me home.

I looked over Jordan,
And WHAT did I see,
Comin' for to carry me home,
A band of angels comin' after me,
Comin' for to carry me home.
If you get there before I do,
Comin' for to carry me home,
Tell all my friends I'm comin' too,
Comin' for to carry me home.

Elijah Rock
(Chorus)
Elijah Rock shout shout
Elijah Rock comin' up Lord
Elijah Rock shout shout
Elijah Rock comin' up Lord
Satan is a liar and a conjure too

If you don't (mind high) watch out
He'll conjure you
If I could I sho'ly would
Stand on the rock where Moses stood

Ezekiel said he saw him
Wheel in the mid' of a wheel
John talked about him
In the book of the 7 seals
Some say the Rose of Sharon
Others say the Prince of Peace
But I can tell everybody (this ol' world)
He been a rock and a shelter for me
Hallelujah

Didn't My Lord Deliver Daniel

(Chorus)
Didn't my Lord deliver Daniel?
Deliver Daniel, deliver Daniel?
Didn't my Lord deliver Daniel?
And why not every man?

He delivered Daniel from the lion's den
And Jonah from the belly of the whale
And the Hebrew children from the fiery furnace
Why not every man?

The moon runs down in a purple stream
And the sun refused to shine
And every star did disappear
Yes, freedom shall be mine

There is a Balm in Gilead

There is a balm in Gilead,
To make the wounded whole;
There's power enough in heaven,
To cure a sin-sick soul.

While European and American Christian missionaries made it their quest to *save the African* as the slaves arrived in America and Europe, the descendants of Cush and Mizraim maintained some actual knowledge of Israel and her God. Like the Israelites' song in the "strange lands" of Babylon and Persia, so Negro Spirituals expressed an unyielding faith in the God of Abraham, Isaac, and Jacob. These songs by Black slaves were also strong statements of identification and solidarity with God's firstborn—Israel. The slave traders' attempts to erase the memory of a biblical past were effective but not final. These songs and their biblical themes would continue to fuel the hopes and aspirations of Black people through slavery, Jim Crow, and the civil rights era of the 1950s and 1960s. It was educator and poet James Weldon Johnson, who, at the turn of the 20th century, admonished the descendants of African slaves to remember from whence they came. The third and final verse of his composition, *Lift Ev'ry Voice and Sing* (the Negro National Anthem), is even more relevant today than when written in 1899.

God of our weary years, God of our silent tears
Thou who has brought us thus far on the way
Thou who has by Thy might
Led us into the light
Keep us forever in Thy path, we pray
Lest our feet stray from the places our God where we met Thee
Lest our hearts drunk with the wine of the world we forget Thee
Shadowed beneath Thy hand
May we forever stand
True to our God

THE AFRICAN BIBLICAL TIE TO ISRAEL

True to our native land[11]

Israel is in the blood of the Africans, both literally and figuratively. From the land of Ham to the New World, Africans retained in-depth knowledge of the God of Israel and His covenant bond with the Jewish people. To this day, the Church remains an integral part of the lives of a large percentage of Black American families. Further, an increased curiosity of the Hebrew roots of the Christian faith throughout the Body of Christ has helped re-energize the subject of Zionism. This is an opportunity for the Black Church to yet, again, provide dynamic and scripturally sound leadership for the world to follow.

Separating the Jewish people from the biblical narrative would be akin to reinterpreting the text to distort its meaning. Biblically literate, intellectually honest Black Christians would have no patience for this. In the Black Church, Shadrach, Meshcah, and Abednego are affectionately called the "Hebrew boys" because that's who they were. David killed Goliath, the Philistine, and led the Israelites to victory because that's what happened. We're "marching to Zion—that beautiful city of God" because that's what the Bible teaches. We want to be ready to "walk in Jerusalem just like John" because Jerusalem is the Holy City. It was established by King David, who "danced before the Lord with all his might," as he inaugurated Zion. We are always glad when someone says to us, "let us go into the house of the Lord," which is in Jerusalem. And Jesus, our Lord, and Savior, is King of Israel and will reign forever in Jerusalem. Through our music, our love of scripture, and our affinity for the Holy Land, Black Christians remain deeply connected to our Jewish brothers and sisters.

Historically, Zionism for the Black Christian comes from a place of deep spiritual heritage. Israel is not merely an intellectual concept; it is an emotional connection. It has been this way since the beginning.

---

[11] The final stanza from "Lift Every Voice and Sing," (1899) commonly referred to as the Black National Anthem and historically as the Negro National Anthem, originally written as a poem by former NAACP leader James Weldon Johnson and set to music by his brother John Rosamond Johnson. The song was first performed in 1900, at a segregated school in Jacksonville, Fla. to celebrate the birthday of President Abraham Lincoln.

CHAPTER 2
THE JEWISH DIASPORA AND PROPHETIC RETURN TO ISRAEL

> Ezekiel 37.3
>
> *Then He said to me; "Son of man, can these bones become alive?" And I answered, "O Lord God, You [alone] know."*
>
> ג וַיֹּאמֶר אֵלַי בֶּן־אָדָם הֲתִחְיֶינָה הָעֲצָמוֹת הָאֵלֶּה וָאֹמַר אֲדֹנָי יֱהֹוִה אַתָּה יָדָעְתָּ:
>
> (The Complete Jewish Bible with Rashi Commentary, Ezekiel 37.3)

Israel, both the State and the people, is a multiethnic nation. The Jewish people were dispersed all over the earth and are returning to their homeland. It is crucial for the Black Church to understand this point for reasons that will become clearer both in this chapter and the ones to follow. Also, this chapter is a prelude to my next work entitled, *The Diaspora: Discovering Israel's Multiethnic Identity & Her Prophetic Return to the Land.*

As we begin this part of our discussion, let us reiterate the importance of language. The term Jew or Jewish came to describe someone from the land of Judah. Today, Jew can generally mean one of two things:

1. A biological descendant of Jacob (an actual Israelite), or
2. A non-Israelite/Gentile convert to Judaism or member of the Jewish faith

We will concern ourselves mainly with the ethnically Jewish (Israelite) people, as

Diaspora chiefly refers to them. This is not to in any way diminish the identity of Jewish converts, as the Torah teaches that they are to be considered Israelites (Leviticus 24.22). Rather, we seek to clarify and focus our topic on the actual seed of Jacob, their origins, their scattering, and their prophetic re-gathering in the land of Israel.

What does a Jew look like? What are the distinguishing physical characteristics of an Israelite? As Christians, many of us grew up with pictures of Jesus in our homes or churches. From where did those pictures come? Depending on the worldview or cultural leaning of your childhood congregation, your Jesus portraits may have been a Black man with long locks or an Afro. More traditionally, your pictures of Jesus were of a White man who looked more like a Swede than a Middle Easterner. Who remembers the felt boards in Sunday School with the paper cut outs of Peter, John, Joshua, or Samson? And does Charlton Heston *really* look like Moses?

Throughout Church history, each civilization received and subsequently told the gospel story from its perspective. Jesus (or Yeshua) and other biblical figures inevitably took on not only the physical likeness of the host country but the peoples' cultural attributes as well. To the Greeks, Jesus was presented as Greek, complete with toga-like apparel. To the ancient Coptic Church in Egypt, Jesus was Nubian with wooly hair. American Jewish professor and theologian Ron Moseley states in his book, *Yeshua: A Guide to the Real Jesus and the Original Church*:

> In the United States, many twentieth-century Protestants picture Jesus according to their successful, middle-class, American lifestyle. Some have even forsaken the darker Jewish look for the blond and tanned Hollywood-like appearance which is often portrayed in modern art.[1]

The land of Israel is in the northeastern region of Africa and the southwestern region of Asia, from where we get the term Afro-Asiatic. Israel is connected by land to Egypt (the land of Ham) via the Sinai Desert. The chief patriarch of the Israelite nation is Abraham, son of Terah. Before following God's leading to Canaan, Abraham lived in Ur, which was in the region of ancient Babylon

---

[1] From "Introduction," by R. Moseley & M. Wilson, 1996, *Yeshua: A Guide to the Real Jesus and the Original Church*, p. 4. Copyright 1996 by Ron Wayne Moseley.

(present-day Iraq). Again, according to modern notions of race, Abraham, Isaac, Jacob and their progeny would all be considered *people of color*. They all originated from the Afro-Asiatic region of the world, and would have ranged in complexion from light to dark just as the people in that region do today. So, it is highly unlikely that a White, almost Nordic Jesus could have originated in the Middle East. However, as mentioned in chapter one, our goal is not to solve all anthropological mysteries or quell centuries-old debates. Our focus here is to attempt to identify the dispersed of Judah from the four corners of the earth (Isaiah 11).

First, we examine scripture and learn how and why the Israelites were indeed dispersed throughout the world.

> Deuteronomy 28.15, 64
> 15 *And it will be, if you do not obey the Lord, your God, to observe to fulfill all His commandments and statutes which I am commanding you this day, that all these curses will come upon you and overtake you.*

> ט וְהָיָ֗ה אִם־לֹ֤א תִשְׁמַע֙ בְּק֔וֹל יְהֹוָ֖ה אֱלֹהֶ֑יךָ לִשְׁמֹ֤ר לַֽעֲשׂוֹת֙ אֶת־כָּל־מִצְוֺתָ֣יו וְחֻקֹּתָ֔יו אֲשֶׁ֛ר אָֽנֹכִ֥י מְצַוְּךָ֖ הַיּ֑וֹם וּבָ֧אוּ עָלֶ֛יךָ כָּל־הַקְּלָל֥וֹת הָאֵ֖לֶּה וְהִשִּׂיג֥וּךָ׃

> 64 *And the Lord will scatter you among all the nations, from one end of the earth to the other, and there you will serve other deities unknown to you or your forefathers, [deities of] wood and stone.*

> סד וֶהֱפִֽיצְךָ֤ יְהֹוָה֙ בְּכָל־הָ֣עַמִּ֔ים מִקְצֵ֥ה הָאָ֖רֶץ וְעַד־קְצֵ֣ה הָאָ֑רֶץ וְעָבַ֤דְתָּ שָּׁם֙ אֱלֹהִ֣ים אֲחֵרִ֔ים אֲשֶׁ֧ר לֹא־יָדַ֛עְתָּ אַתָּ֥ה וַֽאֲבֹתֶ֖יךָ עֵ֥ץ וָאָֽבֶן׃
> (The Complete Jewish Bible with Rashi Commentary, Deuteronomy 28.15, 64)

The Bible tells us that, because of Israel's disobedience to God's commandments, God would ultimately cast them out of Israel. This forced migration happened at three major points in Israel's history:

1. After the Assyrians invaded the Northern Kingdom of Israel in approximately 722 B.C.
2. After the Babylonians invaded the Southern Kingdom of Judah around 586 B.C. (Babylonian king Nebuchadnezzar also destroyed the First

THE JEWISH DIASPORA AND PROPHETIC RETURN TO ISRAEL

Temple in Jerusalem, killed thousands of Israelites, and took the most capable to serve his empire. Among those captives were Daniel and Hananiah, Mishael and Azariah - Shadrach, Meshach and Abednego).
3. After the Romans destroyed the Second Temple (and ultimately, the land of Judah) in A.D. 70.

Another recurring story in the dispersion of the Israelites is the impending civil war between King Rehoboam of Judah and King Jeroboam of Northern Israel (about 930 B.C.). After the death of King Solomon, son of King David, the Kingdom of Israel divided into regions consisting of ten northern tribes under Jeroboam and two southern tribes under Rehoboam, son of Solomon.

> 1 Kings 12.21–24
> *21 And Rehoboam came to Jerusalem, and he assembled all the House of Judah and the tribe of Benjamin, one hundred and eighty thousand chosen warriors, to wage war with the House of Israel, to return the kingdom to Rehoboam, the son of Solomon.*
> *22 And the word of God was to Shemiah, the man of God, saying,*
> *23 "Speak to Rehoboam, the son of Solomon, King of Judah, and to all of the house of Judah and Benjamin, and the rest of the people, saying,*
> *24 "Thus said the Lord: 'You shall not go up and you shall not war with your brothers, the children of Israel; return each man to his home for this thing has been brought about by Me.' "And they heeded the word of the Lord, and they returned to go [home], in accordance with the word of the Lord.*

> כא וַיָּבֹא (כתיב וַיָּבֹאוּ) רְחַבְעָם יְרוּשָׁלַםִ וַיַּקְהֵל אֶת־כָּל־בֵּית יְהוּדָה וְאֶת־שֵׁבֶט בִּנְיָמִן מֵאָה וּשְׁמֹנִים אֶלֶף בָּחוּר עֹשֵׂה מִלְחָמָה לְהִלָּחֵם עִם־בֵּית יִשְׂרָאֵל לְהָשִׁיב אֶת־הַמְּלוּכָה לִרְחַבְעָם בֶּן־שְׁלֹמֹה:
> כב וַיְהִי דְּבַר הָאֱלֹהִים אֶל־שְׁמַעְיָה אִישׁ־הָאֱלֹהִים לֵאמֹר:
> כג אֱמֹר אֶל־רְחַבְעָם בֶּן־שְׁלֹמֹה מֶלֶךְ יְהוּדָה וְאֶל־כָּל־בֵּית יְהוּדָה וּבִנְיָמִין וְיֶתֶר הָעָם לֵאמֹר:
> כד כֹּה אָמַר יְהֹוָה לֹא־תַעֲלוּ וְלֹא־תִלָּחֲמוּן עִם־אֲחֵיכֶם בְּנֵי־יִשְׂרָאֵל שׁוּבוּ אִישׁ לְבֵיתוֹ כִּי מֵאִתִּי נִהְיָה הַדָּבָר הַזֶּה וַיִּשְׁמְעוּ אֶת־דְּבַר יְהֹוָה וַיָּשֻׁבוּ לָלֶכֶת כִּדְבַר יְהֹוָה:

(The Complete Jewish Bible with Rashi Commentary,
1 Kings 12.21-24)

Because of the Israelites' obedience to the prophetic word through Shemiah, they averted war. But, the battle had been anticipated since before Solomon's death, as it was prophesied that Israel would be split when he passed (1 Kings 11). This event is referenced in the history of many African and Asian Israelite tribes. The Igbo of West Africa, the Lemba of Southern Africa, the Ethiopian Jews, and the Pardesi Jews of India are groups whose story involves Solomon and the First Temple period. Some Israelites fled the impending war and were scattered throughout the Middle East and Africa. Many Levites (the priestly tribe) settled in Sanaa, which is in modern-day Yemen. As Islam spread from Arabia throughout East, North, and West Africa, the Israelites on the Continent were either killed, absorbed, or fled westward.

According to Igbo Hebrew author and historian, Remy Ilona, the Igbo of West Africa are possibly the largest Jewish tribe in the world. A percentage of the Africans taken during the Trans-Atlantic Slave Trade were Igbo. This would mean that a significant portion of African slaves brought to Europe, the Americas and the West Indies are Israelite.

The Second Temple period of Israel's history is 530 B.C. to 70 A.D. Before His crucifixion, Jesus prophesied the Roman destruction of the Second Temple and the Holy City (around 35 A.D.).

> Mark 13.1–2
> *1 And as he came out of the temple, one of his disciples said to him, 'Look, Teacher, what large stones and what large buildings!' 2 Then Jesus asked him, 'Do you see these great buildings? Not one stone will be left here upon another; all will be thrown down.'*
> (English Standard Version, Mark 13.1-2)

> Matthew 23.37–38
> *37 "O Jerusalem, Jerusalem, the city that kills the prophets and stones those who are sent to it! How often would I have gathered your children together as a hen gathers her brood under her wings, and you were not willing! 38 See, your house is left to you desolate."*
> (English Standard Version, Matthew 23.37-38)

In the long tradition of Israelite prophets, Jesus calls Israel to repentance and laments her unwillingness to do so. As Jeremiah did before Him, Jesus warns of the destruction of the Holy Temple by the Gentiles. We have no biblical account of the Second Temple's destruction, but it is recorded in extra-biblical history.

In 63 BC, Judaea became a protectorate of Rome. Coming under the administration of a governor, Judaea was allowed a king; the governor's business was to regulate trade and maximize tax revenue. While the Jews despised the Greeks, the Romans were a nightmare. Governorships were bought at high prices; the governors would attempt to squeeze as much revenue as possible from their regions and pocket as much as they could. Even with a Jewish king, the [Jews] revolted in 70 AD, a desperate revolt that ended tragically. In 73 A.D., the last of the revolutionaries were holed up in a mountain fort called Masada; the Romans had besieged the fort for two years, and the 1,000 men, women, and children inside were beginning to starve. In desperation, the Jewish revolutionaries killed themselves rather than surrender to the Romans. The Romans then destroyed Jerusalem, annexed Judea as a Roman province, and systematically drove the Jews from [Judea]. After 73 A.D., Hebrew history would only be the history of the Diaspora as the Jews and their world view spread over Africa, Asia, and Europe.[2]

Some 60 years after the destruction of the Temple, which the Jewish people still mourn to this day, the Jewish people were rallied once more by another leader, Shimon Bar Kokhba. This was known as the Bar Kokhba Revolt (132-135 A.D.). Once again, however, the Romans, led by Emperor Hadrian, defeated the remaining Judaens. Except for a small remnant in Israel, the Jews would go into exile for almost 2,000 years.

Following the battle of Bethar, there were a few small skirmishes in the Judean Desert Caves, but the war was essentially over and Judean independence was lost. The Romans plowed Jerusalem with a yoke of oxen. Jews were sold into slavery and many were transported to Egypt. Judean settlements were not rebuilt. Jerusalem was turned into a pagan city called Aelia Capitolina and the Jews were forbidden to live there. They were permitted to enter only on the 9th of Av to mourn their losses in the revolt. Hadrian changed the country's name from Judea to Syria

---

[2] From "Ancient Jewish History: The Diaspora," by Jewish Virtual Library, n.d., *Jewish Virtual Library*.

Palestina.³

Syria Palestina is the name from which we get *Palestine*. Emperor Hadrian so despised the Jewish people that he changed the name of their country to that of their mortal enemies: the Syrians and the Philistines. For the next two millennia, Palestine would be the possession of foreign powers, including the Roman Empire, the Byzantine Empire, Christian Crusaders, the Ottoman Empire, Great Britain, Muslim rulers, and finally, a protectorate of the League of Nations (United Nations).

Even before the Romans finally destroyed Jerusalem and Judea in post-biblical history (70 A.D.), we see an acknowledgment and inclusiveness of the Israelite Diaspora within New Testament scripture. We see the multiethnic Jewish people in the Pentecost narrative of Acts chapter two.

Acts 2.1-11
1 When the day of Pentecost had come, they were all together in one place.
2 And suddenly from heaven there came a sound like the rush of a violent wind, and it filled the entire house where they were sitting. 3 Divided tongues, as of fire, appeared among them, and a tongue rested on each of them.
4 All of them were filled with the Holy Spirit and began to speak in other languages, as the Spirit gave them ability.
5 Now there were devout Jews from every nation under heaven living in Jerusalem. 6 And at this sound the crowd gathered and was bewildered, because each one heard them speaking in the native language of each.
7 Amazed and astonished, they asked, 'Are not all these who are speaking Galileans? 8 And how is it that we hear, each of us, in our own native language? 9 Parthians, Medes, Elamites, and residents of Mesopotamia, Judea and Cappadocia (Turkey), Pontus and Asia, 10 Phrygia and Pamphylia, Egypt and the parts of Libya belonging to Cyrene, and visitors from Rome, 11 both Jews and proselytes, Cretans and Arabs—in our own languages we hear them speaking about God's deeds of power.'
(English Standard Version, Acts 2.1-11)

---

³ From "Ancient Jewish History: The Bar-Kokhba Revolt (132 - 135 CE)," by Jewish Virtual Library, n.d., *Jewish Virtual Library*.

THE JEWISH DIASPORA AND PROPHETIC RETURN TO ISRAEL

In his only recorded epistle, the Apostle James, brother of Jesus, addresses his letter to the Israelite Diaspora.

> James 1.1–2
> *1 James, a bondservant of God and of the Lord Jesus Christ, To the twelve tribes which are scattered abroad: Greetings. 2 Count it all joy, my brothers, when you meet trials of various kinds.*
> (English Standard Version, James 1.1-2)

But, just as God told the Israelites, they would be scattered for their rebellion, so He promised that at the appointed time, He would gather them again.

> Deuteronomy 30.1–4
> *1 And it will be, when all these things come upon you the blessing and the curse which I have set before you that you will consider in your heart, among all the nations where the Lord your God has banished you, 2 and you will return to the Lord, your God, with all your heart and with all your soul, and you will listen to His voice according to all that I am commanding you this day you and your children, 3 then, the Lord, your God, will bring back your exiles, and He will have mercy upon you. He will once again gather you from all the nations, where the Lord, your God, had dispersed you. 4 Even if your exiles are at the end of the heavens, the Lord, your God, will gather you from there, and He will take you from there.*

א וְהָיָה כִי־יָבֹאוּ עָלֶיךָ כָּל־הַדְּבָרִים הָאֵלֶּה הַבְּרָכָה וְהַקְּלָלָה אֲשֶׁר נָתַתִּי לְפָנֶיךָ וַהֲשֵׁבֹתָ אֶל־לְבָבֶךָ בְּכָל־הַגּוֹיִם אֲשֶׁר הִדִּיחֲךָ יְהֹוָה אֱלֹהֶיךָ שָׁמָּה:
ב וְשַׁבְתָּ עַד־יְהֹוָה אֱלֹהֶיךָ וְשָׁמַעְתָּ בְקֹלוֹ כְּכֹל אֲשֶׁר־אָנֹכִי מְצַוְּךָ הַיּוֹם אַתָּה וּבָנֶיךָ בְּכָל־לְבָבְךָ וּבְכָל־נַפְשֶׁךָ:
ג וְשָׁב יְהֹוָה אֱלֹהֶיךָ אֶת־שְׁבוּתְךָ וְרִחֲמֶךָ וְשָׁב וְקִבֶּצְךָ מִכָּל־הָעַמִּים אֲשֶׁר הֱפִיצְךָ יְהֹוָה אֱלֹהֶיךָ שָׁמָּה:
ד אִם־יִהְיֶה נִדַּחֲךָ בִּקְצֵה הַשָּׁמָיִם מִשָּׁם יְקַבֶּצְךָ יְהֹוָה אֱלֹהֶיךָ וּמִשָּׁם יִקָּחֶךָ:

(The Complete Jewish Bible with Rashi Commentary, Deuteronomy 30.1-4)

> Psalm 147.2–4
> *2 The Lord is the builder of Jerusalem; He will gather the outcasts of Israel.
> 3 Who heals the brokenhearted and binds up their wounds.
> 4 He counts the number of the stars; He calls them all by name.*

ב בֹּנֵה יְרוּשָׁלִַם יְהֹוָה נִדְחֵי יִשְׂרָאֵל יְכַנֵּס:
ג הָרֹפֵא לִשְׁבוּרֵי לֵב וּמְחַבֵּשׁ לְעַצְּבוֹתָם:
ד מוֹנֶה מִסְפָּר לַכּוֹכָבִים לְכֻלָּם שֵׁמוֹת יִקְרָא:

(The Complete Jewish Bible with Rashi Commentary, Psalm 147.2-4)

Jeremiah 31.9-10

9 Hear the word of the Lord, O nations, and declare it on the islands from afar, and say, "He Who scattered Israel will gather them together and watch them as a shepherd his flock.
10 For the Lord has redeemed Jacob and has saved him out of the hand of him who is stronger than he.

ט שִׁמְעוּ דְבַר־יְהֹוָה גּוֹיִם וְהַגִּידוּ בָאִיִּים מִמֶּרְחָק וְאִמְרוּ מְזָרֵה יִשְׂרָאֵל יְקַבְּצֶנּוּ וּשְׁמָרוֹ כְּרֹעֶה עֶדְרוֹ:
י כִּי־פָדָה יְהֹוָה אֶת־יַעֲקֹב וּגְאָלוֹ מִיַּד חָזָק מִמֶּנּוּ:

(The Complete Jewish Bible with Rashi Commentary, Jeremiah 31.9-10)

Not only does God declare that He will redeem His people and bring them back to the Land; He also names the nations from which Israel will come.

Isaiah 11.11–12

11 And it shall come to pass that on that day, the Lord shall continue to apply His hand a second time to acquire the rest of His people, that will remain from Assyria and from Egypt [Mizraim] and from Pathros and from Cush [Ethiopia] and from Elam and from Sumeria [Mesopotamia] and from Hamath and from the islands of the sea.
12 And He shall raise a banner to the nations, and He shall gather the lost of Israel, and the scattered ones of Judah He shall gather from the four corners of the earth.

יא וְהָיָה | בַּיּוֹם הַהוּא יוֹסִיף אֲדֹנָי | שֵׁנִית יָדוֹ לִקְנוֹת אֶת־שְׁאָר עַמּוֹ אֲשֶׁר יִשָּׁאֵר מֵאַשּׁוּר וּמִמִּצְרַיִם וּמִפַּתְרוֹס וּמִכּוּשׁ וּמֵעֵילָם וּמִשִּׁנְעָר וּמֵחֲמָת וּמֵאִיֵּי הַיָּם:
יב וְנָשָׂא נֵס לַגּוֹיִם וְאָסַף נִדְחֵי יִשְׂרָאֵל וּנְפֻצוֹת יְהוּדָה יְקַבֵּץ מֵאַרְבַּע כַּנְפוֹת הָאָרֶץ:

(The Complete Jewish Bible with Rashi Commentary, Isaiah 11.11-12)

Zephaniah 3.10
From the other side of the rivers of Cush, My supplicants, the community of My scattered ones-they shall bring Me an offering.

י מֵעֵ֖בֶר לְנַֽהֲרֵי־כ֑וּשׁ עֲתָרַי֙ בַּת־פּוּצַ֔י יוֹבִל֖וּן מִנְחָתִֽי׃
(The Complete Jewish Bible with Rashi Commentary, Zephaniah 3.10)

Assyria, Egypt, Ethiopia, Mesopotamia . . . and the islands of the sea are either definitive or generic geographical locations. They are neither metaphor nor symbol. So, why would God bother to mention the names of specific countries when identifying the Diaspora? Why did it not suffice to simply say, "I'm gathering my people from where I scattered them?" One possible reason could be to let the world know that the Jewish people would live among them and return to Israel from their midst. Further, according to anthropological science, the human body adapts to its habitation, climate, etc.[4] After 2,000 years of living in foreign lands, physically adapting to different climates, and some intermarriage, people from the Middle East would look like the people in their host countries. The Jews of Europe would look European. The Jews of India would look Indian. The Jews from Ethiopia will look like descendants of Cush.

With this knowledge, let us now consider the Israelite Diaspora, where they are, and from where they have returned to Israel.

THE JEWS OF EASTERN EUROPE

European Jews are considered to be the largest population of Jewish descendants—possibly more than 80% Jews worldwide. I have studied the subject of the Jewish Diaspora for the past 25 years, albeit as a layman, and I am not convinced of this percentage. There seem to be more Jews of African, Asian, and Latino descent than many scholars have acknowledged to this point. But, again, that is a discussion for the sequel to this book.

European Jews, or Jews of European descent, are commonly (generically) referred to as Ashkenazim. Ashkenaz was the grandson of Japheth, and the great-grandson

---

[4] In his influential work *Anthropology and Modern Life (1986)*, physicist and pioneer anthropologist Franz Boas explains that, while still controlled by bodily build, the functions of the human body are influenced by external conditions.

of Noah. He is known as the progenitor of the people of modern-day Europe.

Genesis 10.1–3

1 And these are the generations of the sons of Noah: Shem, Ham, and Japheth, and sons were born to them after the Flood. 2 The sons of Japheth were Gomer and Magog and Madai and Javan and Tubal, and Meshech and Tiras. 3 And the sons of Gomer were Ashkenaz and Riphath and Togarmah.

א וְאֵלֶּה תּוֹלְדֹת בְּנֵי־נֹחַ שֵׁם חָם וָיָפֶת וַיִּוָּלְדוּ לָהֶם בָּנִים אַחַר הַמַּבּוּל:
ב בְּנֵי יֶפֶת גֹּמֶר וּמָגוֹג וּמָדַי וְיָוָן וְתֻבָל וּמֶשֶׁךְ וְתִירָס:
ג וּבְנֵי גֹּמֶר אַשְׁכְּנַז וְרִיפַת וְתֹגַרְמָה:

(The Complete Jewish Bible with Rashi Commentary, Genesis 10.1-3)

Ashkenaz is also a Hebrew designation for German. We learn in the Table of Nations that one of Japheth's sons was Javan, from whom descended the Greeks (Genesis 10). Jewish presence in Greece dates back to the 6th century B.C.

Contact between Greeks and Jews outside of Greece began after the Babylonian exile of 586–539 B.C. When the Persian king Cyrus allowed Jews to return to their homeland after the Babylonian exile, they met Greeks for the first time. The prophet Ezekiel wrote of the Greek traders of "Javan," Ionia, who traded in slaves and worked with bronze. The Greek historian Herodotus knew of the Jews . . . and included them in his list of those serving in the Persian king Xerxes' navy when Xerxes invaded Greece in 480 B.C.

There may have been isolated Jews living in Greek cities as far back as the Babylonian exile, but the first organized Jewish communities in Greece were established in approximately 400 B.C. The communities flourished during the reign of Alexander the Great and the subsequent Hellenistic (Greek) period in around 300 B.C. Jewish immigrants flooded Hellenist cities along the Aegean Coast and the Greek mainland.[5]

Intense debate surrounds the issue of how the Jewish people arrived in Western

---

[5] From "Greece Virtual Jewish History Tour," by Shira Sondberg, n.d., *Jewish Virtual Library*.

Europe. We will adhere to our primary focus and simply summarize the prevailing theory. Through wars, religious and ethnic persecution, slavery, trade and commerce, the Jewish people of Greece and Rome moved north and west, migrating into Eastern as well as Western Europe. Jewish migration into Western Europe was among the latest in world Jewry, around the 5th and 6th centuries A.D.[6] This makes European Jews among the youngest community of the Diaspora.

It would be from within the Ashkenazic community that the *Founding Fathers* of the modern Jewish State would emerge. Leo Pinsker, Theodor Herzl, Max Nordau, Israel Zangwill, and Ze'ev Jabotinsky were all Jews of Eastern and Western Europe.

Ashkenazic, or Jews of European ancestry, are the Jewish people with whom Americans, or Westerners, are most familiar. Because of acculturation, they are the most visible to us. This means that when one hears the word "Jew," the image evoked is usually Ashkenazim. It is important to note this because, when the entire Jewish nation is overwhelmingly identified by a single representation—in this case, the icon of a White/European—there is the danger of missing the diversity of the Jewish people.

Sadly, because of the evil and dogged persistence of antisemitism, the blind hatred of Jews, the term Jew can also mean any and everything negative. That is how a group of people are dehumanized. As Black Americans who are aware of our history, we know this all too well. Once people are reduced to a stereotypical representative, it is much easier to universally ascribe nefarious traits to those people and summarily dismiss them. As Nigerian author, Chimamanda Adichie said, "Show a person as one thing and only one thing, and that is what they become."[7]

---

[6] See *A Historical Atlas of the Jewish People: From the Time of the Patriarchs to the Present*, 1992, in E. Barnavi (Ed.) for more information on the Jewish Diaspora.

[7] In "The Danger of a Single Story," (2009), now one of the most viewed TED talks of all time, author Chimamanda Ngozi Adichie explains how receiving a "single story" creates stereotypes and leads to critical misunderstanding.

JEWS OF THE MIDDLE EAST AND NORTH AFRICA

The Jewish communities of the Middle East and North Africa (Mizrahi Jews) are the most ancient. Mizrahi Jews' connection to the land of Israel goes back to the beginning of the nation over 3,000 years. They are the Jews of Iran, Iraq, Egypt, Syria, Lebanon, Libya, Tunisia, Morocco, Yemen, and Turkey. The vast majority of the Jews from those lands became citizens of Israel after 1948. Iran and Iraq are part of the ancient Persian and Babylonian Empires, respectively, and the Jews of those regions trace their ancestry back to the First Temple period (500 B.C.). An excellent resource on these Jewish communities is JIMENA – Jews Indigenous to the Middle East & North Africa, based in San Francisco.

Today, there are over 8,000 Jews who still live in Iran, ancient Persia. The Iranian government will not allow them to leave. In 2014, it was discovered that several Iranian Jews, whose whereabouts were unknown for twenty years, were killed while attempting to flee Iran for Israel.

> According to Channel 10, the eight Iranian Jews who sought to escape in 1994 were instructed by Israeli officials to travel to the Zahedan region in eastern Iran, where they would meet with a contact from a local tribe who would smuggle them over the Pakistani border. From there they would be flown to Turkey or Cyprus and then Israel.
>
> However, the plan went fatally awry: The eight traveled in three separate groups. Two of these groups were killed by Iranian security forces who believed them to be members of the Mujahedeen-e-Khalq, a group of Iranian dissidents that opposes the clerical regime and has conducted militant operations against its forces.[8]

There are still Jews in Iran who also wish to make *aliyah* (return home to Israel). Over 70 years after Israel's rebirth, there are Jews who are trying desperately to return to their homeland. Yet, their enemies will not allow them to leave.

As the Diversity Outreach Coordinator for Christians United for Israel (CUFI), in 2017, I helped lead the only Christian effort to tell the story of the Mizrahi Jews called *The Mizrahi Project*. The Mizrahi Project is a series of short films

---

[8] From "Missing Iranian Jews were mistaken for rebels, killed by authorities," 2014, by I. Sharon and T. Staff, *The Times of Israel*.

featuring stories of Jews who were expelled or forced to flee from what are now Arabized or Islamic lands. There are nearly one million of these *Forgotten Refugees*. One potential interviewee for the project was an Iranian Jewish woman living in Los Angeles. My team and I were connected to the young lady from the Persian Jewish community there. I'll call her *Riyah*. Riyah thanked us for our efforts but declined to appear in the series as she still has family in Iran. She did not doubt that, once her video was seen, the Iranian regime would imprison or otherwise harm her loved ones.

That moment brought home a sobering reality to me. My colleagues and I were telling the stories of past bondage and freedom, yet there are still thousands of Jews being held against their will in Iran today. While we were free to speak about their suffering, Riyah was not. As a Black American, I am free to protest and even rectify any injustice my community faces. As a Persian Jew with a family still under the yoke of the Iranian regime, Riyah could not tell her story. We became her voice.

JEWS OF SPAIN AND PORTUGAL

This Jewish community from Spain is known as the Sephardim. The history of Spanish Jewry dates back at least two thousand years when the Romans destroyed the Second Temple in Jerusalem and brought Jews back to Europe.[9] The Jewish people of Spain and Portugal experienced virtually the same treatment of their kin worldwide—times of great success and achievement and times of great persecution and death. In 1492, King Ferdinand and Queen Isabella issued the Alhambra Decree expelling all Jews from Spain by July 31st.

> It is estimated that more than 235,000 Jews lived in Spain before the inquisition. Of these, approximately 165,000 immigrated to neighboring countries (mostly to Italy, England, Holland, Morocco, Egypt, France, and the Americas), 50,000 converted to Christianity, and 20,000 died en route to a new location.[10]

The Sephardim are the descendants of those expelled from Spain and survived

---

[9] From "Spain Virtual Jewish History Tour," by Jewish Virtual Library, n.d., *Jewish Virtual Library*.

[10] See previous footnote.

their journey to their next adopted home.

JEWS OF INDIA AND BURMA

From Shavei Israel:

> The B'nei Menashe (sons/children of Manasseh) claim descent from one of the Ten Lost Tribes of Israel, who were sent into exile by the Assyrian Empire more than 27 centuries ago.
>
> Their ancestors wandered through Central Asia and the Far East for centuries, before settling in what is now northeastern India, along the border with Burma and Bangladesh.[11]

Many B'nei Menashe have been returning to Israel over the past few years. Unlike the vast majority of their Diaspora brethren, the Jews of India fared relatively better. Included in the Indian/Burmese Jewish branch are the Jews of Calcutta and the Cochin Jews.

> The first Jews to come to India were the Jews in Cochin in southern India (today, it's the port city of Kochi) were the so-called "Black Jews," who traditionally spoke the Judeo-Malayalam tongue, native to the state of Kerala. Some say that these "Black Jews" settled in the Malabar coast during the times of King Solomon of Israel, and after the Kingdom of Israel split into two. The Pardesi Jews, also called the "White Jews" settled later, coming to India from western European nations such as Holland and Spain, and spoke the ancient Sephardic language of Ladino. A notable settlement of Spanish and Portuguese Jews starting in the 15th century was Goa, but this settlement eventually disappeared. In the 17th and 18th centuries, Cochin had an influx of Jewish settlers from the Middle East, North Africa, and Spain.[12]

JEWS OF CHINA

From Shavei Israel:

---

[11] From "Bnei Menashe," by Shavei Israel, n.d., *Shavei Israel*.

[12] From "India Virtual Jewish History Tour," by Jewish Virtual Library, n.d., *Jewish Virtual Library*.

The first Jews arrived in Kaifeng, one of the capitals of imperial China, over a thousand years ago, when Jewish merchants from Persia settled in the area.

At its height, in the Middle Ages, Kaifeng's Jewish community numbered as many as 5,000 people, with rabbis, synagogues and various communal institutions.

But assimilation eventually began to take its toll. The last rabbi of Kaifeng died two centuries ago, and by the middle of the 19th century, the community was forced to sell the synagogue, Torah scrolls and its other remaining assets.

Until today, however, there are between 500 and 1,000 identifiable descendants of the Jewish community, and in recent years an awakening has been taking place among them, as increasing numbers of young Kaifeng Jews seek to reclaim their heritage.[13]

JEWS OF PERU

There is much speculation about Christopher Columbus' journey to the New World. Some say that Columbus was Jewish and was seeking a new home for the Jews who had been exiled from Spain. Whether or not Columbus was Jewish, we know that Jews were on the vessels with him as they were being expelled by King Ferdinand and Queen Isabella. Those Jews may have settled on the coast of South America near Colombia, Ecuador, and Peru.

There were also Jews who came to Peru during the rubber boom of the 19th century. On June 21, 2009, the New York Times featured the following article on these Sephardic Jews.

> "It was astounding to discover that in Iquitos there existed this group of people who were desperate to reconnect to their roots and re-establish ties to the broader Jewish world," said Lorry Salcedo Mitrani, the director of a new documentary, "The Fire Within," about the Jews of the Peruvian

---
[13] From "The Kaifeng Jews," by Shavei Israel, n.d., *Shavei Israel*.

Amazon.

Scholars compare the Jews here with groups like the Hispanic crypto-Jews of the southwestern United States and northern Mexico, the Lemba of southern Africa or the Bene Israel of India, who in varying ways have sought to reclaim a Jewish identity that had seemingly been weakened through time.[14]

JEWS OF JAMAICA

Like the Jews of Latin America, the Jews of Jamaica are of Sephardic ancestry. Jews have lived in Jamaica since 1530 with their numbers growing to an estimated 400,000. Today their community is notably smaller.

Most of Jamaica's Jews left for Britain, the U.S. and Canada between 1962, when Jamaica became independent, and the 1970s, when political unrest was widespread. This sharply reduced the island's Jewish population, which by 1978 had only 350 remaining.

This sharp reduction in so short a period seems to have lit a desire to survive among those remaining. In 1969 a Hillel School was founded by the United Congregation of Israelites in Kingston as a secular private primary and secondary school.[15]

During the Spanish Inquisition, Jews were forced to convert to Christianity or were killed by the Catholic Church.

JEWS OF AFRICA

In his article, *Choosing to be Chosen: Religious leaders gather to challenge notions of "Who is a Jew?"*, author Don Lattin shared this anecdote.

> A little known story is that of the African Jewish Diaspora, which has received relatively little scholarly attention. When Ethiopian-born

---

[14] From "Adopting forebears' faith and leaving Peru for Israel," by S. Romero, 2009, *New York Times*.

[15] From "Jamaica," by Shavei Israel, n.d., *Shavei Israel*.

Ephraim Isaac is greeted with the question familiar to many diverse Jews, "Are you Jewish? You don't look Jewish," he sometimes responds, "Ethiopia is mentioned in the Bible over 50 times, but Poland not once."[16]

Years ago, I had a friendly debate with a colleague. We were discussing the Israelite Diaspora and the history of African Jews. My colleague was incredulous to the entire notion of non-European Jews, basing his rebuttal almost entirely on pictures and movies about the Bible. At some point, my colleague stopped talking and began staring at the map on the wall in the room. After several moments of silence, he said, "I never realized how close Israel was to Africa. I never realized where Israel was."

Find Cairo in northeastern Egypt and move up to Jerusalem, Israel

I share that story not to ridicule my colleague nor to champion my "knowledge." I share it as a reminder that everyone has a frame of reference, a starting point. Our understanding of something is based first and foremost on how we understand things. Though my colleague was educated, he did not know geography—particularly Africa and the Middle East. Simply seeing Israel on a map was his starting point in understanding Israel's proximity to Africa.

As we discussed in chapter one, Israelites have lived in the land of Ham (ancient Egypt and Cush — Africa) since before Israel became a nation. We recounted

---

[16] From "Choosing to be Chosen: Religious leaders gather to challenge notions of 'Who is a Jew?'" by D. Lattin, 2008, *California Magazine*.

Abraham and Sarah's sojourn through Egypt at the time of famine and how two generations later, Jacob and his sons joined Joseph in Egypt during yet another famine. For 430 years, the children of Jacob/Israel lived among the children of Mizraim (Egypt), much of that time as slaves. And we explained how Jethro's daughters mistook Moses for an Egyptian, suggesting that there was virtually no physical distinction between ancient Hebrews (Semites) and ancient Egyptians (Hamites).

Exploring the African Israelite Diaspora, we must bear in mind that civilization (e.g. education, laws, provinces, commerce, language, culture) started in the East. The Table of Nations lists the descendants of each of Noah's three sons and the lands they established. The first prominent figures in Genesis 10.6-10 are the progeny of Ham and Shem. Ham's grandson, Nimrod, is the first to establish nations as a "mighty hunter."

> Genesis 10.6-10
>
> *6 And the sons of Ham were Cush (Ethiopia) and Mizraim (Egypt) and Put (Libya) and Canaan. 7 And the sons of Cush were Seba and Havilah and Sabta and Raamah and Sabtecha, and the sons of Raamah were Sheba and Dedan. 8 And Cush begot Nimrod; he began to be a mighty man in the land. 9 He was a mighty hunter before the Lord; therefore it is said, "Like Nimrod, a mighty hunter before the Lord." 10 And the beginning of his kingdom was Babylon and Erech and Accad and Calneh, in the land of Shinar.*
>
> ו וּבְנֵי חָם כּוּשׁ וּמִצְרַיִם וּפוּט וּכְנָעַן:
> ז וּבְנֵי כוּשׁ סְבָא וַחֲוִילָה וְסַבְתָּה וְרַעְמָה וְסַבְתְּכָא וּבְנֵי רַעְמָה שְׁבָא וּדְדָן:
> ח וְכוּשׁ יָלַד אֶת־נִמְרֹד הוּא הֵחֵל לִהְיוֹת גִּבֹּר בָּאָרֶץ:
> ט הוּא־הָיָה גִבֹּר־צַיִד לִפְנֵי יְהוָה עַל־כֵּן יֵאָמַר כְּנִמְרֹד גִּבּוֹר צַיִד לִפְנֵי יְהוָה:
> י וַתְּהִי רֵאשִׁית מַמְלַכְתּוֹ בָּבֶל וְאֶרֶךְ וְאַכַּד וְכַלְנֵה בְּאֶרֶץ שִׁנְעָר:
>
> (The Complete Jewish Bible with Rashi Commentary, Genesis 10.6-10)

These nations dominate the pages of the Old Testament and the first chapters of world history books. Next, we read of the descendants of Japheth, Noah's youngest son—Greece (Javan), Rome, Gog, Magog, Ashkenaz, etc., in Genesis 10.2-5. It is in the New Testament that Rome (preceded by Greece) is a world empire. God showed Daniel through Nebuchadnezzar's vision in Daniel 3, world power shifts over thousands of years from East to West (Babylon, Persia,

Greece, Rome).

People driven from their homeland and forced to find ways to survive would naturally flee toward economic opportunity. This is basic human nature. For the ancient Jews, Egypt was the first choice when seeking refuge—a pattern established first by Abraham and facilitated by the wealth and military might of Egypt. As we mentioned in chapter one, the Jews had become so dependent on Egypt that God told the prophet Isaiah to issue this warning:

> Isaiah 30.2–3
> 2 *Those who go to descend to Egypt, and they have not asked of My mouth, to strengthen themselves with the strength of Pharaoh and to take shelter in the shade of Egypt.*
> 3 *And the strength of Pharaoh shall be to you for shame, and the shelter in the shade of Egypt for disgrace.*
>
> ב הַהֹלְכִים֙ לָרֶ֣דֶת מִצְרַ֔יִם וּפִ֖י לֹ֣א שָׁאָ֑לוּ לָעוֹז֙ בְּמָע֣וֹז פַּרְעֹ֔ה וְלַחְס֖וֹת בְּצֵ֥ל מִצְרָֽיִם׃
> ג וְהָיָ֥ה לָכֶ֛ם מָע֥וֹז פַּרְעֹ֖ה לְבֹ֑שֶׁת וְהֶחָס֥וּת בְּצֵל־מִצְרַ֖יִם לִכְלִמָּֽה׃
>
> (The Complete Jewish Bible with Rashi Commentary, Isaiah 30.1-2)

Like their North African and Middle Eastern brethren, the story of the Jews in the African Diaspora is ancient, a saga of more than 3,000-years interwoven in the history of the Motherland. It involves the Israelites' migration through Africa, the rise of Islam, and its effect on the African Jewish Diaspora, as well as the Trans-Atlantic Slave Trade. Again, this is a summarization and will be further detailed in the sequel to this book *The Israelite Diaspora: Understanding Israel's Multiethnic Identity and Her Prophetic Return to The Land*.

An overview of the history of the Jews of Africa suggests the existence of three main branches:

1. Ethiopian - East African
2. Lemba - Southern African
3. Igbo - West African

ETHIOPIAN JEWS

As previously stated, Ethiopia and Egypt's relationship with Israel pre-dates the founding of the ancient Israelite nation. Through the Queen of Sheba's visit to King Solomon (1 Kings 10) and the Ethiopian eunuch's visit to Jerusalem (Acts 8), we have also demonstrated the normalcy of travel between the two regions. Finally, we learned that ancient Ethiopia was not only a much larger territory in antiquity, but it also comprised part of present-day Saudi Arabia near the Horn of Africa.

During the First Temple period (900 B.C.), it is believed that some Israelites, including the priestly Levitical tribe, relocated to Senaah in anticipation of a pending civil war. Senaah is modern day Yemen, part of the region of ancient-day Cush. These Israelites would have been spared during the eventual destruction of Jerusalem by Nebuchadnezzar (586 B.C.). The Bible tells us that at the rebuilding of Jerusalem under Nehemiah's leadership, almost 4,000 of the Levites in Senaah returned.

> Nehemiah 7.6, 38
> *6 These are the people of the province who went up from the captivity of the exile, whom Nebuchadnezzar the king of Babylon had exiled to Babylon, and they returned to Jerusalem and to Judea, each one to his city.*
>
> *38 The children of Senaah were three thousand nine hundred and thirty.*
>
> ו אֵלֶּה | בְּנֵי הַמְּדִינָה הָעֹלִים מִשְּׁבִי הַגּוֹלָה אֲשֶׁר הֶגְלָה נְבוּכַדְנֶצַּר מֶלֶךְ בָּבֶל וַיָּשׁוּבוּ לִירוּשָׁלַם וְלִיהוּדָה אִישׁ לְעִירוֹ:
>
> ל חבְּנֵי סְנָאָה שְׁלֹשֶׁת אֲלָפִים תְּשַׁע מֵאוֹת וּשְׁלֹשִׁים:
>
> (The Complete Jewish Bible with Rashi Commentary, Nehemiah 7.6, 38)

Throughout their long history in Ethiopia, Beta Israel (house of Israel) suffered greatly at the hands of the Ethiopian government and many of its citizens. After several unsuccessful attempts since Israel's independence in 1948, the Ethiopian Jews remained determined to reach their homeland, and set out on foot across the Sudanese border. During the 1980s and 1990s, some 4,000 souls perished in the dangerous journey from Ethiopia and across the border into Sudan, where the Israeli government eventually airlifted them home. Some died of exhaustion, some of starvation. Some were murdered by Sudanese who discovered Jews in the country. Beta Israel gave their lives marching to Zion. Each year, the state of Israel commemorates the sacrifice of the Ethiopian Jews in a special ceremony during Jerusalem Day on the 28th of Iyar (late May-early June).

There are countless testimonies of God's miracle working power within the Ethiopian *aliyah* (immigration or return to their homeland in Israel). In 2013, I had the honor of interviewing Ms. Pnina Tamano-Shata, Israel's newly appointed Aliyah and Integration Minister. Pnina was part of Operation Moses (1984), Israel's secret airlift of the Ethiopian Jews who crossed the border into Sudan. I will never forget what she shared about her story.

> They loaded us up on the trucks in the middle of the night, and the IDF (Israel Defense Forces) loaded us up on the Hercules planes. My father put me and my four siblings on one truck, so my mother and two other siblings ended up on another truck. [Their] truck collapsed during the night, but we weren't told of the accident because it would break the secrecy and endanger the success of the operation. So, they needed to stay behind.[17]

Pnina's mother and two siblings were left in Sudan. The IDF and Israeli secret service (Mossad) spent a year searching for them and found them. The family was reunited in Israel.

LEMBA JEWS

In the mid-1990s the Lemba tribe of southern Africa made headlines for having the DNA of the Levitical tribe, or the cohen gene. Scholars and laymen have been debating the significance of the findings since they were released.

> Recent work has brought the Lemba to international attention. The chief reason for this are genetic studies that have suggested that the Lemba may have something like "Jewish" ancestry. The original research which seemed to be reaching towards this conclusion was carried out

---

[17] Pnina Tamano-Shata during an interview with Institute for Black Solidarity with Israel (IBSI), 2013. Copyright 2013 by IBSI.

by Professor Trefor Jenkins of the South African Institute for Medical Research and the University of the Witwatersrand in Johannesburg. Jenkins had the idea of trying to determine the origin of the Lemba by collecting genetic material from the tribe. The reason for this is that one tribal tradition had it that the original Lemba immigrants from the north, from Sena, were males who subsequently took local African wives. Jenkins argued that if the Y-chromosome of the Lemba, which only passes down the male line, could be shown to originate in some specific part of the world, it might be possible to determine where the Lemba were from.[18]

If one accepts these DNA results, the Lemba are the most genetically authentic Levites in the world.

IGBO JEWS

As we've mentioned, the Igbo of West Africa trace their lineage back to the Israelites who fled the Holy Land before 586 B.C. The Israelite tribes believed to have made the trek westward include Gad, Asher, and Naphtali. Remy Ilona's *The Igbos and Israel: An Inter-cultural Study of the Oldest and Largest Jewish Diaspora* is a thorough and detailed work on the subject.

As varied as each ethnic group we've mentioned, anthropologist Cheikh Diop said this about the Semitic physical features:

> All Semites (Arabs and Jews), as well as the quasi-totality of Latin Americans, are mixed breed of Blacks and Whites. All prejudice aside, this interbreeding can still be detected in the eyes, lips, nails, and hair of most Jews."[19]

Israel's independence in 1948 was the official end to almost two millennia of dispossession. The Jewish people had been without a homeland since the Romans destroyed their place of worship and the Holy City during the First Century A.D.

---

[18] From "Lemba," by Jewish Virtual Library, n.d., *Jewish Virtual Library*.

[19] From "Critical Review of the Most Recent Theses of the Origin of Humanity," by C. A. Diop, 1991, *Civilization or Barbarism: An Authentic Anthropology*, p. 65. Copyright 1991 by Lawrence Hill Books.

God used the Gentile nations to scatter the people of Israel. He is now using them to gather their descendants. Non-Jewish or Christian organizations are helping thousands of diaspora Jews make aliyah.

BLACK HEBREW ISRAELITES

Very generally speaking, the Black Hebrew Israelites (BHI) are three distinct, separate groups. The first group was established in America around the late 1800s by Black preachers like William S. Crowdy. Crowdy taught that Black people were physical descendants of Israel. Some of his followers embraced Judaism and sought to be a part of the broader Jewish community. The second group is the BHI of Dimona, Israel, who moved to the Holy Land from Chicago in the 1960s led by a man named Ben Ammi. The BHI of Dimona have been fully integrated into Israeli society and serve in the Israel Defense Forces (IDF). According to the Israel Ministry of Foreign Affairs:

> In the nearly 40 years since, the community has moved from being unknown, to become kibbutz Shomrei Hashalom (Guardians of Peace), one of the largest urban kibbutzim in Israel. They presently number about 2000 in Dimona, with additional families in Arad, Mitzpe Ramon and the Tiberias area.
>
> The community has become most noted for its healthy holistic lifestyle. All members are vegans, eating no meat, dairy products nor foods with chemical additives. Adult members exercise three times a week and are advised to have at least one full-body massage each month for its health benefits. They do not smoke or drink alcohol, except for naturally fermented wines they produce themselves. The health practices and organic agriculture program of the community have drawn visitors from around the world, especially government officials from Africa.[20]

The third group, and unfortunately the most visible, is a sect that not only teaches that Black Americans (among a few other groups of non-White people) are the true Israelites, but that all others are fake or impostors. This group is hostile toward White people and Ashkenazi Jews in particular. Because of their growing,

---

[20] From "The Hebrew Israelite Community," by Israel Ministry of Foreign Affairs, 2006, *Israel Ministry of Foreign Affairs*.

negative influence, we will discuss this third group in chapter five – *Anti-Zionism: Hatred for Israel*.

Many of the Jewish communities we discussed in this chapter are now home in the Jewish State. Israel is a multiethnic nation. Jews from all four corners of the earth are living together just as God declared they would. An Israeli colleague named Victor Ogbonnaya shared his insights about Israel's pluralism (Victor's father is Igbo and mother a Canadian Jew):

> "[Israel] is a country that went to great lengths to bring Jews of diverse ethnicities into its borders. Operation Solomon to bring Ethiopian Jews to Israel . . . Operation Magic Carpet for the Yemeni Jews, Operation Yachin for Moroccan Jews; the Russian Alia, which saw the immigration of over 1 million Russians to Israel. They are all viewed as Jews first. No country is free of racism, but I strongly believe that in Israel, at least as regarding to Jews of different ethnicities, integration overcomes discrimination. It's not perfect, and it takes time, but there is progress . . . Israel is diverse by choice."[21]

The one thing that separates Israel from any other democracy on earth, that distinguishes her as a light to the nations is the return of the Diaspora, what the Jewish people call The Redemption. No other nation in recorded history has ever actively sought after its people all over the earth and returned them to their home. This is the heart of Zionism—the return of the children of Israel to *Eretz Yisrael* (the land of Israel).

---

[21] From Victor Ogbonnaya on Facebook, 2013.

CHAPTER 3
ZIONISM AND THE HISTORIC BLACK STRUGGLE FOR FREEDOM

Genesis 12.1

And the Lord said to Abram, "Go forth from your land and from your birthplace and from your father's house, to the land that I will show you."

א וַיֹּאמֶר יְהֹוָה אֶל־אַבְרָם לֶךְ־לְךָ מֵאַרְצְךָ וּמִמּוֹלַדְתְּךָ וּמִבֵּית אָבִיךָ אֶל־הָאָרֶץ אֲשֶׁר אַרְאֶךָּ:

(The Complete Jewish Bible with Rashi Commentary, Genesis 12.1)

Zionism is a word with many meanings and applications used for a myriad of purposes. At its root, Zionism is the belief that Israel is the ancestral homeland of the Jewish or Israelite people. Therefore, a Zionist is a proponent of a safe, secure, sovereign Jewish nation. The challenge in offering a short definition to such a broad term is that one is certain to be contradicted or corrected. This book, however, is primarily focused on explaining biblical Zionism and what the implications are within our contemporary *and* political realities.

The Black Church's relationship to Zion is centuries old and symbolically interwoven in our own story of freedom. As mentioned in the first chapter, *Zion* is very frequently used for Black houses of worship. This is true regardless of denomination or specific affiliation. In fact, the principle of Zion as the Jewish homeland is one of the many points of identification between Black Americans and Jews—a homeland and safe haven from our enemies. For the Black Christian, spiritual Zion is the final resting place—heaven. As we discussed, the *Zion* theme is often seen in Black Church music. Though the prevalence of this theme has ebbed and flowed throughout the generations, it has always been present in the Black Church. As late as 1981, gospel music legend James Cleveland was the contributing editor to *Songs of Zion*, a collection of hymns which have been popular in the Black Church for generations.

The name *Zion* (T'ziyon צִיּוֹן) comes from the name of the fortress that King David captured from the Jebusites. He made Zion the spiritual and political capital of the Israelite nation in 900 B.C.

2 Samuel 5.7,9
7 And David conquered the stronghold of Zion which is the city of David.

9 And David dwelt in the stronghold and he called it the city of David. And David built round about from the mound and inward.

ז וַיִּלְכֹּד דָּוִד אֵת מְצֻדַת צִיּוֹן הִיא עִיר דָּוִד׃

ט וַיֵּשֶׁב דָּוִד בַּמְּצֻדָה וַיִּקְרָא־לָהּ עִיר דָּוִד וַיִּבֶן דָּוִד סָבִיב מִן־הַמִּלּוֹא וָבָיְתָה׃
(The Complete Jewish Bible with Rashi Commentary, 2 Samuel 5.7, 9)

1 Chronicles 15.1
And [David] made himself houses in the City of David, and he prepared a place for the Ark of God, and he pitched a tent for it.

א וַיַּעַשׂ־לוֹ בָתִּים בְּעִיר דָּוִיד וַיָּכֶן מָקוֹם לַאֲרוֹן הָאֱלֹהִים וַיֶּט־לוֹ אֹהֶל׃
(The Complete Jewish Bible with Rashi Commentary,
1 Chronicles 15.1)

In scripture, *Zion* is synonymous with Jerusalem (יְרוּשָׁלַיִם). The word appears some 153 times in the Bible. *Jerusalem* appears over 700 times.

Psalm 128.5
May the Lord bless you from Zion, and see the good of Jerusalem all the days of your life.

ה יְבָרֶכְךָ יְהֹוָה מִצִּיּוֹן וּרְאֵה בְּטוּב יְרוּשָׁלָ͏ִם כֹּל יְמֵי חַיֶּיךָ׃
(The Complete Jewish Bible with Rashi Commentary, Psalm 128.5)

Psalm 135.21
Blessed is the Lord from Zion, He Who dwells in Jerusalem. Hallelujah!

כא בָּרוּךְ יְהֹוָה ׀ מִצִּיּוֹן שֹׁכֵן יְרוּשָׁלָ͏ִם הַלְלוּיָהּ׃
(The Complete Jewish Bible with Rashi Commentary, Psalm 135.21)

Joel 3.16 (Joel 4.16 in Jewish Tanakh)
And the Lord shall roar from Zion, and from Jerusalem He shall give forth His voice, and the heavens and earth shall quake, and the Lord is a shelter to His people and a stronghold for the children of Israel.

טז וַיהֹוָה מִצִּיּוֹן יִשְׁאָג וּמִירוּשָׁלַ͏ִם יִתֵּן קוֹלוֹ וְרָעֲשׁוּ שָׁמַיִם וָאָרֶץ וַיהֹוָה מַחֲסֶה לְעַמּוֹ וּמָעוֹז לִבְנֵי יִשְׂרָאֵל׃
(The Complete Jewish Bible with Rashi Commentary, Joel 4.16)

Even during biblical times, the name *Zion* was used to denote a place, an ideal or the Israelite people personified.

Psalm 97.8
Zion heard and rejoiced, and the daughters of Judah exulted, because of Your judgments, O Lord.

ח שָׁמְעָה וַתִּשְׂמַח ׀ צִיּוֹן וַתָּגֵלְנָה בְּנוֹת יְהוּדָה לְמַעַן מִשְׁפָּטֶיךָ יְהֹוָה׃
(The Complete Jewish Bible with Rashi Commentary, Psalm 97.8)

Isaiah 52.1
Awaken, awaken, put on your strength, O Zion; put on the garments of your beauty, Jerusalem the Holy City, for no longer shall the uncircumcised or the unclean continue to enter you.

א עוּרִי עוּרִי לִבְשִׁי עֻזֵּךְ צִיּוֹן לִבְשִׁי ׀ בִּגְדֵי תִפְאַרְתֵּךְ יְרוּשָׁלַ͏ִם עִיר הַקֹּדֶשׁ כִּי לֹא יוֹסִיף יָבֹא־בָךְ עוֹד עָרֵל וְטָמֵא׃
(The Complete Jewish Bible with Rashi Commentary, Isaiah 52.1)

An Israelite is known biblically as a son or daughter of *Zion*.

Song of Solomon 3.11
Go out, O daughters of Zion, and gaze upon King Solomon, upon the crown

with which his mother crowned him on the day of his nuptials and on the day of the joy of his heart.

יא צְאֶינָה ׀ וּרְאֶינָה בְּנוֹת צִיּוֹן בַּמֶּלֶךְ שְׁלֹמֹה בָּעֲטָרָה שֶׁעִטְּרָה־לּוֹ אִמּוֹ בְּיוֹם חֲתֻנָּתוֹ וּבְיוֹם שִׂמְחַת לִבּוֹ:

(The Complete Jewish Bible with Rashi Commentary, Song of Solomon 3.11)

Joel 2.23
And the children of Zion, rejoice and jubilate with the Lord your God, for He gave you the teacher for justification, and He brought down for you rain, the early rain and the late rain in the first month.

כג וּבְנֵי צִיּוֹן גִּילוּ וְשִׂמְחוּ בַּיהֹוָה אֱלֹהֵיכֶם כִּי־נָתַן לָכֶם אֶת־הַמּוֹרֶה לִצְדָקָה וַיּוֹרֶד לָכֶם גֶּשֶׁם מוֹרֶה וּמַלְקוֹשׁ בָּרִאשׁוֹן:

(The Complete Jewish Bible with Rashi Commentary, Joel 2.23)

Christian Zionism is essentially the same as Biblical Zionism, the belief that the land of Israel was given to the Jewish people by God forever. It is an acknowledgment of the same truth found in the Old Testament and continued in the New Testament. Zion is inextricably linked to God's eternal covenant relationship with the Jewish people.

Psalm 69.35–37
35 Heaven and earth will praise Him, the seas and everything that moves therein,
36 When God saves Zion and builds the cities of Judah, and they dwell there and take possession of it. 37 And the seed of His servants inherit it, and those who love His name dwell therein.

לה יְהַלְלוּהוּ שָׁמַיִם וָאָרֶץ יַמִּים וְכָל־רֹמֵשׂ בָּם:
לו כִּי אֱלֹהִים ׀ יוֹשִׁיעַ צִיּוֹן וְיִבְנֶה עָרֵי יְהוּדָה וְיָשְׁבוּ שָׁם וִירֵשׁוּהָ:
לז וְזֶרַע־עֲבָדָיו יִנְחָלוּהָ וְאֹהֲבֵי שְׁמוֹ יִשְׁכְּנוּ־בָהּ:

(The Complete Jewish Bible with Rashi Commentary, Psalm 69.35-37)

Luke 1.54–55
54 He has helped his servant Israel, in remembrance of his mercy, as he spoke

to our fathers, 55 to Abraham and to his offspring forever.
(English Standard Version, Luke 1.54-55)

During Jesus' day, he too regarded Jerusalem as the holy city. He visited the Temple, made pilgrimage during the three annual required times (Passover, Weeks or Pentecost, and Tabernacles), and paid the Temple tax. Zionism was a fundamental principle, a core belief of every Torah-keeping Jew, including Jesus' disciples. After his death and resurrection, Jesus' disciples asked him about the restoration or self-rule to Israel, knowing full well that this was the chief purpose of the Jewish Messiah.

Acts 1.6–7
6 So when they had come together, they asked him, "Lord, will you at this time restore the kingdom to Israel?" 7 He said to them, "It is not for you to know times or seasons that the Father has fixed by his own authority."
(English Standard Version, Acts 1.6-7)

Biblical Zionism contains within it the core teaching that God promised the land of Canaan, later named *Israel* after the Israelite people, to Abram (Abraham) and his descendants. This is where we get the term, *Promised Land*.

Genesis 15.18-21
18 On that day, the Lord formed a covenant with Abram, saying, "To your seed I have given this land, from the river of Egypt until the great river, the Euphrates river.
19 The Kenites, the Kenizzites, and the Kadmonites,
20 And the Hittites and the Perizzites and the Rephaim,
21 And the Amorites and the Canaanites and the Girgashites and the Jebusites.

יח בַּיּוֹם הַהוּא כָּרַת יְהֹוָה אֶת־אַבְרָם בְּרִית לֵאמֹר לְזַרְעֲךָ נָתַתִּי אֶת־הָאָרֶץ הַזֹּאת מִנְּהַר מִצְרַיִם עַד־הַנָּהָר הַגָּדֹל נְהַר־פְּרָת:
יט אֶת־הַקֵּינִי וְאֶת־הַקְּנִזִּי וְאֵת הַקַּדְמֹנִי:
כ וְאֶת־הַחִתִּי וְאֶת־הַפְּרִזִּי וְאֶת־הָרְפָאִים:
כא וְאֶת־הָאֱמֹרִי וְאֶת־הַכְּנַעֲנִי וְאֶת־הַגִּרְגָּשִׁי וְאֶת־הַיְבוּסִי:
(The Complete Jewish Bible with Rashi Commentary,
Genesis 15.18-21)

Though Abraham did not live to see the fulfillment of this promise, Moses and the children of Israel were to physically receive the inheritance.

> Exodus 3.7–8
> *7 And the Lord said, "I have surely seen the affliction of My people who are in Egypt, and I have heard their cry because of their slave drivers, for I know their pains.*
> *8 I have descended to rescue them from the hand of the Egyptians and to bring them up from that land, to a good and spacious land, to a land flowing with milk and honey, to the place of the Canaanites, the Hittites, the Amorites, the Perizzites, the Hivvites, and the Jebusites.*

ז וַיֹּאמֶר יְהֹוָה רָאֹה רָאִיתִי אֶת־עֳנִי עַמִּי אֲשֶׁר בְּמִצְרָיִם וְאֶת־צַעֲקָתָם שָׁמַעְתִּי מִפְּנֵי נֹגְשָׂיו כִּי יָדַעְתִּי אֶת־מַכְאֹבָיו:
ח וָאֵרֵד לְהַצִּילוֹ | מִיַּד מִצְרַיִם וּלְהַעֲלֹתוֹ מִן־הָאָרֶץ הַהִוא אֶל־אֶרֶץ טוֹבָה וּרְחָבָה אֶל־אֶרֶץ זָבַת חָלָב וּדְבָשׁ אֶל־מְקוֹם הַכְּנַעֲנִי וְהַחִתִּי וְהָאֱמֹרִי וְהַפְּרִזִּי וְהַחִוִּי וְהַיְבוּסִי:

(The Complete Jewish Bible with Rashi Commentary, Exodus 3.7-8)

God delivered Moses and the Israelites from slavery in Egypt. After forty years in the wilderness of Sinai, Moses' successor, Joshua, along with Caleb, and the second generation, finally laid claim to the Promise.

> Joshua 1.2–4
> *2 Moses my servant has died; and now arise cross this Jordan, you and all this nation, to the land which I give the children of Israel.*
> *3 Every place on which the soles of your feet will tread I have given to you, as I have spoken to Moses.*
> *4 From this desert and Lebanon to the great river, the Euphrates, all the land of the Hittites to the great sea westward shall be your boundary.*

ב מֹשֶׁה עַבְדִּי מֵת וְעַתָּה קוּם עֲבֹר אֶת־הַיַּרְדֵּן הַזֶּה אַתָּה וְכָל־הָעָם הַזֶּה אֶל־הָאָרֶץ אֲשֶׁר אָנֹכִי נֹתֵן לָהֶם לִבְנֵי יִשְׂרָאֵל:
ג כָּל־מָקוֹם אֲשֶׁר תִּדְרֹךְ כַּף־רַגְלְכֶם בּוֹ לָכֶם נְתַתִּיו כַּאֲשֶׁר דִּבַּרְתִּי אֶל־מֹשֶׁה:
ד מֵהַמִּדְבָּר וְהַלְּבָנוֹן הַזֶּה וְעַד־הַנָּהָר הַגָּדוֹל נְהַר־פְּרָת כֹּל אֶרֶץ הַחִתִּים וְעַד־הַיָּם הַגָּדוֹל מְבוֹא הַשָּׁמֶשׁ יִהְיֶה גְּבוּלְכֶם:

(The Complete Jewish Bible with Rashi Commentary, Joshua 1.2-4)

Joshua led Israel into Canaan around 1400 B.C. After Joshua's death, God instituted a system of judges that ruled over different provinces. The provinces were divided by tribe, with the Levites or priestly tribe being excluded from land ownership. The Hebrew monarchy began around 1050 B.C. with the inauguration of Saul from the tribe of Benjamin. The second king of Israel was David, to whom God promised an eternal kingdom (1 Chronicles 17). For the Christian, Jesus, descendant or son of David, is the fulfillment of this promise—our soon coming King.

The Negro Spirituals about Moses (Let My People Go) and Joshua (Joshua 'Fit the Battle of Jericho) are inspirational songs about the Israelites' victory over their enemies. They are musical stories about God's miraculous works on behalf of his people. Moses was the brave leader who stood up to Pharaoh. Joshua was the warrior who led Israel to victory in the Promised Land. The Israelites were the ultimate underdogs, something Black folk have identified with since being dispossessed in Africa and sold as chattel slavery throughout the New World. For the Black slave, *Zion* became synonymous with freedom. In 1950, Thomas Dorsey, the *father of gospel music*, arranged an old spiritual that captured the layered meaning *Zion* had for Black Americans.

Old Ship of Zion

'Tis the old ship of Zion, 'Tis the old ship of Zion, 'Tis the old ship of Zion, Get on board, get on board

It has landed many a thousand, It has landed many a thousand, It has landed many a thousand, Get on board, get on board

King Jesus is the captain,
King Jesus is the captain
King Jesus is the captain
Get on board, get on board[1]

For the Black Church, Zion is the spiritual focal point. It is home for weary travelers. Zion is the reward after a life of struggle and toil; the reminder of what awaits the man or woman who's been "washed in the blood of the Lamb." This is why "King Jesus is the captain" and will lead us to our place of rest, of victory. The

---

[1] Lyrics from "Old Ship of Zion," written and arranged by T. A. Dorsey and originally recorded in Chicago, Ill., by the Roberta Martin Singers in 1950.

old hymn *We're Marching to Zion* was written by Englishman, Sir Isaac Watts in the early 18th century. It has been a staple in the Black Church for over 200 years.

We're Marching to Zion
Come, we that love the Lord, And let our joys be known; Join in a song with sweet accord, Join in a song with sweet accord, And thus surround the throne, And thus surround the throne

Refrain
We're marching to Zion, Beautiful, beautiful Zion; We're marching upward to Zion, The beautiful city of God[2]

So powerful is the concept of Zion that it transcends the Black Church into the broader community. In her landmark, self-titled hip-hop album, *The Miseducation of Lauryn Hill*, Ms. Hill incorporated a small portion of *We're Marching to Zion* in *To Zion*.

To Zion
Unsure of what the balance held
I touched my belly overwhelmed
By what I had been chosen to perform
But then an angel came one day
Told me to kneel down and pray
For unto me a man-child would be born
Woe this crazy circumstance
I knew his life deserved a chance
But everybody told me to be smart
"Look at your career," they said
"Lauryn, baby use your head"
But instead I chose to use my heart

Chorus
Now the joy of my world
Is in Zion! (Zion, Zion!)
Now the joy of my world

---

[2] Lyrics from "We're Marching to Zion," verses written by I. Watts, 1707, and chorus and composition by R. Lowry, 1867.

Is in Zion! (Zion, uhh, Zion!)

How beautiful if nothing more
Than to wait at Zion's door
I've never been in love like this before
Now let me pray to keep you from
The perils that will surely come
See life for you, my prince has just begun
And I thank you for choosing me
To come through unto life to be
A beautiful reflection of His grace
See I know that a gift so great
Is only one God could create
And I'm reminded every time I see your face

Marching, marching, marching to Zion
Marching, marching
Marching, marching, marching to Zion
Beautiful, beautiful Zion[3]

In keeping with both the ancient biblical and Black traditions, Ms. Hill uses Zion to mean more than one thing. Zion is her son, for whom the song was written. Zion is also a place of joy that God created to where we will march or procession—just like David did.

In what would become his final speech, Dr. King drew on the Zion/Promised Land imagery to encourage himself and his followers. To the uninitiated, his words may have seemed unique, but to Black Church attendees, they were as familiar as an old hymn.

> Well, I don't know what will happen now; we've got some difficult days ahead. But it really doesn't matter with me now, because I've been to the mountaintop . . . Like anybody, I would like to live a long life—longevity has its place. But I'm not concerned about that now. I just want to do God's will. And He's allowed me to go up to the mountain. And I've looked over, and I've seen the Promised Land. I may not get there with

---

[3] Lyrics from "To Zion," written by L. Hill and produced by Ruffhouse Records LP, 1998.

you. But I want you to know tonight, that we, as a people, will get to the Promised Land. And so I'm happy tonight; I'm not worried about anything; I'm not fearing any man. Mine eyes have seen the glory of the coming of the Lord.[4]

Dr. King, aware of his impending death, alluded to himself as Moses, who did not enter the Promised Land with the children of Israel. In his last public address, Dr. King announced the end of his journey, setting the stage for the *Joshua Generation* who would enter and possess Canaan. This is spiritual Zionism deeply embedded in the Black Church tradition.

A portion of Isaiah two verse two is a prophecy sung each week in synagogues all over the world. It is known as the *Key M'ztion* (out from Zion).

Isaiah 2.2–3
2 And it shall be at the end of the days, that the mountain of the Lord's house shall be firmly established at the top of the mountains, and it shall be raised above the hills, and all the nations shall stream to it.
3 And many peoples shall go, and they shall say, "Come, let us go up to the Lord's mount, to the house of the God of Jacob, and let Him teach us of His ways, and we will go in His paths," for out of Zion shall the Torah come forth, and the word of the Lord from Jerusalem.

ב וְהָיָה | בְּאַחֲרִית הַיָּמִים נָכוֹן יִהְיֶה הַר בֵּית־יְהֹוָה בְּרֹאשׁ הֶהָרִים וְנִשָּׂא מִגְּבָעוֹת וְנָהֲרוּ אֵלָיו כָּל־הַגּוֹיִם:
ג וְהָלְכוּ עַמִּים רַבִּים וְאָמְרוּ לְכוּ | וְנַעֲלֶה אֶל־הַר־יְהֹוָה אֶל־בֵּית אֱלֹהֵי יַעֲקֹב וְיֹרֵנוּ מִדְּרָכָיו וְנֵלְכָה בְּאֹרְחֹתָיו כִּי מִצִּיּוֹן תֵּצֵא תוֹרָה וּדְבַר־יְהֹוָה מִירוּשָׁלָיִם:
(The Complete Jewish Bible with Rashi Commentary, Isaiah 2.2-3)

It is from this passage in Isaiah that we find the text for one of the most famous Negro Spirituals, still sung in many Black Churches today: *Down By the Riverside*.

Isaiah 2.4
And he shall judge between the nations and reprove many peoples, and they shall beat their swords into plowshares and their spears into pruning hooks; nation shall not lift the sword against nation, neither shall they learn war

---

[4] From "I've Been to the Mountaintop," by M. L. King, Jr., 1968. Copyright 1968 by the Estate of Dr. Martin Luther King, Jr.

anymore.

ד וְשָׁפַט בֵּין הַגּוֹיִם וְהוֹכִיחַ לְעַמִּים רַבִּים וְכִתְּתוּ חַרְבוֹתָם לְאִתִּים וַחֲנִיתוֹתֵיהֶם לְמַזְמֵרוֹת לֹא־יִשָּׂא גוֹי אֶל־גּוֹי חֶרֶב וְלֹא־יִלְמְדוּ עוֹד מִלְחָמָה:

(The Complete Jewish Bible with Rashi Commentary, Isaiah 2.4)

Down by the Riverside

Gonna lay down my burden, Down by the riverside, Down by the riverside,
Down by the riverside
Gonna lay down my burden, Down by the riverside
[I ain't gonna] study war no more

Chorus

I ain't gonna study war no more, study war no more, ain't gonna study war no more I ain't gonna study war no more, study war no more, ain't gonna study oh war no more

Verses

Gonna lay down my sword and shield, Down by the riverside...

Gonna try on my long white robe, Down by the riverside...

Gonna talk with the Prince of Peace, Down by the riverside...

In the Black gospel tradition, *The River* almost exclusively referred to the Jordan, as in the Spiritual, *Roll Jordan, Roll*. The symbolic Jordan River is where one would cross to get to the Promised Land. The chariot of *Swing Low, Sweet Chariot* came to *carry me home* (Jerusalem). Zionism is found throughout Black Church songs and sermons. Whether the term is *Canaan, Israel, Promised Land, Beulah Land, Jerusalem, the Holy City, Mount Zion*, or the *Holy Hill*; these were all expressions of spiritual Zionism. For Bible-believing Christians, there is a clear line that connects historical/biblical Zion, our future home in glory, where we will be with God forever.

Psalm 132.13–14
13 For the Lord has chosen Zion; He desired it for His habitation.
14 This is My resting place forever; here I shall dwell for I desired it.

יג כִּי־בָחַר יְהֹוָה בְּצִיּוֹן אִוָּהּ לְמוֹשָׁב לוֹ:
יד זֹאת־מְנוּחָתִי עֲדֵי־עַד פֹּה אֵשֵׁב כִּי אִוִּתִיהָ:

(The Complete Jewish Bible with Rashi Commentary, Psalm 132.13-14)

Psalm 48.2–3

2 *The Lord is great and very much praised, in the city of our God, the Mount of His Sanctuary.*

3 *The fairest of branches, the joy of the entire earth- Mount Zion, by the north side, the city of a great king.*

ב גָּדוֹל יְהֹוָה וּמְהֻלָּל מְאֹד בְּעִיר אֱלֹהֵינוּ הַר־קָדְשׁוֹ:
ג יְפֵה נוֹף מְשׂוֹשׂ כָּל־הָאָרֶץ הַר־צִיּוֹן יַרְכְּתֵי צָפוֹן קִרְיַת מֶלֶךְ רָב:

(The Complete Jewish Bible with Rashi Commentary, Psalm 48.2-3)

Revelation 14.1–3

1 Then I looked, and behold, on Mount Zion stood the Lamb, and with him 144,000 who had his name and his Father's name written on their foreheads. 2 And I heard a voice from heaven like the roar of many waters and like the sound of loud thunder. The voice I heard was like the sound of harpists playing on their harps, 3 and they were singing a new song before the throne and before the four living creatures and before the elders. No one could learn that song except the 144,000 who had been redeemed from the earth.

(English Standard Version, Revelation 14.1-3)

Revelation 21.1–2

1 Then I saw a new heaven and a new earth, for the first heaven and the first earth had passed away, and the sea was no more. 2 And I saw the holy city, new Jerusalem, coming down out of heaven from God, prepared as a bride adorned for her husband.

(English Standard Version, Revelation 21.1-2)

It was the Apostle John's writings in the book of Revelation that inspired this timeless Negro Spiritual often sung in more traditional Black churches today.

Chorus
I want to be ready,

I want to be ready
I want to be ready, To walk in Jerusalem just like John
John said the city was just four-square, Walk in Jerusalem just like
John And he declared he'd meet me there, Walk in Jerusalem just like John

Oh, John, oh John, what do you say? Walk in Jerusalem just like John
That I'll be there at the coming day, Walk in Jerusalem just like John
When Peter was preaching at Pentecost, Walk in Jerusalem just like John
He was endowed with the Holy Ghost, Walk in Jerusalem just like John
If you get there before I do, Walk in Jerusalem just like John
Tell all my friends I'm a-comin' too, Walk in Jerusalem just like John

POLITICAL VS. SPIRITUAL

Though the idea of Zionism is originally rooted in scripture, the movement that ultimately saw the reestablishment of the nation of Israel was secular. Five men of the 19th and 20th centuries are known as the founding fathers of modern Zionism. Their ideas would lay the groundwork for the present Jewish State.

> The historical, moral and political arguments developed by Leo Pinsker, Theodore Herzl, Max Nordau, Israel Zangwill and Ze'ev Jabotinsky changed Jewish history. They argued that the Jewish state would save the Jewish people and serve, in the words of the great English writer George Elliott, "as a beacon of freedom amidst the despotisms of the East."
>
> These ideas have withstood the test of time. As the founding fathers predicted, without a Jewish state European Jewry was doomed. Equally, they argued that once the Jews would gather their exiles in the Promised Land and reestablish their sovereignty, they would show remarkable recuperative powers. The founding fathers of Zionism did not think antisemitic attacks would necessarily disappear once the Jews had a state of their own, but they argued presciently that a state would give them the power to defend themselves against such assaults.[5]

In addition to protecting and defending the Jewish people, Theodor Herzl was

---

[5] From "Foreword to the English Edition," by B. Netanyahu, 2012, *The Founding Fathers of Zionism*, (location 48 in Kindle edition). Balfour Books. Copyright 2012 by B. Netanyahu.

concerned with helping the one ethnic group whose historic suffering was more than comparable.

> There is still one other question arising out of the disaster of the nations which remains unsolved to this day, whose profound tragedy only a Jew can comprehend. That is the African question. Just call to mind all those terrible episodes of the slave trade, of human beings who merely, because they were black, were stolen like cattle, taken prisoner, captured and sold. Their children grew up in strange lands, the objects of contempt and hostility because their complexions were different. I am not ashamed to say, though I may expose myself to ridicule in saying so, that once I have witnessed the redemption of Israel, my people, I wish to assist in the redemption of the Africans.[6]

This thinking of a founding member of the Zionist movement is quite telling, as Israel's relationship with its African neighbors has been exemplary. While no government is without flaws or even serious mistakes, Israel's track record of good, respectful relations with African states is unprecedented. Israel has forged alliances with many African nations, including Angola, Ghana, Kenya, Uganda, Senegal, Zambia, Rwanda, Malawi, Nigeria, Ethiopia, and Tanzania. Israeli educational, agricultural, technological, business and financial expertise is at work all over the Continent and has been there for decades.

The idea of political Zionism was heralded by some leading political figures of the Black American community. They drew on the Jewish example of a revived homeland as a parallel for what the African Diaspora must do.

> W.E.B. Du Bois: The African movement must mean to us what the Zionist movement must mean to the Jews, the centralization of race effort, and the recognition of a racial front.[7]

> Malcolm X: Pan Africanism will do for the people of African descent all over the world, the same that Zionism has done for Jews all over the

---

[6] From "We are alone," by G. Meir, 1975, *My Life*, p. 371. G. P. Putnam & Sons. Copyright 1975 by Golda Meir.

[7] From "The Black Civil Rights Movement and Zionism," by L. Brenner, n. d., *The Struggle*.

world.[8]

Marcus Garvey, the father of Black Zionism, conducted his campaigns in the 1920s in the Black ghettos with the slogan, Africa for the Africans, like Asia for the Asians and Palestine [Israel] for the Jews.[9] [10]

How does a Christian reconcile the secular roots of the modern Jewish State with the spiritual promise of a restored Israelite nation? If God is the one who truly engineered Israel's restoration, what are we to do with the non-spiritual impetus of the founding fathers (Theodor Herzl was an atheist)? As Christians, we must start by understanding biblical precedent. We must return to scripture.

The dual book of Ezra-Nehemiah tells the story of Israel's redemption after seventy years of exile. In many respects, it is a foreshadowing of the almost 2,000-year Jewish exile that ended in 1948.

After Israel's 70-year exile as punishment for the sin of idolatry, as spoken by the prophet Jeremiah, God fulfilled His word to His people. He did this by using Gentiles and *secular* institutions. In Ezra, the Persian king, Cyrus, signed an order of emancipation for the Jewish people. He urged them to return to Jerusalem (Zion) and rebuild the Temple destroyed by the Babylonian king, Nebuchadnezzar.

> Ezra 1.1–4
> *1 And in the first year of Cyrus, the king of Persia, at the completion of the word of the Lord from the mouth of Jeremiah, the Lord aroused the Spirit of Cyrus, the king of Persia, and he issued a proclamation throughout his kingdom, and also in writing, saying:*
> *2 "So said Cyrus, the king of Persia, 'All the kingdoms of the earth the Lord God of the heavens delivered to me, and He commanded me to build Him a House in Jerusalem, which is in Judea.*

---

[8] From "Jews, African Americans, and Israel. The Ties That Bind," by H. Brackmon, 2010, p. 1.

[9] See "Black Nationalism, Jews and Zionism," by B. Neuberger (1996) for more information.

[10] In his 1921 speech "If you believe the Negro has a soul," Garvey speaks of an "Africa for Africans" and urges an African American audience to join other members of the Universal Negro Improvement Association and African Communities League (UNIA-ACL) in collectively working toward the establishment of an African nation and government for all members of the African Diaspora.

3 Who is among you of all His people, may his God be with him, and he may ascend to Jerusalem, which is in Judea, and let him build the House of the Lord, God of Israel; He is the God Who is in Jerusalem.

4 And whoever remains from all the places where he sojourns, the people of his place shall help him with silver and with gold and with possessions and with cattle, with the donation to the House of God, which is in Jerusalem.'

א וּבִשְׁנַת אַחַת לְכוֹרֶשׁ מֶלֶךְ פָּרַס לִכְלוֹת דְּבַר־יְהֹוָה מִפִּי יִרְמְיָה הֵעִיר יְהֹוָה אֶת־רוּחַ כֹּרֶשׁ מֶלֶךְ־פָּרַס וַיַּעֲבֶר־קוֹל בְּכָל־מַלְכוּתוֹ וְגַם־בְּמִכְתָּב לֵאמֹר:
ב כֹּה אָמַר כֹּרֶשׁ מֶלֶךְ פָּרַס כֹּל מַמְלְכוֹת הָאָרֶץ נָתַן לִי יְהֹוָה אֱלֹהֵי הַשָּׁמָיִם וְהוּא־פָקַד עָלַי לִבְנוֹת־לוֹ בַיִת בִּירוּשָׁלַ͏ִם אֲשֶׁר בִּיהוּדָה:
ג מִי־בָכֶם מִכָּל־עַמּוֹ יְהִי אֱלֹהָיו עִמּוֹ וְיַעַל לִירוּשָׁלַ͏ִם אֲשֶׁר בִּיהוּדָה וְיִבֶן אֶת־בֵּית יְהֹוָה אֱלֹהֵי יִשְׂרָאֵל הוּא הָאֱלֹהִים אֲשֶׁר בִּירוּשָׁלָ͏ִם:
ד וְכָל־הַנִּשְׁאָר מִכָּל־הַמְּקֹמוֹת אֲשֶׁר הוּא גָר־שָׁם יְנַשְּׂאוּהוּ אַנְשֵׁי מְקֹמוֹ בְּכֶסֶף וּבְזָהָב וּבִרְכוּשׁ וּבִבְהֵמָה עִם־הַנְּדָבָה לְבֵית הָאֱלֹהִים אֲשֶׁר בִּירוּשָׁלָ͏ִם:

(The Complete Jewish Bible with Rashi Commentary, Ezra 1.1-4)

In Nehemiah, it was Persian king Artaxerxes that was instrumental in financing the rebuilding of the walls of the Holy City. After requesting a leave of absence to travel to Judea and secure the well-being of his people, Nehemiah goes even further.

Nehemiah 2.6–8

6 And the king said to me- and the queen was sitting beside him-"How long will your trip take, and when will you return?" And it pleased the king, and he sent me, and I gave him a time.

7 And I said to the king, "If it pleases the king, may letters be given to me to the governors of the land beyond the river, that they escort me through until I come to Judea.

8 And a letter to Asaph, the guardian of the king's orchard, that he give me wood to make beams for the gates of the castle that belongs to the Temple and for the wall of the city and for the house to which I shall go," and the king gave me according to the good hand of my God upon me.

ו וַיֹּאמֶר לִי הַמֶּלֶךְ וְהַשֵּׁגָל | יוֹשֶׁבֶת אֶצְלוֹ עַד־מָתַי יִהְיֶה מַהֲלָכְךָ וּמָתַי תָּשׁוּב וַיִּיטַב לִפְנֵי־הַמֶּלֶךְ וַיִּשְׁלָחֵנִי וָאֶתְּנָה לוֹ זְמָן:
ז וָאוֹמַר לַמֶּלֶךְ אִם־עַל־הַמֶּלֶךְ טוֹב אִגְּרוֹת יִתְּנוּ־לִי עַל־פַּחֲווֹת עֵבֶר הַנָּהָר אֲשֶׁר יַעֲבִירוּנִי עַד אֲשֶׁר־אָבוֹא אֶל־יְהוּדָה:
ח וְאִגֶּרֶת אֶל־אָסָף שֹׁמֵר הַפַּרְדֵּס אֲשֶׁר לַמֶּלֶךְ אֲשֶׁר יִתֶּן־לִי עֵצִים לְקָרוֹת

ZIONISM AND THE HISTORIC BLACK STRUGGLE FOR FREEDOM

אֶת־שַׁעֲרֵי הַבִּירָה אֲשֶׁר־לַבַּיִת וּלְחוֹמַת הָעִיר וְלַבַּיִת אֲשֶׁר־אָבוֹא אֵלָיו וַיִּתֶּן־לִי הַמֶּלֶךְ כְּיַד־אֱלֹהַי הַטּוֹבָה עָלָי:

(The Complete Jewish Bible with Rashi Commentary, Nehemiah 2.6-8)

Nehemiah gave glory to God for favor with the king of Persia. The only previous time the Jewish people returned to their homeland after exile, Gentiles played a key and pivotal role. Historians have made the case that the Persian Empire would have benefitted from a strong ally in the region between them and North Africa as well as the Mediterranean, but this does not change the fact that the God of Israel orchestrated the restoration of Judea. Unlike Nebuchadnezzar (Daniel chapter 4), we read nothing of Cyrus' or Artaxerxes' spiritual conversion, yet they are no less used to accomplish God's will. One does not have to believe in God to be used as His servant.

This analogy is not to say that the secular, Jewish architects of modern Israel were Gentiles. The point is, the story of the latter-day redemption of the Hebrews has God's handprint just as much as Ezra-Nehemiah. There are even more parallels.

When the Israelites set their sights on rebuilding the walls of Jerusalem, in addition to the Temple which Cyrus originally decreed, they were met with fierce resistance from their enemies.

> Ezra 4.5; 11–16
> *5 And [Israel's adversaries] would hire advisors against them to frustrate their plan, all the days of Cyrus, the king of Persia, and until the kingdom of Darius, the king of Persia.*
>
> *11 This is the meaning of the letter that they sent to him, to Artaxerxes the king: "Your servants are the people of the other side of the river and Ke'eneth. 12 Let it be known to the king that the Jews who ascended from you upon us have come to Jerusalem, the rebellious and sinful city they are building, and the walls they have completed, and the walls they have joined. 13 Now let it be known to the king that if this city is built and the walls are founded, they will not give the king's due, the head tax, or the meal tax they will not give, and the tax of the kings will suffer. 14 Now, in view of this, that we wish to destroy the Temple, and it is improper for us to witness the king's disgrace, we have therefore sent and notified the king.*

15 That one should search in the annals of your fathers, and you will find in the annals, and you will know that this city is a rebellious city, and it injures kings and countries, and they have made rebellion in its midst since days of yore; because of this, this city was destroyed. 16 We make known to the king that if this city is built, and its walls founded, because of this, you will have no part in the other side of the river."

ה וְסָכְרִים עֲלֵיהֶם יוֹעֲצִים לְהָפֵר עֲצָתָם כָּל־יְמֵי כּוֹרֶשׁ מֶלֶךְ פָּרַס וְעַד־מַלְכוּת דָּרְיָוֶשׁ מֶלֶךְ פָּרָס:

יא דְּנָה פַּרְשֶׁגֶן אִגַּרְתָּא דִּי שְׁלַחוּ עֲלוֹהִי עַל־אַרְתַּחְשַׁשְׂתְּא מַלְכָּא עַבְדָּיךְ (כתיב עבדיך) אֱנָשׁ עֲבַר־נַהֲרָה וּכְעֶנֶת:
יב יְדִיעַ לֶהֱוֵא לְמַלְכָּא דִּי יְהוּדָיֵא דִּי סְלִקוּ מִן־לְוָתָךְ עֲלֶינָא אֲתוֹ לִירוּשְׁלֶם קִרְיְתָא מָרָדְתָּא וּבְאִישְׁתָּא בָּנַיִן וְשׁוּרַיָּא (כתיב ושורי) שַׁכְלִלוּ (כתיב אשכללו) וְאֻשַּׁיָּא יַחִיטוּ:
יג כְּעַן יְדִיעַ לֶהֱוֵא לְמַלְכָּא דִּי הֵן קִרְיְתָא דָךְ תִּתְבְּנֵא וְשׁוּרַיָּא יִשְׁתַּכְלְלוּן מִנְדָּה בְלוֹ וַהֲלָךְ לָא יִנְתְּנוּן וְאַפְּתֹם מַלְכִים תְּהַנְזִק:
יד כְּעַן כָּל־קֳבֵל דִּי־מְלַח הֵיכְלָא מְלַחְנָא וְעַרְוַת מַלְכָּא לָא אֲרִיךְ לַנָא לְמֶחֱזֵא עַל־דְּנָה שְׁלַחְנָא וְהוֹדַעְנָא לְמַלְכָּא:
טו דִּי יְבַקַּר בִּסְפַר דָּכְרָנַיָּא דִּי אֲבָהָתָךְ וּתְהַשְׁכַּח בִּסְפַר דָּכְרָנַיָּא וְתִנְדַּע דִּי קִרְיְתָא דָךְ קִרְיָא מָרָדָא וּמְהַנְזְקַת מַלְכִין וּמְדִנָן וְאֶשְׁתַּדּוּר עָבְדִין בְּגַוַּהּ מִן־יוֹמָת עָלְמָא עַל־דְּנָה קִרְיְתָא דָךְ הָחָרְבַת:
טז מְהוֹדְעִין אֲנַחְנָה לְמַלְכָּא דִּי הֵן קִרְיְתָא דָךְ תִּתְבְּנֵא וְשׁוּרַיָּה יִשְׁתַּכְלְלוּן לָקֳבֵל דְּנָה חֲלָק בַּעֲבַר נַהֲרָא לָא אִיתַי לָךְ:

(The Complete Jewish Bible with Rashi Commentary, Ezra 4.5; 11-16)

This letter was full of propaganda and distorted facts, something Israel has known all of its existence. While it was true that full sovereignty was the ultimate goal of the Israelite people rebuilding the wall, it was not true that Jerusalem was a *rebellious and sinful city*, at least not rebellious to Persia. Israel had no history of affecting any kingdoms or provinces outside of her God-given boundaries. The wars Israel fought against nations like Syria, Babylon, and Persia were all initiated by those nations—not Israel. Yet the King ordered the Jews to stop rebuilding Jerusalem, which would not resume until Nehemiah came later. However, once Nehemiah did arrive, he too faced bitter opposition from Israel's enemies.

Nehemiah 2.19
Then Sanbalat the Horonite, and Tobiah the Ammonite slave, and Geshem the Arab heard, and they mocked us and despised us, and they said, "What is this thing that you are doing? Are you rebelling against the king?"

יט וַיִּשְׁמַע סַנְבַלַּט הַחֹרֹנִי וְטֹבִיָּה | הָעֶבֶד הָעַמּוֹנִי וְגֶשֶׁם הָעַרְבִי וַיַּלְעִגוּ לָנוּ וַיִּבְזוּ עָלֵינוּ וַיֹּאמְרוּ מָה־הַדָּבָר הַזֶּה אֲשֶׁר אַתֶּם עֹשִׂים הַעַל הַמֶּלֶךְ אַתֶּם מֹרְדִים:

(The Complete Jewish Bible with Rashi Commentary, Nehemiah 2.19)

Nehemiah 3.33–35

33 And it came to pass when Sanballat heard that we were building the wall, he became wroth and was very angry, and he ridiculed the Jews.

34 And he spoke before his brethren and the army of Samaria, and he said, "What are the feeble Jews doing? Will they let them? Will they sacrifice? Will they finish in one day? Will they revive the stones from the heaps of dust, for they are burnt?"

35 And Tobiah the Ammonite was beside him, and he said, "Even what they build, if a fox comes up and breaches the wall of their stones?"

לג וַיְהִי כַּאֲשֶׁר שָׁמַע סַנְבַלַּט כִּי־אֲנַחְנוּ בוֹנִים אֶת־הַחוֹמָה וַיִּחַר לוֹ וַיִּכְעַס הַרְבֵּה וַיַּלְעֵג עַל־הַיְּהוּדִים:
לד וַיֹּאמֶר | לִפְנֵי אֶחָיו וְחֵיל שֹׁמְרוֹן וַיֹּאמֶר מָה הַיְּהוּדִים הָאֲמֵלָלִים עֹשִׂים הֲיַעַזְבוּ לָהֶם הֲיִזְבָּחוּ הַיְכַלּוּ בַיּוֹם הַיְחַיּוּ אֶת־הָאֲבָנִים מֵעֲרֵמוֹת הֶעָפָר וְהֵמָּה שְׂרוּפוֹת:
לה וְטוֹבִיָּה הָעַמֹּנִי אֶצְלוֹ וַיֹּאמֶר גַּם אֲשֶׁר־הֵם בּוֹנִים אִם־יַעֲלֶה שׁוּעָל וּפָרַץ חוֹמַת אַבְנֵיהֶם:

(The Complete Jewish Bible with Rashi Commentary, Nehemiah 3.33-35)

Nehemiah 4.1–2; 5

1 Now it came to pass when Sanballat, and Tobiah, and the Arabs, and the Ammonites, and the Ashdodites heard that the wall of Jerusalem was repaired, that the people who were exposed had commenced to be closed in, that they became very angered.

2 And they all banded together to come to wage war against Jerusalem and to wreak destruction therein.

5 And our adversaries said, "They will not know and they will not see until we come into their midst, and we shall slay them and stop the work."

לג וַיְהִי כַּאֲשֶׁר שָׁמַע סַנְבַלַּט כִּי־אֲנַחְנוּ בוֹנִים אֶת־הַחוֹמָה וַיִּחַר לוֹ וַיִּכְעַס הַרְבֵּה וַיַּלְעֵג עַל־הַיְּהוּדִים:
לד וַיֹּאמֶר | לִפְנֵי אֶחָיו וְחֵיל שֹׁמְרוֹן וַיֹּאמֶר מָה הַיְּהוּדִים הָאֲמֵלָלִים עֹשִׂים

הֶיַעַזְבוּ לָהֶם הַיִזְבָּחוּ הַיְכַלּוּ בַיּוֹם הַיְחַיּוּ אֶת־הָאֲבָנִים מֵעֲרֵמוֹת הֶעָפָר וְהֵמָּה שְׂרוּפוֹת:
לה וְטוֹבִיָּה הָעַמֹּנִי אֶצְלוֹ וַיֹּאמֶר גַּם אֲשֶׁר־הֵם בּוֹנִים אִם־יַעֲלֶה שׁוּעָל וּפָרַץ חוֹמַת אַבְנֵיהֶם:

(The Complete Jewish Bible with Rashi Commentary, Nehemiah 3.33-35)

Nehemiah 6.1–2

1 Now it came to pass, when it was heard by Sanballat, Tobiah, Geshem the Arab, and the rest of our enemies that I had built the wall, and that no breach was left therein; also that until that time I had not erected doors in the gates.

2 Then Sanballat and Geshem sent to me, saying, "Come and let us meet together in Kefirim in the Valley of Ono"; and they were plotting to do me harm.

א וַיְהִי כַאֲשֶׁר נִשְׁמַע לְסַנְבַלַּט וְטוֹבִיָּה וּלְגֶשֶׁם הָעַרְבִי וּלְיֶתֶר אֹיְבֵינוּ כִּי בָנִיתִי אֶת־הַחוֹמָה וְלֹא־נוֹתַר בָּהּ פָּרֶץ גַּם עַד־הָעֵת הַהִיא דְּלָתוֹת לֹא־הֶעֱמַדְתִּי בַשְּׁעָרִים:
ב וַיִּשְׁלַח סַנְבַלַּט וְגֶשֶׁם אֵלַי לֵאמֹר לְכָה וְנִוָּעֲדָה יַחְדָּו בַּכְּפִירִים בְּבִקְעַת אוֹנוֹ וְהֵמָּה חֹשְׁבִים לַעֲשׂוֹת לִי רָעָה:

(The Complete Jewish Bible with Rashi Commentary, Nehemiah 6.1-2)

The biblical story of the rebuilding of Jerusalem is also the story of Israel's enemies opposing it at every turn. From the Amalekites, Moabites, and Ammonites of the Bible, to the Muslim Brotherhood, Hezbollah, and Iranian Ayatollahs of today, Israel has always been threatened by those who hate her. Some believe that the lack of *peace in the Middle East* is a sign that God did not author the reestablishment of the Jewish State. On the contrary, it confirms it, and we have biblical precedent to attest to it. Peace will ultimately happen in the region and the world when the Messiah comes—on this, both Jews and Christians agree.

We also have biblical precedent for understanding God's heart and mind concerning the Jewish people. God's promise to Abraham that those who blessed him and his seed would be blessed, and those who cursed him would be cursed is echoed far beyond Genesis 12. The same God who consistently identifies Himself as the *God of Abraham, Isaac and Jacob* is the protector and defender of the Jewish people today. Black Christians have always known this; we've always

ZIONISM AND THE HISTORIC BLACK STRUGGLE FOR FREEDOM

known the *people of the Book* are God's chosen. This is especially true in America, as evidenced in our songs, our sermons, our struggle, our pain, and our triumphs. We have always identified with the people who have been persecuted from their beginning. *Zionism* represents peace and security for the Israelites and refuge from their enemies.

Joel 3.1-7 (Joel 4.1-7 in the Jewish Tanakh)
1 For behold, in those days and in that time when I return the captivity of Judah and Jerusalem,
2 I will gather all the nations and I will take them down to the Valley of Jehoshaphat, and I will contend with them there concerning My people and My heritage, Israel, which they scattered among the nations, and My land they divided.
3 And upon My people they cast lots, and they gave a boy for a harlot, and a girl they sold for wine, and they drank.
4 And also, what are you to Me, Tyre and Sidon and all the regions of Philistia? Are you paying Me recompense? And if you are recompensing Me, I will swiftly return your recompense upon your head.
5 For My silver and My gold you took, and My goodly treasures you have brought into your temples.
6 And the children of Judah and the children of Jerusalem you have sold to the children of the Jevanim, in order to distance them from their border.
7 Behold I arouse them from the place where you sold them, and I will return your recompense upon your head.

א כִּי הִנֵּה בַּיָּמִים הָהֵמָּה וּבָעֵת הַהִיא אֲשֶׁר אָשִׁיב (כתיב אָשׁוּב) אֶת־שְׁבוּת יְהוּדָה וִירוּשָׁלִָם:
ב וְקִבַּצְתִּי אֶת־כָּל־הַגּוֹיִם וְהוֹרַדְתִּים אֶל־עֵמֶק יְהוֹשָׁפָט וְנִשְׁפַּטְתִּי עִמָּם שָׁם עַל־עַמִּי וְנַחֲלָתִי יִשְׂרָאֵל אֲשֶׁר פִּזְּרוּ בַגּוֹיִם וְאֶת־אַרְצִי חִלֵּקוּ:
ג וְאֶל־עַמִּי יַדּוּ גוֹרָל וַיִּתְּנוּ הַיֶּלֶד בַּזּוֹנָה וְהַיַּלְדָּה מָכְרוּ בַיַּיִן וַיִּשְׁתּוּ:
ד וְגַם מָה־אַתֶּם לִי צֹר וְצִידוֹן וְכֹל גְּלִילוֹת פְּלָשֶׁת הַגְּמוּל אַתֶּם מְשַׁלְּמִים עָלָי וְאִם־גֹּמְלִים אַתֶּם עָלַי קַל מְהֵרָה אָשִׁיב גְּמֻלְכֶם בְּרֹאשְׁכֶם:
ה אֲשֶׁר־כַּסְפִּי וּזְהָבִי לְקַחְתֶּם וּמַחֲמַדַּי הַטֹּבִים הֲבֵאתֶם לְהֵיכְלֵיכֶם:
ו וּבְנֵי יְהוּדָה וּבְנֵי יְרוּשָׁלִַם מְכַרְתֶּם לִבְנֵי הַיְּוָנִים לְמַעַן הַרְחִיקָם מֵעַל גְּבוּלָם:
ז הִנְנִי מְעִירָם מִן־הַמָּקוֹם אֲשֶׁר־מְכַרְתֶּם אֹתָם שָׁמָּה וַהֲשִׁבֹתִי גְמֻלְכֶם בְּרֹאשְׁכֶם:

(The Complete Jewish Bible with Rashi Commentary, Joel 1.1-7)

Psalm 121.4
Behold the Guardian of Israel will neither slumber nor sleep.

ד הִנֵּה לֹא יָנוּם וְלֹא יִישָׁן שׁוֹמֵר יִשְׂרָאֵל:
(The Complete Jewish Bible with Rashi Commentary, Psalm 121.4)

2 Chronicles 20.21–24
21 And [Jehoshaphat, king of Judah] took counsel with the people, and he set up singers to the Lord that they should praise the beauty of holiness, when they went out before the advance guard and said, "Give thanks to the Lord, for His kindness is eternal."
22 And at the time they commenced with song and praise, the Lord placed liers-in-wait against the children of Ammon, Moab, and Mount Seir, who were coming to Judah, and they were struck down.
23 And the children of Ammon and Moab rose up against the inhabitants of Mount Seir to destroy and annihilate, and when they finished with the inhabitants of Seir, each one helped his friend to destroy.
24 And the Judeans came upon the place overlooking the desert, and they turned to the multitude, and behold they were corpses falling to the ground, with no survivors.

כא וַיִּוָּעַץ אֶל־הָעָם וַיַּעֲמֵד מְשֹׁרְרִים לַיהֹוָה וּמְהַלְלִים לְהַדְרַת־קֹדֶשׁ בְּצֵאת לִפְנֵי הֶחָלוּץ וְאֹמְרִים הוֹדוּ לַיהֹוָה כִּי לְעוֹלָם חַסְדּוֹ:
כב וּבְעֵת הֵחֵלּוּ בְרִנָּה וּתְהִלָּה נָתַן יְהֹוָה ׀ מְאָרְבִים עַל־בְּנֵי עַמּוֹן מוֹאָב וְהַר־שֵׂעִיר הַבָּאִים לִיהוּדָה וַיִּנָּגֵפוּ:
כג וַיַּעַמְדוּ בְּנֵי עַמּוֹן וּמוֹאָב עַל־יֹשְׁבֵי הַר־שֵׂעִיר לְהַחֲרִים וּלְהַשְׁמִיד וּכְכַלּוֹתָם בְּיוֹשְׁבֵי שֵׂעִיר עָזְרוּ אִישׁ־בְּרֵעֵהוּ לְמַשְׁחִית:
כד וִיהוּדָה בָּא עַל־הַמִּצְפֶּה לַמִּדְבָּר וַיִּפְנוּ אֶל־הֶהָמוֹן וְהִנָּם פְּגָרִים נֹפְלִים אַרְצָה וְאֵין פְּלֵיטָה:

(The Complete Jewish Bible with Rashi Commentary, 2 Chronicles 20.21-24)

In chapter two, we discussed the destruction of Judah and the scattering of the Jewish people by the Romans (70 A.D. and 132 A.D.). Though there was always a remnant of Jews in the land that became known as Palestine, the sovereign nation of Israel would not exist again until May 14, 1948. During almost 2,000 years of exile, the Jewish people were indeed pursued, attacked, and killed. While some Jewish men or women rose to places of prominence in their host countries, they were often the exception to the rule. That was true throughout the Diaspora, but especially in Arab or Muslim lands. This is not to say that the Jewish people did not also suffer terribly under oppressive Christian rule. They did. In fact, it can be said that no other organization was more responsible for the persecution of the Jewish people than the Christian Church. We mention Arab Muslim antisemitism for two main reasons:

1. It is in Islamic nations today that Christians and other Muslims are being slaughtered. The number of deaths is unprecedented in history.
2. Early in Islam's history, there was a discriminatory system against non-Muslims known as *dhimmi*. *Dhimmi* laws are remarkably similar to the Jim Crow laws of the south and are still in effect in some Muslim countries today.

The organization, JIMENA (Jews Indigenous to the Middle East & North Africa), explains the concept of *Dhimmi*.

A Dhimmi is a historical term referring to a non-Muslim member of a Muslim society. Under Islamic (Sharia) law non-Muslims living in Muslim majority societies were given a special status of "residency in exchange for taxes." For Jews living in Muslim societies as Dhimmi, they were afforded a protected status provided they recognized the supremacy of Islam expressed in the payment both of poll taxes and obedience to a series of restrictions. These restrictions usually involved the clothing worn by Jews, the animals they were allowed to ride and the prohibition of their ability to bear arms. Synagogues were not permitted to be built higher than the mosques nearby. An example of a restriction put on a Jewish community due to it's Dhimmi status was the first yellow stars worn by the Jews of Baghdad in the 9th century imposed on them by a local Caliph, or Muslim ruler.[11]

In addition to my friends at JIMENA, I've spoken with many Jews whose families lived in the Arabized lands of North African and the Middle East. These Jews are called *Mizrahi* (from the east). One of my good friends from the Mizrahi community also recommended that I read Sir Martin Gilbert's, *In Ishmael's House: A History of Jews in Muslim Lands*. From study and conversation, I learned that dhimmi laws include prohibitions like:

---

[11] From "FAQ on Jews From Arab Countries," by JIMENA, n.d., *JIMENA*.

- Jews (non-Muslims) are forbidden to leave their houses when it rains or snows (to prevent the "impurity" of the Jews from being transmitted to Muslims).
- Jewish men must not wear fine clothes.
- Jewish women are obliged to expose their faces in public (like prostitutes).
- A Jew must never overtake a Muslim on a public street.
- A Jew must never speak loudly to a Muslim.
- If a Muslim insults a Jew, the latter must drop his head and remain silent.
- A Jew who buys meat must wrap and conceal it carefully from Muslims.
- It is forbidden for a Jew to have a house higher than his Muslim neighbor's.
- It is forbidden for a Jew to leave his town or enjoy the fresh air of the countryside.
- It is forbidden for Jews to ride on horseback.
- Jewish/non-Muslim Weddings must be celebrated in the greatest secrecy.
- Jews must not consume good fruit.
- A Jew cannot serve as a witness in a Muslim court involving another Muslim.

Now, consider the Jim Crow laws of the segregated south.

- A black male could not offer his hand (to shake hands) with a white male because it implied being socially equal.
- Blacks and whites were not supposed to eat together. If they did eat together, whites were to be served first, and some sort of partition was to be placed between them.
- Blacks were not allowed to show public affection toward one another in public, especially kissing, because it offended whites.
- Jim Crow etiquette prescribed that blacks were introduced to whites, never whites to blacks.
- Whites did not use courtesy titles of respect when referring to blacks, for example, Mr., Mrs., Miss., Sir, or Ma'am. Instead, blacks were called by their first names. Blacks had to use courtesy titles when referring to whites, and were not allowed to call them by their first names.

- If a black person rode in a car driven by a white person, the black person sat in the back seat, or the back of a truck.
- Never assert or even intimate that a white person is lying.
- Never impute dishonorable intentions to a white person.
- Never suggest that a white person is from an inferior class.
- Never lay claim to, or overly demonstrate, superior knowledge or intelligence.
- Never curse a white person.
- Never laugh derisively at a white person.
- Never comment upon the appearance of a white female.[12]

Of course, if a Jew failed to comply with any of the *dhimmi* laws, it meant imprisonment, torture or death. Black people who did not comply with Jim Crow laws met the same fate, particularly death by hanging. These executions were called *Jim Crow lynchings*.

Likewise, in Christian lands, Jews were often harassed, beaten, and murdered. Jews suffered at the hands of misguided Christians worldwide from Spain to Russia to Ethiopia. From 1966 to 1970, the Igbo Jews of Nigeria were systematically killed by their own government in what is known as the Biafra War. Israel was among the only nations to assist the Igbo by airdropping food and medicine to the people. By the end of the conflict, some three million Igbo had perished. After the war, a group of Igbo emigrated to Israel and live in Tel Aviv today. There in Tel Aviv, the Igbo commemorate the Biafra War every year with surviving Israeli pilots who flew the aid missions to Nigeria.

Throughout the centuries of suffering in exile, the Jewish people held onto the belief that one day, they would return to *Zion*. At the end of each Passover celebration in Jewish homes and synagogues, the people declare *l'shana haba bi-Yerushalayim* (next year in Jerusalem). Today, Israel is a reality, a fulfillment of biblical prophecy. We live in the day of the Israelite Redemption and the return from the four corners of the earth—biblical *Zionism*.

---

[12] Retrieved from "What was Jim Crow," by the Jim Crow Museum of Racist Memorabilia at Ferris State University, 2000. Originally published in *Jim Crow Guide* by S. Kennedy, 1990, by Florida Atlantic University Press.

ZIONISM AND THE BLACK CHURCH

From the Holocaust of Nazi Europe to the *farhuds*[13] of the Middle East to the oppression in African and Asian lands, the Jewish people have emerged. As God promised, He is returning them to Israel from the north, south, east, and west. As the psalmist said, *this is the Lord's doing, and it is marvelous in our eyes.* Although Israel has gained independence, and many Jews are returning, Israel's enemies haven't stopped their pursuit. While the modern Jewish state is a leader in many technologies and provides life-saving, life-improving inventions for the world, she has never been more marginalized and vilified. Zionism today includes defending Israel's right to live in peace. It is standing in solidarity with the only viable democratic nation in the Middle East while innocent people are dying all over the region. Zionism does not mean ignoring Israel's flaws. Like any government, it has them. But Zionism does mean actively seeking the "peace of Jerusalem" as God spoke through King David. It means letting our Jewish brothers and sisters know, "you are not alone," and that we remember our biblical mandate as well as our shared struggle for peace and freedom.

On college campuses and state governments across the country, Zionism means fighting against the Boycott, Divestment, and Sanction (BDS) measures that only seek to destroy Israel, not bring peace to the region. It means speaking against antisemitism and Jew-hatred in our community—wherever we find it. It means pastors and preachers teaching our biblical mandate and not replacing it with manmade agendas. It means Black Church leaders reaching out to the rabbis and Jewish leaders in their cities who are like-minded, remembering our mutual path of struggle. Zionism means forging real, mutually respectful relationships with those Jewish leaders so that hate and misinformation will not sidetrack us—again. Decades of violence against the Jewish State have resulted in procedures that may inconvenience everyone. Zionism means not confusing Israel's stringent security measures with the unfair treatment of people. It means acknowledging the oppression of Arabs in the Palestinian territories and holding accountable everyone responsible for their suffering.

Admittedly, for most Black Christians, or any Westerner, Israel or the Middle East is simply not on the radar. There are too many pressing matters we must deal with right here, right now—jobs, finances, housing, education, and healthcare, to name a few. How do we prioritize something as seemingly idealistic as support

---

[13] Pogrom or "violent dispossession" enacted against the Jewish population of Baghdad, Iraq from June 1-2, 1941.

for Israel and the Jewish people? Scripture explains the importance of Israel, but scripture underscores many vital issues for Christians, first and foremost, the spreading of the gospel of Jesus Christ. Why *should* we prioritize Israel? Why did Dr. Martin Luther King prioritize Israel? What did he know in the 1960s that does not seem to be common knowledge today? What can we learn from his model?

Dr. King's example is as powerful today as ever. The more one considers his words and actions, the more evident it becomes that they were prophetically instructive for such a time as this. It is no accident that the most significant civil rights figure of the 20th century was a Black American, Baptist preacher from the segregated South. It is equally providential that he was an outspoken, fearless supporter of Israel and loyal friend to the Jewish people. Dr. King's example set a high bar, not only for the Black Church, but for all Christians—one we are still trying to reach more than fifty years after his death. Next, we examine Dr. King's pro-Israel legacy and view Zionism through the lens of the struggle for Black civil rights.

CHAPTER 4
THE PRO-ISRAEL LEGACY OF THE REVEREND DR. MARTIN LUTHER KING, JR.

Isaiah 62.1
For the sake of Zion, I will not be silent, and for the sake of Jerusalem I will not rest, until her righteousness comes out like brilliance, and her salvation burns like a torch.

א לְמַעַן צִיּוֹן לֹא אֶחֱשֶׁה וּלְמַעַן יְרוּשָׁלַםִ לֹא אֶשְׁקוֹט עַד־יֵצֵא כַנֹּגַהּ צִדְקָהּ וִישׁוּעָתָהּ כְּלַפִּיד יִבְעָר:

(The Complete Jewish Bible with Rashi Commentary, Isaiah 62.1)

Many groups have attempted to invoke the late Reverend Dr. Martin Luther King, Jr. as a champion of their cause. His image will forever symbolize hope and strength to every person or group fighting for freedom. He is quoted as a modern-day prophet as his timeless words are applied to all things related to justice, equality, and civil rights. After his death, one could go into many Black American homes and see him virtually enshrined on souvenir plates or pillowcases, right along with Jesus and John F. Kennedy. Some Black Christians believe Dr. King is almost too revered, rising to the level of a deity, or at least a "perfect" man, while others feel that all of the accolades and superlatives are more than justified. Regardless of one's opinion of him, Dr. King's civil rights legacy and impact beyond the 20th century is undeniable.

In addition to being a beacon for human rights, he forged relationships with Jews involved in the civil rights movement. His friendship with Rabbi Abraham Joshua Heschel remains an icon of Black-Jewish cooperation today. Dr. King knew and underscored the parallel struggles of the two peoples.

> There isn't anyone in this country more likely to understand our struggle than Jews. Whatever progress we've made so far as a people, their support has been essential.[1]

> Probably more than any other ethnic group, the Jewish community has been sympathetic and has stood as an ally to the Negro in his struggle for justice.[2]

Sadly, Dr. King's solidarity with Israel and the Jewish people has not stopped anti-Zionists from claiming him as *their* champion. Some persons with an anti-Israel agenda will make statements like, "If Dr. King were here today, he would not support Israel because it has become an 'occupying power.'" This view is expressed by academics and intellectuals but is fueled by anti-Israel rhetoric and propaganda. Further, as we will see, nothing about this debate and controversy is new.

There are significant Israel-related events that occurred at different junctures during Dr. King's life. Martin Luther King, Jr. was born in Atlanta, Georgia, on January 15, 1929. Also, in 1929 was the *Hebron Massacre*. Arabs rioted and killed some sixty Jewish men, women, and children in Hebron as well as over forty in Jerusalem. It was the worst violence perpetrated on the Jews of Palestine (historic Israel) since the 19th century, further emphasizing the need for a sovereign Jewish homeland. This violence was spurred in large part by the Muslim Brotherhood, founded in Egypt in 1928.

> A populist movement with a strong Islamic fundamentalist message, the Muslim Brotherhood stirred up hatred not only against Zionism as a political and national movement, but against Jews as bearers of an alien and destructive religion and ideology. Its very first topic for debate

---

[1] King to former lawyer and adviser, Clarence B. Jones. Quote retrieved from "King and the Jews," by C. B. Jones, 2008, *Wall Street Journal*.

[2] From "Conversation with Martin Luther King," by M. L. King, E. Gendel, and A. J. Heschel, 1968, *Conservative Judaism*, 22(3) (https://www.rabbinicalassembly.org/sites/default/files/public/resources-ideas/cj/classics/1-4-12-civil-rights/conversation-with-martin-luther-king.pdf.). Copyright 1968 by the Rabbinical Assembly.

was 'The Subject of Palestine and the necessity of Jihad.'[3]

In the Spring of 1948, Reverend King graduated from Morehouse College at the age of 19. Also, in the Spring of 1948, Israel declared its independence from Great Britain, becoming a sovereign Jewish State for the first time in almost 2,000 years. On January 18, 1953, Reverend King married Coretta Scott, a student at the New England Conservatory of Music. Later, they had four children together—Dexter, Bernice, Yolanda, and Martin Luther III.

Reverend King earned his doctorate in systematic theology from Boston University in 1955. The Southern Christian Leadership Conference (SCLC) was launched directly following the successful Montgomery Bus Boycott in Alabama (1955-56). This was the unofficial beginning of Dr. King's role as a national spokesman for the Black Civil Rights Movement. Also in 1956, Israel fought its second major conflict, the Suez War.

The last 15 months of Dr. King's life (January 1967–April 1968) showed an increasing interest in and connection to Israel. Official documents reveal he was planning what former Israeli Prime Minister, David Ben Gurion, called the "first mass pilgrimage of the American Negro Community to the Holy Lands of Israel." It was to be Dr. King's second trip to the Holy Lands as he and Coretta had gone eight years prior.

> He had visited the Jordanian side of Jerusalem in 1959. Organizers of the 1967 trip hoped to attract at least 5,000 people to make the pilgrimage to Israel with Dr. King to raise money for the Southern Christian Leadership Conference. King planned to preach on the Mount of Olives, in what was then Jordanian East Jerusalem . . . and then again near Capernaum in Israel.[4]

Ben Gurion sent his letter in January 1967. The Israel tour was scheduled for November of that year.

---

[3] From "Jewish and Arab nationalism: The first world war and after," by M. Gilbert, 2011, *In Ishmael's house: A history of Jews in Muslim lands*, p. 157. Copyright 2010 by Martin Gilbert.

[4] From "Black-Jewish relations: Martin Luther King & Israel," by Jewish Virtual Library, n.d., *Jewish Virtual Library*.

I would like to congratulate you on your decision, which will encourage people of all races to revive the old tradition of making pilgrimage to the Bible lands. Your contribution of spiritual leadership to your people will definitely find its fulfillment in such a pilgrimage.

I am planning a trip to the United States in the very near future, and I hope I have an opportunity to meet, so that I may convey these thoughts in person.

With SHALOM greetings,
D. Ben-Gurion

Dr. King received Ben-Gurion's letter on February 1st. He also received a similar letter from then Prime Minister, Levi Eshkol.

Both David Ben-Gurion and Levi Eshkol received Dr. King's reply in early May.

My Dear Prime Minister:

Please pardon my delay in acknowledging receipt of your very kind letter. I take this means to express my deep appreciation to you for the invitation you extended me to come to your wonderful country. I am certainly looking forward to the trip with great enthusiasm. As I have spoken around the country, I have been gratified at the response I have received regarding the Pilgrimage.

I am delighted to have an opportunity to lead a pilgrimage to the Holy Land. I feel that it will be a very meaningful and memorable experience for each participant. World travel is quite significant and has proven effective in our constant quest for Brotherhood.

Again, I reiterate my deep appreciation to you for your interest and cooperation and I look forward to greeting you personally in the near future.

Faithfully,
Martin Luther King, Jr.

ZIONISM AND THE BLACK CHURCH

Tel-Aviv, January 20, 1967.

Dear Rev. Dr. King,

I have learnt with great pleasure of your declared intention to lead the first mass pilgrimage of the American Negro community to the Holy Lands of Israel and Jordan, this coming November.

I would like to congratulate you on your decision, which will encourage people of all races to revive the old tradition of making a pilgrimage to the Bible lands. Your contribution of spiritual leadership to your people will definitely find its fulfilment in such a pilgrimage.

I am planning a trip to the United States in the very near future, and I hope that we will have the opportunity to meet, so that I may convey these thoughts in person.

With Shalom greetings,

D. Ben-Gurion.

The Rev. Dr. Martin Luther King, Jr.
Southern Christian Leadership Conference,
334 Auburn Ave., N.E.,
Atlanta, Georgia 30303

Letter from David Ben Gurion to Dr. King Received from Ben Gurion archives, Ben-Gurion University of the Negev

---

Southern Christian Leadership Conference
334 Auburn Ave., N.E.
Atlanta, Georgia 30303
Telephone 522-1420

Martin Luther King Jr., *President* Ralph Abernathy, *Treasurer* Andrew J. Young, *Executive Director*

May 9, 1967

Mr. David Ben-Gurion
P. O. Box 4476
Tel-Aviv, Isreal

Dear Mr. Ben-Gurion:

Please pardon my delay in acknowledging receipt of your very kind letter. I take this means to express my deep appreciation to you for the invitation you extended me to come to your wonderful country. I am certainly looking forward to the trip with great enthusiasm. As I have spoken around the country, I have been gratified at the response I have received regarding the Pilgrimage.

I am delighted to have an opportunity to lead a pilgrimage to the Holy Land. I feel that it will be a very meaningful and memorable experience for each participant. World travel is quite significant and has proven effective in our constant quest for Brotherhood.

Again, I reiterate my deep appreciation to you for your interest and cooperation and I look forward to greeting you personally in the near future.

Faithfully,

Martin Luther King, Jr.

Kn

Letter from David Ben Gurion to Dr. King Received from Ben Gurion archives, Ben-Gurion University of the Negev

THE PRO-ISRAEL LEGACY OF THE REVEREND DR. MARTIN LUTHER KING, JR.

Less than a month after the Prime Minister received Dr. King's reply (June 6, 1967), the Six Day War broke out, and Israel was, once again, defending itself against the Arab armies of Egypt, Iraq, Syria, Lebanon, and Jordan. Israel miraculously won the battle, which was only the beginning of a new ideological war against her. For Israel's enemies, her victory in June 1967 merely codified her title as *imperialist*. For many, Israel was no longer seen as the underdog. As with the wars of 1948 and 1956, the Arabs were the aggressors in 1967. Israel did preemptively strike Egypt and Syria, but only as a strategic move to take the enemy coalition off guard.

Again, Israel's victory in 1967 was nothing short of miraculous as the Jewish State was severely outnumbered and outgunned. In response to their defeat, the Arab League met in Khartoum, the capital of Sudan. The League consisted of Egypt, Iraq, Lebanon, Saudi Arabia, Syria, Transjordan (Jordan), and Yemen. Rather than discuss Israel's offer of peace, the Arab states condemned the Israelis as occupiers and issued the infamous *Khartoum No's*:

1. No peace with Israel.
2. No recognition of Israel.
3. No negotiations with Israel.

The former Soviet Union walked in lock-step with the Arab League, having supplied "massive amounts of arms to the Arabs."[5] In his book, "The Making of Black Revolutionaries" pro-Arab civil rights activist, James Forman, said after the 1967 War:

> I knew that we had to support the people of the Arab world in their fight to restore justice to the Palestinian people... Our position against Israel, as I saw it, took us one step further along the road to revolution. For (the Student Non-Violent Coordinating Committee) SNCC to see the struggle against racism, capitalism, and imperialism as being indivisible made it inevitable to take a position against the greatest imperialist power in the Middle East, and in favor of liberation and dignity for the

---

[5] See "The six-day war: Background & overview," by Jewish Virtual Library, n.d. *Jewish Virtual Library*.

Arab people."[6]

James Forman made his comments after attending the National Conference on New Politics (NCNP) in Chicago, July 1967. Dr. King and members of the Southern Christian Leadership Conference (SCLC) also attended the conference, but not as delegates. Dr. King delivered the opening address then left for another appointment, leaving other SCLC members to observe. The NCNP adopted a resolution condemning Israel in the wake of the Six Day War and expressing solidarity with the Arabs. When the press reported on the conference and the groups who signed the anti-Zionist resolution, they stated that Dr. King and the SCLC were in agreement. Rabbi Maurice Eisendrath, president of the Union of American Hebrew Congregations, wrote a letter to Dr. King asking for clarification. Two months later, Dr. King replied.

Dr. Maurice N. Eisendrath
Union of American Hebrew Congregations
838 5th Avenue
New York, New York

Dear Dr. Eisendrath:

I am in receipt of your letter making inquiry of SCLC's position on antisemitism. First, let me apologize for being rather tardy in my reply. Absence from the city and accumulation of a huge volume of mail account for the delay.

Serious distortions by the press have created an impression that SCLC was part of a group at the Chicago Conference of New Politics which introduced a resolution condemning Israel and unqualifiedly endorsing all the policies of the Arab powers. The facts are as follows:

The staff members of SCLC who attended the conference (not as official delegates) were the most vigorous and articulate opponents of the simplistic resolution on the Middle East question. As a result of this opposition, the Black caucus modified its stand and the convention voted

---

[6] From "The Arab-Israeli dispute," by J. Forman, 1972, *The making of Black revolutionaries*, pp. 496-497. Copyright 1985 by James Forman.

to eliminate references to Zionism and referred to the executive board the matter of final wording . . . I had no part in planning the structure or the policy of the conference, nor was I a delegate. If I had been at the conference during the discussion of the resolutions, I have made it crystal clear that I could not have supported any resolution calling for black separatism or calling for condemnation of Israel and an unqualified endorsement of the policy of the Arab powers. I later made this clear to the press but a disclaimer seldom gets the attention that an original sensation attack receives.

SCLC has expressly, frequently and vigorously denounced antisemitism and will continue to do so. It is not only that antisemitism is immoral - though that [alone] is enough. It is used to divide Negro and Jew, who have effectively collaborated in the struggle for justice. It injures Negroes because it upholds the doctrine of racism which they have the greatest stake in destroying.[7]

With rising international controversy after the 1967 War, Dr. King was under tremendous pressure from Arab leaders and portions of the Black militant civil rights movement to cancel his Holy Land pilgrimage. For his part, Dr. King did not want to appear biased in his desire to see peace between the Arabs and Israelis. Also, many conflicting reports were coming in regarding the battle and its aftermath. This included Israel's offer of peace, which the Arabs misrepresented and declined. In July 1967, one month after the War, Dr. King said in a private, secretly recorded meeting:

I just think that if I go, the Arab world, and of course Africa and Asia for that matter, would interpret this as endorsing everything that Israel has done, and I do have questions of doubt.[8]

Israel critics attempt to use this statement of Dr. King's to prove he was not supportive of the Jewish State after the 1967 War. Nothing could be further from the truth. Dr. King was sorting through information and made his independent

---

[7] King's letter to Eisendrath, 1967. Copyright by the Estate of Dr. Martin Luther King, Jr.

[8] From a transcript of an FBI-wiretapped conference call from the King-Levison File, July 24, 1967. Retrieved from "In the words of Martin Luther King," 2016, *The War on Error: Israel, Islam, and the Middle East*, p. 259.

assessment of the facts. Though he ultimately canceled his group visit to Israel, planning to postpone it until 1968, we have no record of him ever condemning Israel, publicly or privately. What's more, Israel offered to return captured land to the Arabs in exchange for peace. Again, the Arab League met in Khartoum, Sudan, and issued a resounding, three-fold *NO*.

In 1977, Egyptian President Anwar Sadat was invited by the Israeli government to speak in the Knesset, where he called for peace. Sadat's negotiations with Israeli Prime Minister Menachem Begin would eventually lead to the signing of an official peace treaty in 1979. The peace treaty came twelve years after the 1967 War; twelve years after the Arab League, led by Egypt, issued the infamous Khartoum No's. As part of the treaty, Israel returned the Sinai to Egypt in April 1982. For his efforts towards peace with Israel, Anwar Sadat was assassinated by an Islamic extremist. Some believe Sadat's killer was an ex-member of the Muslim Brotherhood.

Seeing dark-skinned, kinky-haired Anwar Sadat on the news in the 1970s, I remember my mother saying, "Egypt's president is a Black man!" It was the first time I recall paying attention to world events. It was then that Israel and Africa captured my young mind.

After Israel's victory in the 1967 War, other influential Black militant voices were solicited by Israel's enemies to condemn the Jewish State. One of those voices was the Minister of Information for the Black Panthers, Eldridge Cleaver.

> The [American Jewish] Committee study quotes . . . Eldridge Cleaver, in a December 1969 interview in Algiers [Algeria], as stating that "Zionists, wherever they may be, are our enemies. We totally support the armed struggle of the Palestinian people against the watchdogs of imperialism." The report also quotes a news story from the International edition of the Herald Tribune, which reported on December 29, 1969 in a story from Algiers that El Fatah leader Yassir Arafat and Cleaver hugged and kissed each other at a meeting with Palestine refugees here, then Cleaver climbed the rostrum to deliver a fierce attack on American Zionists. The study quotes the Jan. 30, 1970 report of CBS correspondent Richard C. Hottelet from Algiers on an El Fatah-Black Panther alliance. The El Fatah guerrilla organization, Mr. Hottelet declared, "is discussing training Black Panthers in actual combat against Israel to prepare them

Eldridge Cleaver (r), Yasser Arafat (second from r), and two other men, 1969.
Photo credit: unknown

for a sabotage and assassination campaign in the United States."[9]

However, after living for several years in Arab lands where he saw the Arab enslavement of Africans firsthand, Eldridge Cleaver returned to the U.S., a vocal supporter of Israel and the Jewish people.

> Cleaver, who's book, "Soul on Ice, made him the darling of revolutionaries of the 1960s, first indicated his changed outlook, after his return, in a Boston Herald-American article in which he condemned "Communist dictatorship" and "black African dictatorships."

> He denounced the (1975) United Nations resolution equating Zionism with racism as a "travesty of the truth," saying "Jews have done more than any other people to expose and condemn racism."[10]

After learning the truth, Black Panther Eldridge Cleaver became a Zionist.

---

[9] From "Aj committee charges Black Panther's anti-Zionist statements close to anti-Semitism," 1970, *Jewish Telegraphic Agency*.

[10] From "He chose to switch than fight," 1976, *The Free Lance-Star*.

ZIONISM AND THE BLACK CHURCH

The preferred ideological target of terrorists and anti-Israel propagandists was young, Black, gifted, passionate yet misinformed pursuers of justice who, like the Apostle Paul said, "had a zeal" that was "not according to knowledge." These talented yet naïve young people were quickly manipulated with Marxist-inspired teachings that oversimplified the real, complex struggle for justice by assigning virtue to someone based on their skin color or socioeconomic class—the way that White racists do to people of color. The Israeli-Arab conflict was sold as one in which the Jews ("White people") were oppressing and exploiting the Arabs ("Colored people"), and that *intersectionality* demanded young, Black seekers of justice vehemently oppose the Jewish State. Another young, Black freedom fighter exploited by anti-Zionist deception was Stokely Carmichael (aka, Kwame Toure). Born in 1941, Kwame Toure was a contemporary of Dr. King and passed away in 1998. Toure remained an anti-Zionist his entire career stating in 1996, "I'm against Zionism . . . The only good Zionist is a dead Zionist."[11]

By the spring of 1968, Israel's friends were few and dwindling. The hard left was increasing its takeover of American liberal politics, and anti-Zionism/antisemitism was its calling card. The *Khartoum No's* of the Arab League could arguably be seen as the precursor to today's global Boycott, Divestment, and Sanction (BDS) campaign against Israel. Young, Black militants were increasingly anti-Zionist, becoming more dismissive of Dr. King and the largely pro-Israel leaders of the Civil Rights Movement.

On March 25, 1968, ten days before his assassination, Dr. King was the honored guest of the 68th Annual Convention of the Rabbinical Assembly for Conservative Judaism. Rabbi Heschel gave him an illustrious introduction. The following is an excerpt:

> Where does moral religious leadership in America come from today? The politicians are astute, the establishment is proud, and the market place is busy. Placid, happy, merry, the people pursue their work, enjoy their leisure, and life is fair. People buy, sell, celebrate and rejoice. They fail to realize that in the midst of our affluent cities there are districts of despair, areas of distress.

---

[11] From "Conversations/Kwame Ture; formerly Stokely Carmichael and still ready for the revolution," by K. de Witt, 1996, *New York Times*.

Martin Luther King is a voice, a vision and a way. I call upon every Jew to harken to his voice, to share his vision, to follow in his way. The whole future of America will depend upon the impact and influence of Dr. King.

May everyone present give of his strength to this great spiritual leader, Martin Luther King.[12]

Dr. King's response was equally gracious:

> I need not pause to say how very delighted I am to be here this evening and to have the opportunity of sharing with you in this significant meeting, but I do want to express my deep personal appreciation to each of you for extending the invitation. It is always a very rich and rewarding experience when I can take a brief break from the day-to-day demands of our struggle for freedom and human dignity and discuss the issues involved in that struggle with concerned friends of good will all over our nation. And so I deem this a real and a great opportunity.
>
> I've looked over the last few years, being involved in the struggle for racial justice, and all too often I have seen religious leaders stand amid the social injustices that pervade our society, mouthing pious irrelevancies and sanctimonious trivialities. All too often the religious community has been a tail light instead of a head light.
>
> But here and there we find those who refuse to remain silent behind the safe security of stained glass windows, and they are forever seeking to make the great ethical insights of our Judeo-Christian heritage relevant in this day and in this age. I feel that Rabbi Heschel is one of the persons who is relevant at all times, always standing with prophetic insights to guide us through these difficult days.
>
> He has been with us in many of our struggles. I remember marching from Selma to Montgomery, how he stood at my side and with us as we faced that crisis situation. I remember very well when we were in Chicago for the Conference on Religion and Race. Eloquently and profoundly he

---

[12] See footnote #2.

> spoke on the issues of race and religion, and to a great extent his speech inspired clergymen of all the religious faiths of our country; many went out and decided to do something that they had not done before. So I am happy to be with him, and I want to say Happy Birthday, and I hope I can be here to celebrate your one hundredth birthday.[13]

With the opening remarks concluded, moderator Rabbi Gendler began reading the prepared questions for Dr. King to answer. A series of queries revealed the rabbis' attempt to understand the mixed signals coming from Black Americans. There was great synergy between the Black American and Jewish communities, but things seemed to be changing quickly; the spring of 1968 was a turbulent time in America and the world.

The Vietnam War gained both momentum and media scrutiny while claiming a disproportionate number of young Black American lives. John F. Kennedy had been killed by Lee Harvey Oswald in 1963. Elijah Muhammed loyalists gunned down Malcolm X in 1965. The Black Civil Rights Movement was intensely debated within the Black community, as the younger, more aggressive Black leaders were impatient with the older guard's non-violent approach. They were no longer willing to await the slow process of change. Malcolm's words, "by any means necessary," had become their mantra. Many of these younger Black leaders wrongly believed that given the U.S.-Israel alliance, Zionism was simply an extension of Western colonialism and imperialism. In their confusion, they were vehement in their opposition to Israel and wholly sided with the Soviet-backed Arabs powers.

Rabbi Gendler continued with his questions for Dr. King:

> "Would you please comment on Congressman [Adam Clayton] Powell's charge that you are a moderate, that you cater to Whitey, and also his criticism that you do not accept violence?"[14]

Dr. King:

> On the question of Congressman Powell and his recent accusation, I

---

[13] See previous footnote.

[14] See previous footnote.

must say that I would not want to engage in a public or private debate with Mr. Powell on his views concerning Martin Luther King. Frankly, I hope I am so involved in trying to do a job that has to be done that I will not come to the point of dignifying some of the statements that the Congressman has made.

On the question of appealing to "Whitey," I don't quite know what the Congressman means. But here again I think this is our problem which must be worked out by all people of good will, black and white. I feel that at every point we must make it very clear that this isn't just a Negro problem, that white Americans have a responsibility, indeed a great responsibility, to work passionately and unrelentingly for the solution of the problem of racism, and if that means constantly reminding white society of its obligation, that must be done. If I have been accused of that, then I will have to continue to be accused.[15]

Rabbi Gendler:

"What steps have been undertaken and what success has been noted in convincing anti-Semitic and anti-Israel Negroes, such as [H] Rap Brown, Stokely Carmichael [Kwame Ture], and [Congressman Dwight] McKissick, to desist from their anti-Israel activity? What effective measures will the collective Negro community take against the vicious antisemitism, against the militance and the rabble-rousing of the Browns, Carmichaels, and Powells?

Have your contributions from Jews fallen off considerably? Do you feel the Jewish community is copping out on the civil rights struggle?

What would you say if you were talking to a Negro intellectual, an editor of a national magazine, and were told, as I have been, that he supported the Arabs against Israel because color is all important in this world? In the editor's opinion, the Arabs are colored Asians and the Israelis are white Europeans. Would you point out that more than half of the Israelis are Asian Jews with the same pigmentation as Arabs, or would you suggest that an American Negro should not form judgments on the basis

---

[15] See previous footnote.

of color? What seems to you an appropriate or an effective response?"[16]

The issue of race would, and continues to, permeate discussions about the Middle East for many in the Black community and, by default, in the Black Church. This was due largely to the Arab and Soviet propaganda machines relentlessly twisting the narrative (more on this in chapter five). From their Afro-Asiatic origins to their worldwide presence throughout the Diaspora, Jews are a multiethnic group. But, men like the PLO's Yasser Arafat and Egyptian Premier Gamal Nasser exploited the fact that the stereotypical image of a Jew in the Western world was a White European banker, landlord, lawyer, or store owner.

Israel's enemies told the world that the Jews of European descent were not the Jews of the Bible. They led many to believe the Jews came from Europe as conquerors and colonizers in the Western imperialist tradition. They contended the Arabs in Palestine, by contrast, were *people of color*, and all people of color should stand in solidarity with their Arab brothers against the *evil, White, racist Zionists*. The most ironic part of this false narrative is that by the eighth century, Arabs had colonized all of North Africa under the banner of an imperial Islam. To this day, the African lands of Egypt, Libya, Morocco, Algeria, Tunisia, North Sudan, and Mauritania are strictly under Arab Islamic control. To further dispel this false narrative, the colonization was hardly amicable. The Arab subjugation and enslavement of Africans is 1400 years old and counting, as parts of the Middle East still participate. Today, there are an estimated one million African slaves in Libya alone.[17]

At the Rabbinical Assembly, the question of race, Israel, and Black-Jewish relations was posed directly and solely to Dr. King. Standing as a mediator between the Black and Jewish communities, Dr. King served as *The* Spokesman— America's pastor and sage. His divine assignment often had him explaining Black Americans to Jews and vice versa, even though neither group is a monolith and, at times, exhibits behavior that is inexplicable. Dr. King was looked upon as an ambassador, always expected to bring peace. He began answer to the tough question:

---

[16] See previous footnote.

[17] See "Libyan slave trade has shocked the world. Here's what you should know," by C. Quackenbush, 2017, *TIME* for more information.

> On the Middle East crisis, we have had various responses. The response of some of the so-called young militants again does not represent the position of the vast majority of Negroes. There are some who are color-consumed and they see a kind of mystique in being colored, and anything non-colored is condemned. We do not follow that course in the Southern Christian Leadership Conference, and certainly most of the organizations in the civil rights movement do not follow that course.[18]

Dr. King explained to the rabbis that within the Black community, there were those whose worldview was guided by disdain and distrust of all things white and blind veneration of all things black. Consider his word choice of some being "color-consumed" or the feeling of a "mystique in being colored." These are psychological terms, and Dr. King was psycho-analyzing. Many in the Black militant movement were so preoccupied with "Whitey" that they could not see clearly or think rationally. Accepting the propaganda of Israelis as "colonizers" led Black militants to be deceived into thinking that Israeli Jews were "Whitey" despite Rabbi Gendler's statement that "more than half of the Israelis are Asian Jews with the same pigmentation as Arabs." Black militants were also ignoring the shared legacy of slavery and dispossession among Blacks and Jews. Again, many Arab Islamic nations still practice some of the most despicable forms of African hatred—including slavery.

What was King's reply to the errant call of racial solidarity between the "colored" Arabs and Black Americans? In a word—nonsense. He echoed his 1963 landmark speech, *I Have a Dream*, "not by the color of their skin, but by the content of their character." Dr. King understood that the Arab-Israeli conflict could not be reduced to colorism. He and the Black community would judge the situation in the Middle East on its merits. He told the rabbis, and the world, though there were some who were "color-consumed," he was not, and there was no "mystique" in being colored. This was not the position of a self-hating Black man, but a strong, courageous man unafraid to say what was unpopular among grossly misinformed detractors.

Dr. King continued:

> I think it is necessary to say that what is basic and what is needed in the

---

[18] See footnote #2.

Middle East is peace. Peace for Israel is one thing. Peace for the Arab side of that world is another thing. Peace for Israel means security, and we must stand with all of our might to protect its right to exist, its territorial integrity. I see Israel, and never mind saying it, as one of the great outposts of democracy in the world, and a marvelous example of what can be done, how desert land almost can be transformed into an oasis of brotherhood and democracy. Peace for Israel means security and that security must be a reality.[19]

Dr. King's words were powerful at face value. What is even more powerful is that he spoke these words almost a full year after the 1967 War. At this time, Israel was still in possession of Judea and Samaria (West Bank), Gaza, and the Sinai desert. Dr. King dismissed the notion of Israel being a colonizing, imperialistic power. Instead, he recognized the truth and called for protection of Israel's "territorial integrity." Israel, an "occupying power?" Clearly, Dr. King disagreed.

Demonstrating that one does not have to be anti-Arab to be pro-Israel, Dr. King continued:

On the other hand, we must see what peace for the Arabs means in a real sense of security on another level. Peace for the Arabs means the kind of economic security that they so desperately need. These nations, as you know, are part of that third world of hunger, of disease, of illiteracy. I think that as long as these conditions exist there will be tensions, there will be the endless quest to find scapegoats. So there is a need for a Marshall Plan for the Middle East, where we lift those who are at the bottom of the economic ladder and bring them into the mainstream of economic security.[20]

In 1968, Dr. King called for a *Marshal Plan* for the Arabs living in Palestine. He suggested, just as the international community rebuilt Europe after World War II, so should there be an effort to lift the Arabs, "... at the bottom of the economic ladder and bring them into the mainstream of economic security." A Zionist who truly desires peace in the Middle East is equally concerned about the well-being of the Israelis and the Arab Palestinians.

---

[19] See previous footnote.

[20] See previous footnote.

By 2014, the combined Palestinian aid from the United Nations Relief Works Agency (UNRWA) and the European Union was over $2 billion annually.[21] According to the Jerusalem Institute of Justice, the Palestinian Authority has received the per capita equivalent of 25 *Marshall Plans* over the past two decades alone.[22] Tens of billions of dollars have gone to precisely what Dr. King advocated, yet poverty in the Palestinian Territories persists. In the 2013 report by the European Court of Auditors, the Palestinian Authority was accused of wasting $3.1 billion dollars.

> According to The Sunday Times, which got an early glimpse of the report, "EU investigators who visited sites in Jerusalem, Gaza and the West Bank noted 'significant shortcomings' in the management of funds sent to Gaza and the West Bank."[23]

In the Palestinian territory of Gaza (population 2 million), there are hundreds of millionaires, all members of the Hamas ruling party.[24] Yet, Gaza's infrastructure is sorely lacking in meeting the needs of its citizens.[25]

Israel's critics generally blame these improprieties on the Jewish State and its manipulation of the Palestinian economy. The Israeli government's involvement with Gaza and the West Bank is a long and challenging issue. It is under constant scrutiny by Israelis, as well as others. However, Israel does not control international economic aid to the Palestinians. Israel's implied guilt for Palestinian suffering was no doubt something else Dr. King anticipated when he said, "I think that as long as these (Arab poverty) conditions exist there will be tensions; there will be the endless quest to find scapegoats." In other words, if the Arab plight does not improve, Israel would be consistently and relentlessly blamed.

---

[21] See "Palestinian authority's 2013 budget passed despite political rift," by O. Shabban, 2013, *Al-Monitor*.

[22] See "The UNRWA Dilemma," by T. Dias, 2013, *Gatestone Institute* for more information.

[23] From "Report: Billions of Dollars of Aid to Palestinian Authority Lost to Corruption," by Z. Pontz, 2013, *The Algemeiner*.

[24] See "How Many Millionaires Live in the 'Impoverished' Gaza Strip?," by K. A. Toameh, 2012, *Gatestone Institute* for more information.

[25] See "Hamas Considers Economic Reforms as Gaza's Economic Activity Plummets," by Reuters, 2014, *Haaretz*.

By the spring of 1968, Israel was on trial in the world court of opinion, and Dr. King was one of her character witnesses. He did not flinch. He did not waver. Regardless of the barrage of antisemitic, anti-Zionist declarations that poured out of Arab and Communist countries as well as the United Nations, Dr. King remained a faithful friend to Israel and the Jewish people. He spoke truth to power. He stood by the only viable democracy in the Middle East while maintaining his integrity as a true champion of human rights.

In *Letter from a Birmingham Jail*, Dr. King used the analogy of Hitler's persecution of the Jewish people to explain his willingness to disobey unjust laws. In his analogy, he also revealed his empathy for the Jewish people and his assurance that he would have tended to their plight.

> We should never forget that everything Adolf Hitler did in Germany was "legal" and everything the Hungarian freedom fighters did in Hungary was "illegal." It was "illegal" to aid and comfort a Jew in Hitler's Germany. Even so, I am sure that, had I lived in Germany at the time, I would have aided and comforted my Jewish brothers. If today I lived in a Communist country where certain principles dear to the Christian faith are suppressed, I would openly advocate disobeying that country's antireligious laws.[26]

It was not only the Holocaust but the historic persecution of the Jewish people around the world that dictated the need for a sovereign Jewish State. Dr. King knew this as well as anyone. His statement, "we must stand with all of our might to protect its right to exist, its territorial integrity," spoke to an active role in Israel's safety. From where did this *brothers-in-arms* mentality come? I submit it was a quintessential blending of Christian Zionism and social activism. Just as Dr. King applauded Rabbi Heschel for "refusing to remain silent behind the safe security of stained glass windows," so was he unwilling to remain silent while Israel and the Jewish people were being physically attacked, politically isolated, and morally vilified.

So significant and effective was Dr. King's support of Israel, that Israel's enemies took note and lamented it. In 1993, Edward Said, Palestinian American Professor

---

[26] From "Letter from a Birmingham Jail," by M. L. King, 1963. Copyright by the Estate of Dr. Martin Luther King, Jr.

and anti-Israel activist, stated:

> With the emergence of the civil rights movement in the middle '60s – and particularly in '66-'67 – I was very soon turned off by Martin Luther King, who revealed himself to be a tremendous Zionist, and who always used to speak very warmly in support of Israel, particularly in '67, after the war.[27]

In researching this book, I came across an article written by history professor and author Gil Troy. In the piece, Professor Troy mentioned Bayard Rustin and an organization called BASIC (Black Americans to Support Israel Committee). Bayard Rustin was a civil rights warrior and a close friend and colleague of Dr. King. Mr. Rustin was also Dr. King's coach in non-violent protests inspired by Gandhi. Continuing Dr. King's pro-Israel, pro-peace legacy after his death, his associates, Bayard Rustin and A. Philip Randolph, formed BASIC to galvanize Black American solidarity with Israel and the Jewish people.

Until reading Gil Troy's article, I had never heard of BASIC. The discovery was a very emotional experience for me. I was personally relieved to learn that amid the exploitation of the Black struggle for justice and the international condemnation of Israel, many Black Americans defended their heritage and stood by their Jewish brothers. They refused to forget the shared legacy of oppression and the need to band together when attacked. Though I was heartened to learn of post-Dr. King efforts like BASIC, I was also disappointed that this information was not common knowledge, especially with the global rise of antisemitism disguised as *justice*. That is much of the reason I was inspired to write this book.

Up to this point, we have focused exclusively on Dr. King's moral and political support for Israel. We have analyzed some of his most powerful words advocating for the Jewish State, and there was not one Bible verse among them. However, Dr. King was a doctor of biblical theology and pastor of a Baptist church. He honed his great oratory skill within the Black Church framework, he loved gospel music and his favorite singer was the incomparable Mahalia Jackson. Born and raised in the southern, Black Baptist ethic, Dr. King understood the spiritual significance of Israel, the Jewish people, and biblical Zionism. Surely, he knew every Negro

---

[27] Quote by Edward Said during an interview with Peter Osborne and Anne Beezer (1993). Retrieved from *Radical Philosophy Archive*.

Spiritual we listed in chapter one and then some. Surely, he knew every biblical text we cited in chapter three, and then some. Yet, we have no record of him making a public case for biblical Zionism or arguing the validity of the State of Israel based on biblical history.

One can only surmise his reasons. Perhaps Dr. King was too wise to argue spiritual matters with those who did not share a Christian worldview. Perhaps he saw no need to preach Israel's biblical rights to the Land when a non-religious case could be made just as effectively. Perhaps an Israel solidarity built on a Christian biblical and spiritual tradition of the Black Church had morphed into an intellectually articulated case for the Jewish State. Whatever his reasons for not quoting the Bible in his defense of Israel's right to exist, his model is once again prophetically instructive, for there are two entirely different, yet related arguments that the Church must make for Israel—the biblical and the moral.

Israel has the right to live in peace with its Arab neighbors. Likewise, the Arab Palestinian people have the right to live free of oppression and dictatorial rule. Legitimate criticism of any government is the sign of a healthy democracy—if it is a democracy. Israel is a democracy. Gaza and the Palestinian Authority (also known as the West Bank) are ruled by leaders responsible for consistent human rights violations. Honor killings, torture, suicide bomber training for children, and religious persecution all exist in the Palestinian territories. On May 8, 2014, the Los Angeles Times published a piece entitled, *Human rights complaints rise in Palestinian Territories*.

> Complaints of torture and other mistreatment rose by 50% last year in areas governed by the Palestinian Authority, according to a report by the Ramallah-based Independent Commission for Human Rights.
>
> The report notes, "a remarkable increase in the number of complaints received on alleged cases of torture and violations involving the right to physical safety in the West Bank and the Gaza Strip."
>
> It says that 497 allegations of torture and ill treatment were received by the commission in 2013, compared with 294 cases in 2012. Most of the cases, 347, were in the Hamas-ruled Gaza Strip.

The Palestinian watchdog group established by the president of the Palestinian Authority 20 years ago said it had also registered a "noticeable increase" in arbitrary detentions in the West Bank and Gaza. It attributed the rise "to the political variables and the continuation of the internal political division" between the Ramallah-based Palestinian Authority and Hamas, the Islamist movement that has ruled Gaza since 2007.[28]

Like the current leaders of the Palestinian people, former PLO head, Yasser Arafat, ruled with an iron fist. As we will examine in chapter five, Arafat spoke about human rights but was no humanitarian. Dr. King spoke out in favor of the well-being of Jews and Arabs as well as Israel and the Palestinian Territories. Applying his example, the Black Church should be concerned with peace for all people in the Middle East. This would include strongly condemning the human rights abuses perpetrated on the Arab Palestinian people by their leaders.
The moral case for the state of Israel, therefore, includes a genuine concern for the plight of the Arab Palestinians. Israel is the only viable democracy in the Middle East. While Palestinians in the West Bank and Gaza do not enjoy political, economic, or religious freedom, their condition would be even worse without Israel to help care for the oppressed. Israel has a governmental and judicial system that includes Arabs, Muslims, Christians, Jews, women, and other diverse members of society. Israel is a multiethnic, inclusive country, with a government that serves and protects its people from its many enemies.

Israeli compassion means that medical and emergency services are available to both Israelis and Palestinians. The wife of Palestinian Authority, President Mahmoud Abbas, was treated at Assuta Medical Center in Ramat Hachayal, near Tel Aviv.[29] In 2013, Hamas Party leader Ismail Haniyeh took his granddaughter to Israeli doctors at Schneider Medical Center in Petah Tikva.[30] Shortly after the hospital visit for his granddaughter, Haniyeh was filmed at a rally calling for Israel's destruction.[31] Afterward, Haniyeh also took his mother-in-law to Augusta

---

[28] From "Human rights complaints rise in Palestinian territories, group says," by M. Abukhater, 2014, *Los Angeles Times*.

[29] See "Mahmoud Abbas's wife undergoes surgery in Israel," by S. Winer, 2014, *Times of Israel* for more information.

[30] See "Hamas PM Haniyeh's granddaughter transferred to Israeli hospital for treatment," by K. A. Toameh, 2013, *The Jerusalem Post* for more information.

[31] See "Hamas PM Ismail Haniyeh calls for Israel's destruction," by Video Manager, 2014, *Israel 365 News*.

Victoria Hospital in East Jerusalem for cancer treatment.[32] These events occurred within seven months of each other.

Israel's compassion and care, even for its enemies, is the type of compassion worthy of Dr. King's faith and advocacy. For years, Israel has provided medical assistance to its enemy to the north, Syria. Engulfed in a bloody civil war since 2011, over half a million people have died—both fighters and civilians. Israel has tended to the wounded without question or discrimination. Many of the Syrians that Israeli doctors have aided would not hesitate to kill them if given the opportunity.

When Israel withdrew from Gaza in 2005, Hamas and Fatah began fighting and killing each other to establish who would rule. The war was brutal and featured soldiers shooting their enemy in the knee caps and leaving them alive as a form of humiliation. Hamas won the fight and now rules Gaza. Fatah soldiers fled into the West Bank, and the wounded were treated in a state-of-the-art Israeli facility. They received prostheses that cost $45,000 per limb and rehabbed with Israeli physical therapists. "A person is a person. A soldier is a soldier. It doesn't matter where he comes from," said Dr. Tzaki Siev Ner, head of Orthopedic Rehabilitation at Tel Hashomer Hospital in Tel Aviv.[33]

Israel is the nation that Dr. King described as an "oasis of brotherhood and democracy." A light in the midst of darkness. Hope in a sea of despair.

Many scriptures attest to God's eternal covenant with the Jewish people and their right to the land of Israel. There is not one scripture that transferred the title of the land of Israel to the Palestinians or any other people. However, many scriptures teach us to care for the broken and defend the weak.

> Isaiah 1.17
> *Learn to do good, seek justice, strengthen the robbed, perform justice for the orphan, plead the case of the widow.*

> יז לִמְדוּ הֵיטֵב דִּרְשׁוּ מִשְׁפָּט אַשְּׁרוּ חָמוֹץ שִׁפְטוּ יָתוֹם רִיבוּ אַלְמָנָה׃

---

[32] See "Ismail Haniyeh's mother-in-law admitted to Israeli hospital," by TheTower.org staff, 2014, *The Tower* for more information.

[33] See "Palestinian Fatah fighters rehabilitate in Israel," by TIME, 2013, *TIME*.

THE PRO-ISRAEL LEGACY OF THE REVEREND DR. MARTIN LUTHER KING, JR.

(The Complete Jewish Bible with Rashi Commentary, Isaiah 1.17)

Zechariah 7.10
Do not oppress the widow, the orphan, the stranger, or the poor man. Neither shall any of you think evil against his brother in your heart.

י וְאַלְמָנָה וְיָתוֹם גֵּר וְעָנִי אַל־תַּעֲשֹׁקוּ וְרָעַת אִישׁ אָחִיו אַל־תַּחְשְׁבוּ בִּלְבַבְכֶם:

(The Complete Jewish Bible with Rashi Commentary, Zechariah 7.10)

The Black Church tradition is defined by concern for the broken, relief for the oppressed. Dr. King embodied these principles. Because of Israel's outstanding humanitarian work around the world, support of the Jewish State means helping those in need—including the Palestinians. Unfairly criticizing Israel does nothing to defend Palestinian human rights. On the contrary, it only hinders the Palestinians' best hope for real democracy and lasting peace.

As a Christian Zionist and one truly concerned for humanity, Dr. King stood with Israel and sought to relieve the suffering of the Arabs. Support of the Jewish State is not a lack of concern for the Arab Palestinians. It acknowledges that the best hope for peace in the region is a strong, prosperous, secure state of Israel.

Psalm 125.4–5
*4 Be good, O Lord, to the good and to the upright in their hearts.
5 And those who turn their crooked ways-may the Lord lead them away with the workers of iniquity, [and may there be] peace on Israel.*

ד הֵיטִיבָה יְהֹוָה לַטּוֹבִים וְלִישָׁרִים בְּלִבּוֹתָם:
ה וְהַמַּטִּים | עֲקַלְקַלּוֹתָם יוֹלִיכֵם יְהֹוָה אֶת־פֹּעֲלֵי הָאָוֶן שָׁלוֹם עַל־יִשְׂרָאֵל:

(The Complete Jewish Bible with Rashi Commentary, Psalm 125.4-5)

Dr. King's close friend and attorney, Dr. Clarence Jones, stated on February 28, 2014:

> Anybody can stand with you in the warm summer sunlight of an August summer. But only a winter soldier stands with you at midnight in the alpine chill of winter.
>
> From the standpoint of someone who has represented the great legacy

> of this extraordinary man, Martin Luther King Jr . . . I say to my African American brothers and sisters . . . the time is now for every African American person, every person of stature in the African American community, to come forward and stand with Israel in the alpine chill of winter, to show that we are wintertime soldiers.[34]

It is said that the Jewish people never forget a friend, and Israel remembers Dr. King's steadfastness to this day. The only street in the entire Middle East named after the civil rights legend is in one of the best areas of Jerusalem, near the Prime Minister's residence and Liberty Bell Park.

Martin Luther King Street in Jerusalem

Coretta Scott King acknowledged Israel's efforts to commemorate her late husband.

> On April 3, 1968, just before he was killed, Martin delivered his last public address. In it he spoke of the visit he and I made to Israel.
>
> Moreover, he spoke to us about his vision of the Promised Land, a land of justice and equality, brotherhood and peace. Martin dedicated his life to the goals of peace and unity among all peoples, and perhaps nowhere in the world is there a greater appreciation of the desirability and necessity of peace than in Israel.[35]

Mrs. King remained a faithful supporter of Israel and advocated for peace in the region until her passing in 2006. In 2007, the Israelis planted a forest in her honor

---

[34] From "Dr. King's aide Clarence B. Jones honored in Harlem," by Autodidact 17, 2014, *Amsterdam News*.

[35] From "Remembering MLKs ties to Israel, Promised Land vision," by M. Schneier, 1998, *The Jewish News of Northern California*.

in the Galilee region of Northern Israel. My first trip to the Holy Land was part of the African-American Pastors Tour with Christians United for Israel (CUFI) in 2012. Our tour leader, Dr. Michael Stevens, took us to the Coretta Scott King Forest.

CUFI African-American Pastors Israel Mission at Coretta Scott King Forest in the Galilee, 2012

An accurate account of history is the most effective defense against the bondage of disinformation and false narratives. As Jesus said, "the truth will make you free." Black American leaders were historically targeted with anti-Zionist messaging by Israel's enemies. It is still happening today. One goal of this deception is to drive a wedge between Blacks and Jews and between Africa and Israel. In so doing, Israel's enemies seek to paint Israel as an oppressive, imperialist regime determined to rule the world. In reality, Israel is the homeland of the Jewish people who were without one for nearly 2,000 years. This is the essence of Zionism—reclaiming the Jewish homeland, and it has inspired Black leaders for decades.

Civil rights legends like Dr. Martin Luther King, Jr. and Bayard Rustin stood in solidarity with Israel and the Jewish people. They also advocated for the just treatment of the Arab Palestinian people, which included speaking truth to Palestinian leadership—not irresponsibly blaming Israel. This is the type of Zionism that has always been the mark of knowledgeable leaders in the Black community. This is the legacy of Black support for the nation of Israel, for the Jewish people, and for a strong Africa-Israel alliance. This is the truth that must be taught to young Black and African men and women. This is restoration.

CHAPTER 5
ANTI-ZIONISM: HATRED FOR ISRAEL

Psalm 3.2–4
2 O Lord, how many have my adversaries become! Great men rise up against me.
3 Great men say concerning my soul, "He has no salvation in God to eternity."
4 But You, O Lord, are a shield about me, my glory and He Who raises up my head.

ב יְהֹוָה מָה־רַבּוּ צָרָי רַבִּים קָמִים עָלָי׃
ג רַבִּים אֹמְרִים לְנַפְשִׁי אֵין יְשׁוּעָתָה לּוֹ בֵאלֹהִים סֶלָה׃
ד וְאַתָּה יְהֹוָה מָגֵן בַּעֲדִי כְּבוֹדִי וּמֵרִים רֹאשִׁי׃

(The Complete Jewish Bible with Rashi Commentary, Psalm 3.2-4)

If Zionism is a word that has multiple meanings and applications, the same is even more true for *anti-Zionism*. As the term suggests, anti-Zionism is a negative stance toward the Jewish homeland. One who is anti-Zionist believes that for any number of reasons, Israel's sovereignty is wrong. Usually, this sentiment is expressed by casting Zionism in a negative light. This includes accusations of Israeli imperialism, colonialism, and racism. Most conscientious people would never oppose someone else's right to live in peace. However, most people *would* oppose stealing someone else's land to achieve that peace. It is a sign of our God-given humanity to desire justice for ourselves and others.

There is a more sinister definition of anti-Zionism: the outright hatred of Israel or the Jewish people (antisemitism). Anti-Zionism, at its core, is a denial of the

103

right for Israel or the Jewish people to exist. As we stated, most people would never wish to see an entire ethnic group removed from the earth. Such attitudes are the stuff of monsters like Adolph Hitler, who murdered over six million Jews of Europe during his maniacal reign. As another example of the shared struggle between Black and Jewish people, Hitler also persecuted and annihilated an untold number of Afro-Germans.

After World War I, the Allies stripped Germany of its African colonies. The German military stationed in Africa, known as the Schutztruppen, as well as missionaries, colonial bureaucrats, and settlers, returned to Germany with racist attitudes. Separation of white people and Black people was mandated by the Reichstag (German parliament), which enacted a law against mixed marriages in the African colonies.

Following World War I and the Treaty of Versailles (1919), the victorious Allies occupied the Rhineland in western Germany. The use of French colonial troops, some of whom were Black, in these occupation forces heightened anti-Black racism in Germany. Racist propaganda against Black soldiers depicted them as rapists of German women and carriers of venereal and other diseases. The children of Black soldiers and German women were called "Rhineland Bastards."

The Nazis, at the time a small political movement, viewed the "Rhineland Bastards" as a threat to the purity of the Germanic race. In his autobiography, Mein Kampf (My Struggle), Hitler charged that "the Jews had brought the Negroes into the Rhineland with the clear aim of ruining the hated white race by the necessarily-resulting bastardization."

African German mulatto (a person of mixed white and Black ancestry) children were marginalized in German society, isolated socially and economically, and not allowed to attend university. Racial discrimination prohibited them from seeking most jobs, including service in the military. With the Nazi rise to power they became a target of racial and population policy. By 1937, the Gestapo had secretly rounded up and forcibly sterilized many of them. Some were subjected to medical experiments; others mysteriously "disappeared."[1]

From the opening pages of the book of Exodus to the end of the Bible, we see Israel dealing with her foes—Egyptians, Assyrians, Amalekites, Philistines, Moabites, Midianites, Ammonites, Syrians, Romans, and more. The Babylonians destroyed the Temple in Jerusalem, took many Jews as slaves, and killed even more. Israel was also sold in slavery to the Greeks (Joel 3.4-6). During Jesus' day, the Romans were the antagonists and occupiers of Judah. It was the Romans who ultimately destroyed the second Temple and eventually renamed the Jewish homeland, *Palestine*.

Within the synagogue liturgy is a portion called the *Emet V'emunah*, meaning True and Faithful.

Emet V'emunah

True and faithful is all this, and firmly established for us that He is the Lord our God, and there is none besides Him, and that we, Israel, are His people

He is our King, who redeems us from the hand of kings, and delivers us from the grasp of tyrants.

He is our God, who on our behalf repays our foes and brings just retribution on our mortal enemies; who performs great deeds beyond understanding and wonders beyond numbers; who kept us alive, not letting our foot slip; who led us on the high places of our enemies raising our pride above all our foes; who did miracles for us and brought vengeance against Pharaoh; who performed signs and wonders in the land of Ham's children;

Who smote in His wrath all the firstborn of Egypt, and brought His people Israel from their midst into everlasting freedom; who led His children through the divided Reed Sea, plunging their pursuers and enemies into the depths.

When His children saw His might they gave praise and thanks to His name, and willingly accepted His Sovereignty.

---

[1] From "Afro-Germans during the Holocaust," by the United States Holocaust Memorial Museum in the *Holocaust Encyclopedia*, n. d.

Moses and the children of Israel then sang a song to You with great joy, and they all exclaimed:

"Who is like You, Lord, among the mighty?
Who is like You, majestic in holiness,
awesome in praises, doing wonders?"

Your children beheld Your majesty
as you parted the sea before Moses.
"This is my God!" they responded, and then said:

"The Lord shall reign for ever and ever."

And it is said, "For the Lord has redeemed Jacob and rescued him from the power stronger than his own."
Blessed are You, Lord, who redeemed Israel.

These are the words of a people who have known generations of violence and hatred, a people familiar with subjugation, abuse, and being pursued. These are also the words of victory and triumph, of deliverance in the face of death and destruction. Black and Jewish people share a number of common threads. One that may bind them together above all others is an ongoing history of facing relentless enemies. This is another reason for the historic synergy and mutual respect between the two peoples in the United States.

If Christians are to truly understand the spiritual battle involved in standing with Israel and the Jewish people, they must first understand this—Israel and the Jewish people have, and have always had, many enemies. As Christians, we know the root of this opposition is demonic, and like anything spiritual, there will be physical (human) evidence. Whether that human form is an Egyptian Pharaoh throwing Hebrew babies into the Nile River or a German dictator burning Jewish families in ovens, Israel has always had enemies—powerful enemies.

It is a testimony to the covenant-keeping power of God that the Jewish people have survived thousands of years of attack. They have survived and thrived. Through his prophets, God declares that the Israelite people will always exist.

Jeremiah 31.34–35

34 So said the Lord, Who gives the sun to illuminate by day, the laws of the moon and the stars to illuminate at night, Who stirs up the sea and its waves roar, the Lord of Hosts is His name.

35 If these laws depart from before Me, says the Lord, so will the seed of Israel cease being a nation before Me for all time.

לד כֹּה ׀ אָמַר יְהֹוָה נֹתֵן שֶׁמֶשׁ לְאוֹר יוֹמָם חֻקֹּת יָרֵחַ וְכוֹכָבִים לְאוֹר לָיְלָה רֹגַע הַיָּם וַיֶּהֱמוּ גַלָּיו יְהֹוָה צְבָאוֹת שְׁמוֹ:
לה אִם־יָמֻשׁוּ הַחֻקִּים הָאֵלֶּה מִלְּפָנַי נְאֻם־יְהֹוָה גַּם זֶרַע יִשְׂרָאֵל יִשְׁבְּתוּ מִהְיוֹת גּוֹי לְפָנַי כָּל־הַיָּמִים:

(The Complete Jewish Bible with Rashi Commentary, Jeremiah 31.34-35)

The two realities of Israel's enemies and God's protection set the stage for the conflict. Israel has many foes, and God will always defend Israel; God will use people to accomplish His purposes.

The physical, violent opposition to the Jewish State begins with anti-Zionist rhetoric and propaganda or false narratives. False narratives about Israel seek to deny its right to exist and are as old as the Scriptures.

BIBLICAL EXAMPLE OF FALSE NARRATIVE

There is a fascinating and relevant story recorded in Judges 11. It happened around 1080 B.C. The Ammonites were attacking the Israelites, and a man named Jephthah was selected to be the commander of Israel's fighting forces. Like a wise warrior, Jephthah sent a letter to the Ammonite king to see if there could be a diplomatic solution to the conflict. The rational assumption was that the king of Ammon was fighting Israel for a valid reason.

Judges 11.12–13

12 And Jephthah sent messengers to the king of the children of Ammon, saying, "What is (between) me and you, that you have come to me to fight in my land?"

13 And the king of the children of Ammon said to the messengers of Jephthah, "Because Israel took away my land, when they came out of Egypt, from Arnon and up to the Jabbok, and up to the Jordan; and now restore them peacefully."

יב וַיִּשְׁלַח יִפְתָּח מַלְאָכִים אֶל־מֶלֶךְ בְּנֵי־עַמּוֹן לֵאמֹר מַה־לִּי וָלָךְ כִּי־בָאתָ אֵלַי לְהִלָּחֵם בְּאַרְצִי:
יג וַיֹּאמֶר מֶלֶךְ בְּנֵי־עַמּוֹן אֶל־מַלְאֲכֵי יִפְתָּח כִּי־לָקַח יִשְׂרָאֵל אֶת־אַרְצִי בַּעֲלוֹתוֹ מִמִּצְרַיִם מֵאַרְנוֹן וְעַד־הַיַּבֹּק וְעַד־הַיַּרְדֵּן וְעַתָּה הָשִׁיבָה אֶתְהֶן בְּשָׁלוֹם:

(The Complete Jewish Bible with Rashi Commentary, Judges 11.12-13)

The Ammonite king was referring to events that had taken place more than 300 years earlier (Numbers 20). The problem was that the Ammonite king had every fact wrong. Nothing happened the way he said. Israel had not taken *Ammonite* land at all. Israel was in possession of formerly *Amorite* land, but there was a reason for this. Jephthah attempted to set the record straight by giving a complete, accurate rendering of the events in question. The story was somewhat complicated but was the truth.

After leaving Egypt, the king of Edom would not allow Moses and the children of Israel to pass through his land. Moses and the Israelites went around Edom and Moab, a dual kingdom with Ammon, to avoid trouble. Sichon, king of the Amorites, not only refused passage to the Israelites; he decided to launch an attack against them. God gave Israel victory over the Amorites, and they took possession of the Amorites' land. The children of Israel had not stolen Ammonite land, and the Ammonites were not even involved in the original battle. Moses and the children of Israel fought the Amorites, which was a battle of self-defense. Somehow, the king of Ammon and his people had a false narrative. They had been victimized by propaganda. Further, the Ammonites believed their version wholeheartedly and were willing to fight because of it. They fought the Israelites and suffered a crushing defeat (Judges 11.15-27). The more elements of truth contained in a false narrative, the more difficult it is to unravel. I share that ancient story to illustrate what Israel contends with to this day.

Anti-Zionists who base their opposition to the Jewish State on the false narrative that Israel stole Arab land are the modern-day Ammonites. Just like the example in Judges, the truth can sometimes be a complicated story. However, it is no less the truth. The partition of British Mandate Palestine separating Arab and Jewish territory was done legally and with the consent of the international community. Besides, Arab violence against the Jews living in Palestine was one of the key reasons partitioning the land was necessary. Not only are the Jewish people indigenous to the land of Israel with a historical tie that goes back over 3,000 years, but they have also had a continual presence there—even during the exile imposed by the Romans.

Saudi Arabian author Abdulateef Al-Mulhim explains why so many anti-Israel Palestinians and their supporters embrace the false narrative of Israel's rebirth.

> Since 1948 it is not considered appropriate to read or translate a book written by an Israeli author that could help us understand Israel. So, what happened on May 14, 1948?
>
> It was the day when the state of Israel emerged on the world map. Do we know the rest of the story? No. We don't know the entire story because we are wont of dealing with events with emotions. One day after the United Nations mandate (May 15), a long and bloody conflict broke out and after the dust settled, the Arabs called it Nakba or the Day of Catastrophe. It was a defeat but the Arabs chose to call it a catastrophe. Many Palestinians were displaced from their homeland and were promised that they would return to their homes soon. Despite the passage of over six decades, the promise has yet to be delivered. The thousands of Palestinians who fled their homes have turned into millions.
>
> The question now is what if those Palestinians had accepted the mandate and decided to live side by side with the Israelis? I ask the readers to please note that I am just asking a question. So, would the fate of the Palestinians be the same? The reason I am asking is that we read reports that the Palestinian refugees are not allowed fleeing the atrocities in Syria and seeking refuge in Lebanon. That is double the agony.[2]

Christian anti-Zionists, sometimes known as Christian Palestinianists, generally embrace this Nakba narrative. Prominent within this group are people like Stephen Sizer, vicar of the Anglican parish of Christ Church; Virginia Water of Surrey, England; Gary Burge, New Testament scholar at Wheaton College in Illinois; and Naim Ateek, Palestinian priest in the Anglican Church as well as the founder of the Sabeel Ecumenical Liberation Theology Center in Jerusalem.

---

[2] From "May 15: Nakba or defeat?" by A. Al-Muhim, 2014, *Arab News*. https://www.arabnews.com/news/570476.

Naim Ateek is also one of the authors of the *Kairos Palestine Document*, a manipulative work which falsely accuses Israel of "apartheid," and never once mentions the corrupt Palestinian leadership.

In his presentation at the 2011 Berean Call Conference, Dr. Paul Wilkinson outlined the core beliefs within Christian Palestinianism or anti-Zionism:

> The Bible—Christian, not Jewish
> The Church—New Israel, not a new people
> The Land—Palestine, not Israel
> The Holocaust—Resented, not remembered
> May 14, 1948—A catastrophe (Nakba), not a miracle
> State of Israel—Illegitimate, not prophetic
> Israeli Jews—Illegal occupiers
> Bible Prophecy—Moral manifesto
> The Lord Jesus— Palestinian, not Jewish[3]

On a television program in Malaysia called *Viva Palestina*, anti-Zionist Stephen Sizer explained the State of Israel, and Zionism, in these terms:

> The idea of Zionism goes back to empire building, colonialism, and the concept of ethnically pure races. So it's a form of racism. And [Zionists] are going back to the Bible to justify it; 3000–4000 years. What about the people who've lived there since then who can also quote from the scriptures about their justification for being there too? So Zionism is a form of racism today. And Israel's really got to decide whether it wants to be an inclusive, modern society that's multi-faith, multi-ethnic . . . or does it want to go down the route of South Africa and apartheid—and separate Whites from Blacks.[4]

Such distortion of historical facts and dismissing of the Israelite return to the Land help create confusion about Christian Zionism. Calling Zionism racism is a method of manipulation and misrepresents the Black struggle for justice. As is

---

[3] From "Christian Palestinianism," by P. Wilkinson, 2011, *The Berean Call Conference*. https://www.youtube.com/watch?v=osIx3tmvioY.

[4] Stephen Sizer during an interview with news anchor Kamarul Bahrin Hanson and professor Achin Vanaik on *Astro Awani*, 2011.

typically done with religious anti-Zionism, Mr. Sizer is making false arguments and irrelevant statements to prove an invalid point. That other ancient peoples may be able to trace their ancestry to the land of Israel does not change that it is the land of Israel. Archeologists are still uncovering evidence of the Jewish people that goes back more than three millennia. Statements like, "Israel going down the route of South Africa and apartheid" are beyond dishonest. Black South African and Parliament Member Rev. Kenneth Meshoe was asked about the Israel apartheid comparison.

> Anyone who knows what apartheid really is and still makes such a claim [about Israel] should be told to their faces that they are lying. If [what happened] in South Africa... was the same as what's happening in Israel, then definitely there would not have been any need for an armed struggle [in South Africa]."

> He explained that there was an armed struggle because South Africans were denied basic rights such as the right to vote. "Arab-Israelis," Meshoe noted, "do not struggle with the right to vote and have the choice to go to the schools and hospitals of their choice."

> "Apartheid was very painful," Meshoe recalls, "anyone who claims Israel is an apartheid state is actually minimizing the pain of apartheid."[5]

Israel critics point to the Israeli government's relationship with apartheid South Africa as proof that Black people should have nothing to do with the Jewish State. This is a gross oversimplification of what was a challenging situation. Yes, the Israeli government did business with the apartheid government of South Africa, as did many other countries. However, Israel did not do business with apartheid South Africa to show support for the racist regime. Israel voted to condemn[6] apartheid South Africa at the United Nations in 1962. Israel's relationship with South Africa developed particularly during the 1970s after the Yom Kippur War when Israel was isolated from much of the world, especially Africa. It is important to note here that explanation is not justification. To this day, many Israelis lament

---

[5] By K. Meshoe during an interview with *Artuz Sheva* (2013). See "'Israeli apartheid? I know what apartheid is," by K. Rozenbaum, 2013, *Artutz Sheva.*

[6] See "Daily News Bulletin," by Jewish Telegraph Agency, 1962, *Jewish Telegraphic Agency* for more information.

the fact that Israel had anything at all to do with the racist government of South Africa. But, to claim that Jerusalem partnered with Pretoria to oppress Black South Africans is simply not true.

False narratives have been the most consistent form of slander against the Jewish State. This was especially true in the retelling of the Arab-Israeli wars in which Israel was defending its right to exist. Just as Jephthah provided an accurate account to the Ammonite king of Israel's right to be in the land, here is an accurate account of the pivotal Arab-Israeli wars of 1948, 1967, and 1973.

1948: TRAGEDY OR TRIUMPH

For the Christian Zionist, May 14, 1948, Israel's Independence Day, was the beginning of the fulfillment of prophecy. God said He would gather the Jewish people and return them to the Land. The day Israel was reborn was also the official beginning of the Arab-Israeli wars. Outnumbered, outgunned, and on the heels of the Holocaust, the Jewish people fought for their survival. As He did in the Bible, God gave Israel victory over the combined forces of Egypt, Saudi Arabia, Jordan, Syria, and Lebanon. What the Jewish people called a triumph, the Arabs called *Nakba* (tragedy or catastrophe). To this day, Israeli independence is seen from this victory-versus-defeat perspective.

The Israeli government immediately offered citizenship to all Arabs living within the new Jewish State. There were Arab members of the Knesset, the Israeli parliament, from the beginning. Some Arabs decided to stay, and their progeny remain in Israel today. Approximately 750,000 Arabs left the Jewish State, some fleeing the war; however, many left because their leaders told them the Jews would quickly be destroyed. The idea was that they would return once the Jews were driven out or killed. When the Arabs were defeated, those who fled became refugees as their Arab kinsmen refused to absorb them into their countries.

1967: IMPERIALISM OR SELF-DEFENSE

We have already looked at the events of June 1967 and discussed how the Arab League attempted to remove the Jewish State a second time. The Arab forces of Egypt, Syria, Jordan, Saudi Arabia, and Iraq came together so confident of their success; they began celebrating beforehand. The presumptuousness of the Arab states in 1967 was also reminiscent of an exchange between Ben-Hadad, king of Syria, and Ahab, king of Israel (1 Kings 20). Ben-Hadad built a coalition of thirty-two kings to come against Ahab and the children of Israel. The Syrian king was so assured of his triumph that he felt the actual fighting was unnecessary. Ben-Hadad sent messengers to Ahab and told him to surrender his gold, silver, wives, and children. Ahab responded, "one who puts on his armor should not boast as one who takes it off."

The Six Day War is also reminiscent of 2 Chronicles 20. The Judean king, Jehoshaphat, was being threatened by the combined forces of Moab, Ammon, and Mount Seir. Jehoshaphat called for a national day of fasting and prayer, after which the Israelites gathered in the Temple. The king made this petition to God in the presence of all the people:

2 Chronicles 20.6–12
6 "...O Lord, God of our fathers, is it not so that You are God in heaven, and that You rule over all the kingdoms of the nations, and in Your hand is strength and might, and no one can stand with You?
7 Have you, our God, not driven out the inhabitants of this land from before Your people Israel and given it to the seed of Abraham, who loved You, forever?
8 And they dwelt therein and therein they built You a Sanctuary for Your name, saying:
9 Should evil come upon us, whether sword, judgment, pestilence, or famine, we shall stand before this House and before You, for Your name is in this House, and we shall cry out to You from our distress, and You will hear and save.
10 And now, behold the children of Ammon and Moab and Mount Seir, against whom You did not permit Israel to come when they came out of the land of Egypt, for they turned away from them and did not destroy them.
11 And behold they are repaying us by coming to drive us out of Your inheritance, which You caused us to inherit.
12 Our God, will You not execute judgment upon them? For we have no strength before this great multitude that is coming upon us, and we know not what to do, but our eyes are upon You."

ו וַיֹּאמַר יְהוָה אֱלֹהֵי אֲבֹתֵינוּ הֲלֹא אַתָּה־הוּא אֱלֹהִים בַּשָּׁמַיִם וְאַתָּה מוֹשֵׁל בְּכֹל מַמְלְכוֹת הַגּוֹיִם וּבְיָדְךָ כֹּחַ וּגְבוּרָה וְאֵין עִמְּךָ לְהִתְיַצֵּב:

ANTI-ZIONISM: HATRED FOR ISRAEL

ז הֲלֹא ׀ אַתָּה אֱלֹהֵינוּ הוֹרַשְׁתָּ אֶת־יֹשְׁבֵי הָאָרֶץ הַזֹּאת מִלִּפְנֵי עַמְּךָ יִשְׂרָאֵל וַתִּתְּנָהּ לְזֶרַע אַבְרָהָם אֹהַבְךָ לְעוֹלָם:
ח וַיֵּשְׁבוּ־בָהּ וַיִּבְנוּ לְךָ ׀ בָּהּ מִקְדָּשׁ לְשִׁמְךָ לֵאמֹר:
ט אִם־תָּבוֹא עָלֵינוּ רָעָה חֶרֶב שְׁפוֹט וְדֶבֶר וְרָעָב נַעַמְדָה לִפְנֵי הַבַּיִת הַזֶּה וּלְפָנֶיךָ כִּי שִׁמְךָ בַּבַּיִת הַזֶּה וְנִזְעַק אֵלֶיךָ מִצָּרָתֵנוּ וְתִשְׁמַע וְתוֹשִׁיעַ:
י וְעַתָּה הִנֵּה בְנֵי־עַמּוֹן וּמוֹאָב וְהַר־שֵׂעִיר אֲשֶׁר לֹא־נָתַתָּה לְיִשְׂרָאֵל לָבוֹא בָהֶם בְּבֹאָם מֵאֶרֶץ מִצְרָיִם כִּי סָרוּ מֵעֲלֵיהֶם וְלֹא הִשְׁמִידוּם:
יא וְהִנֵּה־הֵם גֹּמְלִים עָלֵינוּ לָבוֹא לְגָרְשֵׁנוּ מִיְּרֻשָּׁתְךָ אֲשֶׁר הוֹרַשְׁתָּנוּ:
יב אֱלֹהֵינוּ הֲלֹא תִשְׁפָּט־בָּם כִּי אֵין בָּנוּ כֹּחַ לִפְנֵי הֶהָמוֹן הָרָב הַזֶּה הַבָּא עָלֵינוּ וַאֲנַחְנוּ לֹא נֵדַע מַה־נַּעֲשֶׂה כִּי עָלֶיךָ עֵינֵינוּ:

(The Complete Jewish Bible with Rashi Commentary,
2 Chronicles 20.6-12)

Just as God delivered Jehoshaphat and the children of Israel from Moab, Ammon, and Mount Seir, so did He deliver them from Egypt, Jordan, Syria, Saudi Arabia, and Iraq. Yet, there was something else miraculous and prophetic about the Six Day War of 1967. When the fighting stopped, Israel had access to all of Jerusalem, the Holy City. In the original partitioning of land in 1947, Jerusalem was under international control. Beginning with the Arab-Israeli War in 1948, Jordan occupied East Jerusalem. As a result of the Arab states' aggression toward Israel in 1967, Israel eventually took back and reunified Jerusalem for the first time in almost 2,000 years. This was evidence of prophecy unfolding as Psalm 147 says, "the Lord rebuilds Jerusalem. He gathers the outcasts of Israel."

THE 1973 YOM KIPPUR WAR

The 1973 War was arguably the most brutal and traumatic for the Israelis.

> On October 6, 1973—Yom Kippur . . . Egypt and Syria launched a coordinated surprise attack against Israel. The equivalent of the total forces of NATO in Europe was mobilized on Israel's borders. On the Golan Heights (north), approximately 180 Israeli tanks faced an onslaught of 1400 Syrian tanks. Along the Suez Canal, fewer than 500 Israeli defenders with only 3 tanks were attacked by 600,000 Egyptian soldiers, backed by 2,000 tanks and 550 aircraft.
>
> Caught by surprise, in the war's initial days, Israel suffered severe losses of life, military equipment, and territory, abruptly shattering the euphoria

the country had experienced since its show of strength in the Six Day War. Following an Egyptian refusal to accept a cease-fire and a Soviet airlift of military equipment to bolster Egyptian forces, the United States sent an airlift to Israel enabling her to recover from the first blow and inflict damage on Egypt and Syria. In response, Saudi Arabia led the Arab world in an oil embargo directed against the United States and other western nations. The war officially ended with a U.N.-declared cease-fire, but fighting continued.[7]

By all military accounts, the Jewish State almost fell during the Yom Kippur War. However, once again, Israel prevailed with help in large part from U.S. President Richard Nixon, to whom Prime Minister Golda Meir appealed personally. In the war's aftermath, some Israelis decided their homeland was too dangerous and vulnerable, so they left the country. Israel survived, but at a very high price.

After Israel's victory in the 1973 Yom Kippur War, the Arabs states, with continued financial support from the Soviet Union, changed their strategy. What the Arabs could not accomplish on the battlefield, they attempted in the arena of ideas. They decided to use the language of civil rights—freedom and justice— lifted straight out of the Black "handbook" and called themselves the oppressed. The Arab Palestinians became the new disenfranchised people of color. The strategy systematically targeted Black leaders, distorting the meaning of justice— this had the most significant impact on Africans and Black Americans.

THE "ZIONISM IS RACISM" LIE

After the 1973 War, the Arab nations could not believe they lost again. With significant help from the Soviet Union and another confederacy of anti-Israel Arab comrades, they had every reason to feel confident. They forgot the God of Israel has the final say. Convinced they could not defeat Israel in a military battle, the Arab States and the Soviet Union chose politics and propaganda. They began an international campaign of delegitimization of Israel and sought to pass a United Nations resolution condemning the very ideology of Jewish sovereignty— Zionism.

---

[7] From "Yom Kippur War 1973," by Anti-Defamation League, n. d., *ADL*.

In his book *Moynihan's Moment: America's Fight Against Zionism as Racism*, Professor Gil Troy wrote:

> Criminalizing Zionism turned David into Goliath, deeming Israel the Middle East perpetual villain with the perennial victims. This great inversion culminated a process that began in 1967 with Israel's imposing Six-Day War victory, followed by the Arab shift from conventional military tactics to guerrilla and ideological warfare, especially after the 1973 Yom Kippur War.[8]

The Arab states usurped the role of oppressed indigenous peoples to win international sympathy. They used Israel's victory over them to their advantage and cast themselves as the victims of Israel's "White European" colonization and imperialism. They also sought to dismantle the flourishing alliance between Israel and Africa. The Arab desire to destroy Israel-Africa relations was not new in 1973; its origins began in the 1950s. Yet, after another defeat at the hands of the Israelis, the Arabs decided to expand on the idea.

Again, Professor Gil Troy:

> Many African leaders . . . appreciated Israel's help in the 1960s and early 1970s - and resented that the Arabs had not offered compensation for the oil price jump (after the Arab oil embargo of 1973). Israelis, especially Labor Zionists like David Ben-Gurion and Golda Meir, felt a sense of "historical mission" to fulfill Theodor Herzl's dream of helping African countries. By the early 1970s, Israel had diplomatic ties with thirty-two African countries, more African embassies than any country other than the United States. Tanzania's president Julius Nyerer called Meir, Israel's prime minister from 1969 to 1974, "the mother of Africa."

> The Arab nations recognized the point. Shortly after seizing power in 1952, Egypt's Gamel Abdul Nasser vowed to run Israel out of Africa. The Arab League appealed to the new African nations in their language, calling Israel's help a "façade for neocolonialism trying to sneak through the back window after the old well-known colonialism had been driven

---

[8] From "Introduction: 'Just a matter of decency'," by G. Troy, 2013, *Moynihan's moment: America's fight against Zionism as racism*, p. 4. Copyright 2013 by Gil Troy.

out through the front door.'" Israel's 1967 triumph unsettled relations with Black Africa. Some countries succumbed to the Arab and now Soviet entreaties, too, but relations thrived with most. The rupture came with the 1973 Yom Kippur War, when [Libyan president] Muammar Qaddafi, the Saudis, and other Arab leaders bullied and bribed twenty-one (African) countries in October and November 1973 alone to sever diplomatic ties with Israel.[9]

I have spoken with Nigerian pastors and leaders who remember a thriving economy in the 1970s. Partnership with Israel empowered many Black African nations to emerge from the devastating effects of real European colonialism. Dr. Saviour Chishimba is a Christian leader in Zambia who recalled his country's progress during the height of its relationship with Israel.

Between 1964 and 1974, Zambia was among the richest countries in Africa and Asia. Countries like Singapore and Malaysia were far poorer than Zambia during the same period. Our nation's prosperity was driven by the ingenuity of the Jews. Israelis built the first, and still the biggest, university in Zambia called University of Zambia in 1966. Israelis also built the biggest hospital in Zambia called University Teaching Hospital.[10]

In the United Nations, the Soviets were attempting to marginalize America and her global influence. Of course, the Arab states were trying to destroy Israel, America's number one ally in the Middle East. The two entities combined forces, pivoted on the *Jews are colonizers*, false narrative and spearheaded U.N. Resolution 3379—Zionism is Racism. This agenda-laden effort turned on its head the very concept of people being protected from racism. Zionism, the belief in and advocacy for a homeland for the Jewish people, was called the opposite— hatred of everyone not Jewish. What's more, *Zionism is Racism* made a complete mockery of the centuries of racial hatred and oppression endured by people of color. The fact that the resolution was championed by some of the most racially oppressive regimes on earth added further insult to injury.

---

[9] From "Moynihan on the move, October 1975,'" by G. Troy, 2013, *Moynihan's moment: America's fight against Zionism as racism*, p. 100. Copyright 2013 by Gil Troy.

[10] From "Israel Should be Zambia's Closest Ally," by A. Barak, 2018, *Mida*.

ANTI-ZIONISM: HATRED FOR ISRAEL

Russia's role in spreading anti-Zionist, antisemitic propaganda cannot be overstated. Joseph Stalin was the communist dictator of the Soviet Union from 1929 to 1953. After the United States formed the North Atlantic Treaty Organization (NATO) to stop the worldwide spread of communism, Stalin launched an anti-Democracy, anti-Zionist countermeasure that still continues. In his book *Disinformation: Former Spy Chief Reveals Secret Strategy for Undermining Freedom, Attacking Religion, and Promoting Terrorism*, Lt. General Ion Mihai Pacepa wrote:

> By mid-1949 [Stalin] was faced with a Western Europe firmly bonded to the United States, and he knew that the Soviet Union did not have the military strength to break up that unity by force. Realizing that his strong-arm methods would no longer work, Stalin turned his thoughts to an old Russian weapon of the emotions that had so successfully been wielded by him and all the [Czars] before him: anti-Semitism. He was convinced that the hatred for the Jews had deep roots in Europe, and he wanted to turn that hatred against his new enemy. Thus, Stalin decided to portray the United States as a Zionist realm owned by Jewish money and run by a greedy "Council of the Elders of Zion" (Stalin's derisive epithet for the US Congress), whose militaristic sharks wanted to transform the rest of the world into a Jewish fiefdom. At that time, Western Europe was grateful to the United States for restoring its freedom and economic prosperity. Stalin, however, was convinced that it could be changed by exploiting Europe's historical anti-Semitism and fear of a new war.[11]

Arguably, the most effective form of Soviet anti-Zionist deception and propaganda targeting the Black community was embodied by the Egyptian-born, self-proclaimed leader of the Arab Palestinian people. His name was Mohammed Yasser Abdel Rahman Abdel Raouf Arafat al-Qudwa al-Husseini, better known as Yasser Arafat, leader of the Palestine Liberation Organization (PLO).

Again, former KGB spy chief, Lt. General Pacepa:

> The KGB had a penchant for "liberation" movements. The Palestinian

---

[11] From "Global war on religion," by R. J. Rychlak and I. M. Pacepa, 2013, *Disinformation: Former spy chief reveals secret strategy for undermining freedom, attacking religion, and promoting terrorism*, p. 94. Copyright 2013 by Ion Mihai Pacepa and Ronald J. Rychlak.

Liberation Organization (PLO), the National Liberation Army of Columbia (FARC), and the National Liberation Army of Bolivia were just a few of the liberation movements born at the KGB.[12]

Regardless of its name, the PLO was not interested in Palestinian liberation. It was a terrorist organization, which, among other things, refused to acknowledge Israel's right to exist and did not officially do so until 1993.[13]

Tamar Pileggi, breaking news editor at The Times of Israel, reported:

> Romanian Lt. General Pacepa told US officials that in 1972 that then-PLO leader Yasser Arafat closely collaborated with the KGB and the Romanian Securitate service, and PLO guerrilla fighters were secretly trained by Soviet intelligence agents.[14]

On the KGB-created liberation movement, Pacepa continued:

> [Several] years ago a black version of liberation theology began growing in a few radical-leftist black churches in the United States. Black liberation theologians James Cone, Cornel West, and Dwight Hopkins have explicitly stated their preference for Marxism because Marxist thought is predicated on a system of oppressor class (whites) versus victim class (blacks), and it sees just one solution: the destruction of the enemy.
>
> The predominantly black Trinity United Church of Christ in Chicago is part of this . . . movement. Its pastor, Reverend Jeremiah Wright . . . became famous [in 2008] for screaming out "not God bless America, but God damn America!"
>
> By 2011 . . . Reverend Wright was touring the United States to preach in packed-full black churches, that "the state of Israel is an illegal, genocidal

---

[12] From "Liberation theology," by R. J. Rychlak and I. M. Pacepa, 2013, *Disinformation: Former spy chief reveals secret strategy for undermining freedom, attacking religion, and promoting terrorism*, p. 106. Copyright 2013 by Ion Mihai Pacepa and Ronald J. Rychlak

[13] See "Did the Palestinians ever really recognize Israel?" by A. Baker, 2018, *The Algemeiner* for more information.

[14] From "Soviet documents 'show Abbas was KGB agent'; Fatah decries 'smear campaign,'" by T. Pileggi, 2016, *Times of Israel*.

... place," and to "equate Judaism with the state of Israel is to equate Christianity with [rapper] Flavor Flav."[15]

Jeremiah Wright has also stated on multiple occasions that "Jesus was a Palestinian."[16] Yet another false teaching and deception designed to delegitimize the Jews of Israel.

Jeremiah Wright's good friend and colleague is Minister Louis Farrakhan of the Nation of Islam. Farrakhan's views on Jews and Israel are well known to those aware of his decades-long career. Louis Farrakhan has joined conspiracy theorists who falsely blame the Jews for the September 11, 2001 (9/11) terrorists attacks on America. He also claims the Jews were the architects of the TransAtlantic Slave Trade, a lie refuted by many, including Professor Henry Louis Gates.[17] We will return to the subject of Louis Farrakhan later in this chapter.

During the relentless campaign of anti-Zionist deception, the Arab leaders used the language of civil rights, justice, human dignity, the rule of law, and other terms, accusing Israel of violating them all. Israel's victories in the wars that her enemies initiated became the "evidence" of her criminal actions. By virtue of the fact that Israel refused to die at the hand of her enemies, she was now slandered as colonial and imperialist. In 1974, Yasser Arafat gave an extensive speech to the General Assembly of the United Nations in which he reframed the entire Israeli-Palestinian debate:

> The Zionist entity clings tenaciously to occupied Arab territory; zionism persists, in its aggressions against us and our territory. New military preparations are feverishly being made. These anticipate another, fifth war of aggression to be launched against us. Such signs bear the closest possible watching, since there is a grave likelihood that this war would forebode nuclear destruction and cataclysmic annihilation.

The world is in need of tremendous efforts if its aspirations to peace,

---

[15] From "Liberation theology," by R. J. Rychlak and I. M. Pacepa, 2013, *Disinformation: Former spy chief reveals secret strategy for undermining freedom, attacking religion, and promoting terrorism*, pp. 108-109. Copyright 2013 by Ion Mihai Pacepa and Ronald J. Rychlak.

[16] See "Jeremiah Wright: 'Jesus was a Palestinian'," by B. Richardson, 2015, *The Hill*.

[17] See "Black demagogues and pseudo-scholars," by H. L. Gates, 1992, *The New York Times*.

> freedom, justice, equality and development are to be realized if its struggle is to be victorious over colonialism, imperialism, neo-colonialism and racism in all its forms, including zionism. Only by such efforts can actual form be given to the aspirations of all peoples, including the aspirations of peoples whose States oppose such efforts. It is this road that leads to the fulfillment of those principles emphasized by the United Nations Charter and the Universal Declaration of Human Rights. Were the status quo simply to be maintained, however, the world would instead be exposed to prolonged armed conflict, in addition to economic human and natural calamity.[18]

Arafat and other enemies of the Jewish State consistently used words like justice, equality, and peace, precisely as the KGB designed. The problem is that Israel's enemies believed those words only applied to themselves, not Israel. The Israelis made multiple offers of peace but were viciously, repeatedly attacked in response. Yasser Arafat *spoke* of peace, but in reality, stood as the leader of a terrorist organization determined to annihilate the Jewish people. Compare Arafat's claims of "Zionist aggression" at the United Nations in 1974 to what stated in a speech less than two weeks before the General Assembly.[19]

> We shall never stop until we can go back home and Israel is destroyed . . . The goal of our struggle is the end of Israel, and there can be no compromises or mediations . . . the goal of this violence is the elimination of Zionism from Palestine in all its political, economic and military aspects . . . We don't want peace, we want victory. Peace for us means Israel's destruction and nothing else.

Reportedly, Arafat also declared, "We will not bend or fail until the blood of every last Jew from the youngest child to the oldest elder is spilt to redeem our land!"[20]

---

[18] From Yasser Arafat's address at the 29th session of the United Nations General Assembly, 1974. Speech transcription retrieved from the United Nations Digital Library.

[19] Quote by Yasser Arafat from November 1974. Retrieved from "The fourth postwar era," by M. Gilbert, 2008, *Israel: A History*, p. 467. Copyright 2008 by Martin Gilbert.

[20] See "Quoting Arafat, Palestinian mission in Colombia calls for Israel's destruction," by TOI Staff, 2017, *Times of Israel*.

With carefully crafted words and a media campaign of deception, Arafat and the PLO boldly exploited Black leaders' lack of knowledge about the Arab-Israeli conflict. He received rockstar treatment in the press, donning the cover of magazines like TIME and LIFE. The Palestine Liberation Organization, responsible for countless deaths of Israeli civilian men, women, and children, was presented to the world as *resistance* fighters. The Wu-Tang Clan is one of the most successful, influential hip hop groups of all time. One of Wu-Tang's hit songs in 1994 was *PLO-Style* because, according to Wu Tang's Method Man, "they freedom fighters and we felt like we was fighting for our freedom everyday too."[21] [22] For Arafat and the PLO beginning in the 1960s, perception eventually became a reality, and anti-Zionism became the default position of anyone in the world truly fighting injustice. Black anti-Zionist, "pro-Palestinian" efforts prove that this terrorist Blaxploitation is still happening today.

Ugandan President Idi Amin, once enjoyed a peaceful relationship with the Israeli government but fell out of favor as his rule descended into the brutalization and slaughtering of his people. He was incensed that Israel refused to sell him helicopters and other tools, which he intended to use against his citizens. Amin befriended the Arab nations and joined the verbal assault against Israel. He also assisted German and Palestinian terrorists who hijacked an Air France plane carrying 100 Israelis in 1976. Israeli commandos led by Jonathan Netanyahu (brother of Israeli Prime Minister, Benjamin Netanyahu), successfully rescued the hostages in *Operation Thunderbolt*, also known as the *Raid on Entebbe*. Jonathan Netanyahu was the only commando killed during the rescue effort. The only Israeli hostage not rescued was 74-year-old Dora Bloch, who fell sick and had been taken to a hospital. Amin reportedly had her shot and killed.

To Black Americans, Idi Amin was a symbol of Black independence and prosperous post-colonial Africa. Many saw him as a rising star who represented hope for a continent that had suffered centuries of subjugation. A Black political leader of that time told me when Idi Amin was scheduled to address the U.N. General Assembly in 1975, there was a great swell of pride among his colleagues. Even though Amin's atrocities against his own people were well known by 1975, no Black American leader would condemn his actions. They reasoned that White

---

[21] See "Method Man Talks 'P.L.O Style' | @SamaanAshrawi," by S. Ashrawi, 2015.

[22] See "Method Man speaks out on 'P.L.O. style' & Black-Palestinian solidarity in a new interview," by S. Heins, 2015, *Okayplayer* for more information.

leaders had terrorized Africa for centuries. To those Black leaders, criticizing Amin was tantamount to being a race-traitor. The silence of Black American leaders in the face of Uganda's tragedy would prove devastating for both the Ugandans and the cause of Africa-Israel solidarity.

Like Yasser Arafat, Idi Amin attacked Israel at the United Nations. His status as a celebrated African head-of-state gave him great credibility among Black American leaders.

> We condemn any form of territorial aggrandizement as practised by the Zionists in the Middle east. We condemn any perpetration of illegalities in the United Nations or sustenance of the bogus State of Israel. Until 1947 there was no State of Israel, but Palestine. The colonial Powers, for their imperialistic motives, created Israel, carved out of the State of Palestine, thus causing upheaval which, if it is not settled immediately, may throw the world into conflagration.[23]

The words were high and lofty—and lies. There has never in history been a *State of Palestine*. Like Arafat, Idi Amin was persecuting his people while intentionally misrepresenting the Israeli's constant fight for survival. For many who were unaware of the facts on the ground, the words of ruthless people like Arafat and Amin were valiant. In the Black community, where the fight for civil rights and human dignity was very real, this was especially true as some were swayed by the self-serving speeches of racial justice and equality. In heartfelt, albeit misguided solidarity, they took up the Palestinian cause against Israel—against Zionism.

Zionism is *not* racism, but anti-Zionism is antisemitism. One cannot oppose the Jewish State and not oppose the Jewish people any more than one can oppose the Kenyan State and not oppose the Kenyan people.

For the Black community and the Black Church, the pivotal moment involving the Israeli-Arab conflict was when Andrew Young resigned his position as U.S. Ambassador to the United Nations in 1979. So controversial was this move that the details are debated to this day. However, certain facts are not in dispute. Ambassador Young had an unauthorized meeting with the PLO's U.N.

---

[23] From Idi Amin's address at the 30th session of the United Nations General Assembly, 1975. Speech transcription retrieved from the United Nations Digital Library.

representative, Zehdi Terzi, "a meeting which violated an American agreement with Israel not to deal with the PLO until it recognized Israel's right to exist and accepted Security Council Resolution 242."[24] Once it became public, news of the meeting caused great controversy among the Israelis and some in the American Jewish community. During that controversy, Ambassador Young resigned. Many Black supporters of Ambassador Young believed that the Israelis and American Jews, forced Young to resign. This belief, coupled with rising tensions between the Black and Jewish communities, exposed a large and growing rift.

> During the course of the affair, charges were leveled against Jews which went well beyond the specific claim that they were responsible for Young's resignation. They were accused, among other things, of obstructing black economic and social progress through their opposition to racial quotas and affirmative-action programs. They were also accused of opposing human rights for Palestinians, and of holding a dual loyalty in their commitment to Israel which led them to support a foreign policy that jeopardized vital American interests, including the need to retain access to Arab oil supplies.[25]

Perhaps the most iconic Middle East moment for Black America was when Dr. King's former protégé, Rev. Jesse Jackson, met with Yasser Arafat to declare his solidarity with the PLO in 1979. The photo of Arafat smiling and hugging Jackson was a perfect example of Arafat's exploitation of Black Americans. The meeting was not particularly effective, and most Black Americans continued to side with Israel over the Palestinian terrorist organization. However, Jackson's efforts would raise the bar for anti-Israel activism, not only within the Black political class but in the academic world. His misguided attacks on U.S. support and military aid for Israel were PLO talking points aimed at separating America from its greatest ally in the Middle East.

> Jackson's tour resulted in considerable publicity for himself and the PLO, but did not produce even a gesture by the PLO indicating a possible interest in renouncing terrorism or recognizing Israel. Jackson announced dramatically that the PLO was declaring a cease-fire in

---

[24] See "The Andrew Young affair," by C. Gershman, 1971, *The Commentary* for more information.

[25] From "The Andrew Young affair," by C. Gershman, 1971, *The Commentary*.

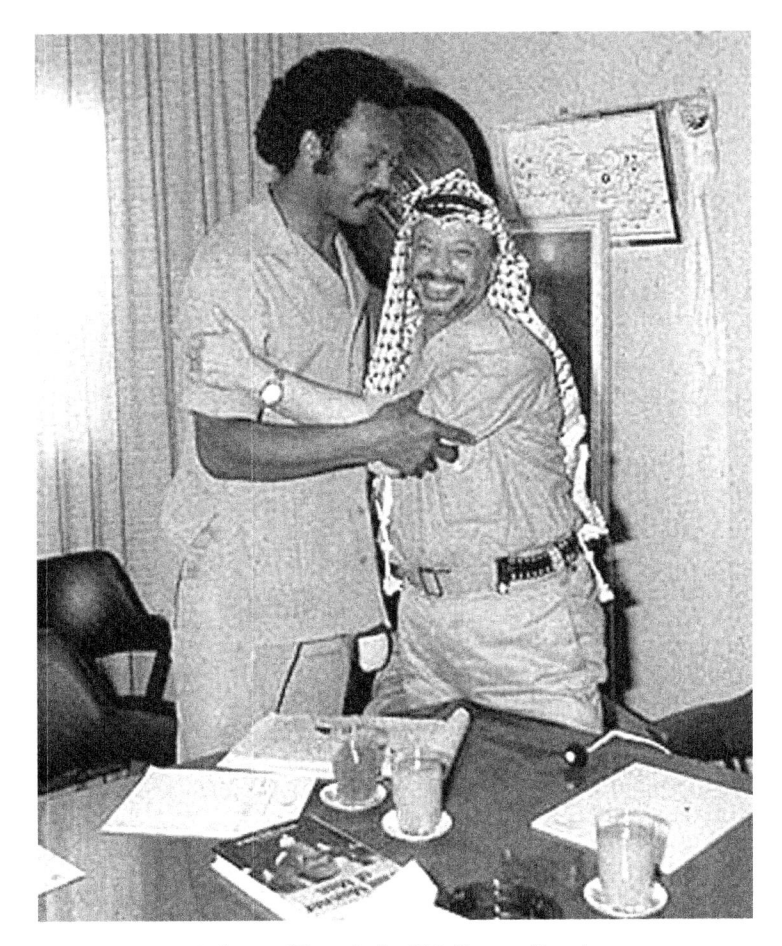

Jesse Jackson and Yasser Arafat, 1979. Photo credit: unknown

Lebanon, but the cease-fire had already been agreed to weeks earlier and a PLO spokesman, upon being questioned as to what had changed, smiled and said that "We will now respect it more." Moreover, for all the support and sympathy Jackson heaped on the PLO, he left, according to a report in the New York *Times*, "a negative impression" on a number of Palestinians themselves. "He didn't do his homework, and he got his geography mixed," said Salim Tamari, a professor at Bir Zeit University on the West Bank. The Times reported that Jackson "apparently thought the Jordan River divided Israel from Lebanon, and spoke several times about stopping the violence on 'both sides' of the Jordan. In fact, the

Israeli-Jordanian border is peaceful now."

Despite the failure of the PLO to move toward either a renunciation of terrorism or the recognition of Israel, and despite his own demonstrated ignorance of the politics of the conflict, Jackson announced he would campaign for U.S. recognition of the PLO and against U.S. military aid to Israel.[26]

Dr. King's close friend and founder of BASIC, Bayard Rustin, led the Black American response to this travesty of true justice. He wrote prolifically on the Arab-Israeli conflict as well as the Arab attempts to co-opt the legacy of the Black struggle for freedom. Regarding Yasser Arafat's 1974 U.N. speech and the PLO, Rustin wrote a reply in January 1975:

> What, then of the PLO's charge that Israel is a "racist" nation. This accusation has been repeated so often - Arafat made numerous references to Israeli "racism" and "colonialism" in his U.N. Address - that it has achieved a measure of acceptance worldwide, and in the American black community.
>
> The question is what do the Arabs mean by "racism?" The standard definition is the systematic oppression of an ethnic or racial minority, very often justified on the grounds that the minority is inherently less intelligent, less clean, less pure or in some way inferior to the majority.
>
> Applying this measurement, it is apparent that some of the most blatant "racist" regimes are in Arab lands. In Iraq, Jews were hanged in a public square, while today napalm is employed against the dissident Kurdish minority. Syria rivals Nazi Germany in its brutal treatment of its Jewish citizens, who are confined to a cramped quarter of Damascus, prevented from emigrating, and from time to time murdered with official sanction. And in the Sudan, it was non-Moslem blacks who were the target of a genocidal war in which 500,000 were killed and many thousands more forced to flee their homes.[27]

---

[26] See previous footnote.

[27] From, "The PLO: Freedom fighters or terrorists," by B. Rustin, 1975, *The Chicago Defender*. Retrieved from Institute for Black Solidarity with Israel (IBSI).

Bayard Rustin also spoke to the dangers of the international community ignoring the terrorism and violence Yasser Arafat was inflicting on the Israelis. Like Dr. King's almost prophetic call to stand with Israel in 1968, Rustin correctly predicted what would happen if the world turned a blind eye to the slaughtering of Israeli civilians. "By embracing the PLO, the United Nations has given a solemn amen to organized brutality, encouraging along the way no one knows how many other extremist organizations with a grudge against society"[28]

Rustin foresaw what we know today as *global terrorism*—Palestinian-style violence against Israel exported internationally. This is being done by an untold number of "extremist organizations with a grudge against society." What the Palestinians exacted against Israeli men, women, and children in the name of *justice*—car-ramming, shooting, stabbing, suicide bombing, plane hijacking—is no longer merely an Israeli problem. As the world allowed terrorism to happen to Israel, it is now happening to the world. Could there be a more vivid application of Genesis 12.3? The rabbis teach that one interpretation of the Hebrew word curse is to "esteem lightly."

"I will bless those who bless you, and whoever *curses* you (esteems you lightly) will be *cursed*." (KJV; emphasis mine)

Some of the most powerful and effective calls to stand with Israel and the Jewish people—to stand on the side of justice—came from the Black community. Likewise, it was the Black community that gave the most accurate predictions and sober warnings of what would happen if we failed to do so. This is what has been referred to as the *Black prophetic voice*, and it has been embodied by Black American leaders throughout history. There must be a new generation of Black Israel-supporters in which that prophetic voice is heard again.

In response to attempts to delegitimize Israel and in defense of the Black struggle for justice, Bayard Rustin started a movement. The day after U.N. Resolution 3379 passed on November 10, 1975, Rustin led a pro-Israel rally of about 100,000 people in downtown Manhattan.

On Sunday, November 23, 1975, BASIC took out a full-page ad in the New York Times, detailing a seven-part declaration of solidarity with Israel. It was endorsed

---

[28] See previous footnote.

by 200 prominent Black Americans from virtually every facet of society, including Coretta Scott-King, Martin Luther King, Sr., Mrs. Medgar Evers, Andrew Young, David Dinkins, Rosa Parks, Arthur Ashe, and opera star Leontyne Price.

We, black Americans, have been guided throughout our long struggle for racial equality by certain fundamental principles. These include:

A. a commitment to democracy;
B. opposition to all forms of racial, religious and sex discrimination;
C. the conviction that denial of equal rights to any minority threatens not only every other minority but democracy itself.

These principles have led us to the following conclusions concerning the Israeli-Arab conflict and its bearings on American society:

1. We condemn the anti-Jewish "blacklist."
   We have fought too long and too hard to root out discrimination from our land to sit idly while foreign interests import bigotry into America. Having suffered so greatly from such prejudice, we consider most repugnant efforts by Arab states to use the economic power of their newly acquired oil wealth to boycott business firms that deal with Israel or that have Jewish owners, directors or executives and to impose anti-Jewish preconditions for investments in this country.

2. We believe blacks and Jews have common interests in democracy and justice.
   In the fight against discrimination, black Americans and American Jews have shared profound and enduring common interests that far transcend any differences between us. Jews through individuals and organizations have been among the most staunch allies in the struggle for racial justice, sharing with us the conviction that equality is indivisible and that no minority is secure in its rights if the rights of any are impaired.

3. We support democratic Israel's right to exist.
   The democratic values that have sustained our struggle in America

are also the source of our admiration for Israel and her impressive social achievements. No nation is without imperfections. But Israel's are far outweighed by the freedom of her democratic society. Only in Israel, among the nations of the Middle East, are political freedoms and civil liberties secure. All religions are free and secure in their observance. Education is free and universal. Social welfare is highly advanced. Her communal farms (Kibbutzim) are models of social idealism, creative innovation, cooperative spirit. Israel's labor movement, the Histadrut, has earned the deep respect of freed trade unionists throughout the world.

4. Arab oil prices have had disastrous effects upon blacks in America and in Africa.

The impact of the massive increases in the price of oil has fallen disproportionately on the shoulders of black Americans. But we are not alone in our suffering. Millions of men, women, and children in Black Africa face starvation because the economies of their countries, already crippled by drought, were further weakened because of oil price increases. The chief cause of Black Africa's disastrous economic situation is the price that the Arabs are exacting for oil - at the same time that they give lip service to their commitment to "African solidarity." The Arab oil-producing states have offered only small loans to the Black African nations, and then only in return for humiliating political concessions.

Israel, small and isolated as it is, has done much to aid the economic development of Black Africa through creative technical programs.

5. We support peace through mutual recognition.

All of us long to see an end to the tragic Arab-Israeli conflict. We have learned from our struggle here in America that the only way to resolve a conflict of nationalities is through mutual acceptance and reconciliation. The Arabs have refused to accept the legitimacy of the state of Israel. Israel consistently demonstrated the desire to make concessions in the interest of peace with her Arab neighbors. But she has refused to accept the conditions that would threaten

ANTI-ZIONISM: HATRED FOR ISRAEL

THE NEW YORK TIMES, SUNDAY, NOVEMBER 23, 1975

Black Americans to Support Israel Committee

"Zionism is not racism, but the legitimate expression of the Jewish people's self determination... From our 400 year experience with slavery, segregation, and discrimination we know that Zionism is not racism." (From a column by Bayard Rustin, Director of Black Americans to Support Israel Committee)

We, black Americans, have been guided throughout our long struggle for racial equality by certain fundamental principles. These in

- ☐ a commitment to democracy;
- ☐ opposition to all forms of racial, religious and sex discrimination;
- ☐ the conviction that denial of equal rights to any minority threatens not only every other minority but democracy itself.

These principles have led us to the following conclusions concerning the Israeli-Arab conflict and its bearings on American soci

1. We condemn the anti-Jewish "blacklist."

We have fought too long and too hard to root out discrimination from our land to sit idly while foreign interests import bigotry into America. Having suffered so greatly from such prejudice, we consider most repugnant efforts by Arab states to use the economic power of their newly acquired oil wealth to boycott business firms that deal with Israel or that have Jewish owners, directors or executives, and to impose anti-Jewish preconditions for investments in this country.

2. We believe blacks and Jews have common interests in democracy and justice.

In the fight against discrimination, black Americans and American Jews have shared profound and enduring common interests that far transcend any differences between us. Jews through individuals and organizations have been among the most staunch allies in the struggle for racial justice, sharing with us the conviction that equality is indivisible and that no minority is secure in its rights if the rights of any are impaired.

3. We support democratic Israel's right to exist.

The democratic values that have sustained our struggle in America are also the source of our admiration for Israel and her impressive social achievements. No nation is without imperfections. But Israel's are far outweighed by the freedom of her democratic society. Only in Israel, among the nations of the Middle East, are political freedoms and civil liberties secure. All religions are free and secure in their observance.

Education is free and universal. Social welfare is highly advanced. Her communal farms (Kibbutzim) are models of social idealism, creative innovation, and cooperative spirit. Israel's labor movement, the Histadrut, has earned the deep respect of free trade unionists throughout the world. Together with other Americans, we enthusiastically join in reaffirming the rights of Israel to exist as a sovereign state.

4. Arab oil policies have had disastrous effects upon blacks in America and in Africa.

The impact of the massive increases in the price of oil has fallen disproportionately on the shoulders of black Americans. But we are not alone in our suffering. Millions of men, women, and children in Black Africa face starvation because the economies of their countries, already crippled by drought, were further weakened because of oil price increases. The chief cause of Black Africa's disastrous economic situation is the price that the Arabs are exacting for oil—at the same time that they give lip service to their commitment to "African solidarity." The Arab oil-producing states have offered only small loans to the Black African nations, and then only in return for humiliating political concessions.

Israel, small and isolated as it is, has done much to aid the economic development of Black Africa through creative technical assistance programs.

5. We support peace through mutual recognition.

All of us long to see an end to the tragic Arab-Israeli conflict. We have learned from our struggle here in America that the only way to resolve a conflict of nationalities is through mutual acceptance and reconciliation. The Arabs have refused to accept the legitimacy of the state of Israel.

Israel has consistently demonstrated the desire to concessions in the interest of peace with her Arab But she has refused to accept the conditions that threaten her existence as an independent sovereig

6. We support genuine Palestinian self-determ

We support the rights of the Palestinians to genu determination, but not at the expense of the righ independence and statehood, and not at the com economic backwaters or of terrorists who woul own "solution" at the point of a gun.

We have compassion for all who have suffered i not least for the Palestinian refugees. But who c why so many of these people continue to live in in the midst of Arab oil wealth?

The spokesmen for the goal of self-determinatio Palestinians through the so-called Palestinian L Organization (PLO) have not been elected. The themselves. The PLO, like all terrorist groups, their unbridled violence against anyone who get including Palestinians, and who disagree with t can forget the murder of Israeli athletes at the the bomb letters, the airplane hijackings and at ground, the sudden massacre of the innocent ch the Tel Aviv airport?

Regardless of what the Arab world calls it, in th shock of the people it is indiscriminate murder

7. We will work for pea

In the months ahead we will work for a just an a peace that will not be a prelude to a new war b beginning of an era of cooperation and good w Israel and her Arab neighbors.

BASIC
Black Americans to Support Israel Committee
260 Park Avenue South, New York, N.Y. 10010

A. Philip Randolph	Bayard Rustin	Lionel Hampton
Chairman	Director	Treasurer

Original BASIC document from the New York Times

Original BASIC document from the New York Times

her existence as an independent sovereign nation.

6. We support genuine Palestinian self-determination.
   We support the rights of the Palestinians to genuine self-determination, but not at the expense of the rights of Jews to independence and statehood, and not at the command of economic blackmailers or of terrorists who would force their own "solution" at the point of a gun.

   We have compassion for all who have suffered in this conflict, not least for the Palestinian refugees. But who can avoid asking why so many of these people continue to live in poverty in the midst of Arab wealth?

   The spokesmen for the goal of self-determination for the Palestinians through the so-called Palestinian Liberation Organization (PLO) have not been elected. They represent only themselves. The P.L.O., like all terrorist groups, have turned their unbridled violence against anyone who gets in their way, including Palestinians, and who disagree with them. Who can forget the murder of Israeli athletes at the Olympic games, the bomb letters, the airplane hijackings and attacks on the ground, the sudden massacre of the innocent civilians at the airport in Tel Aviv?

   Regardless of what the Arab world calls it, in the horrified shock of the people it is indiscriminate murder of innocents.

7. We will work for peace.
   In the months ahead we will work for a just and stable peace, a peace that will not be a prelude to a new war but the beginning of an era of cooperation and good will between Israel and her Arab neighbors.[29]

Following Bayard Rustin's lead, Black American civil rights and political leaders used their influence and raised their voices in support of Israel and the Jewish

---

[29] From "Black Americans to Support Israel Committee," by BASIC, 1975, *The New York Times*. See photocopies on next page.

people.

Texas Congresswoman, Barbara Jordan:

> The dream of Zionism and the existence of the State of Israel will not be swept away into the dustbin of history because a resolution was passed in an ill-considered way. Much more is required to extinguish the dream that we have about democracy, and much more than a resolution is required to destroy a country.
>
> As an American I regret this resolution, but I don't let that piece of paper deter my commitment to the survival of freedom and liberty and democracy in Israel. That resolution is bothersome, it is a problem, but it doesn't have anything to do with the substance or the content of our belief. As a Black American, who understands racism, I know that it makes no sense to equate it with Zionism.[30]

NAACP President, Roy Wilkins:

> The United Nations is composed largely of dictatorial regimes, which test whether the system or combination of systems will accomplish a particular task. The particular task in this instance was to line up solidly with the Arabs against Israel.
>
> Equating Zionism with race discrimination enlisted support for the resolution. The black African nations gobbled it down and now must whistle for the little money they will get from the Arabs.[31]

National Urban League President, Vernon Jordan:

> Black people, who recognize code words since we've been victimized by code words like 'forced busing,' 'law and order,' and others, can easily

---

[30] From "Excerpts from a major address by Barbara Jordan: Congress of the United States, Texas," by the Public Affairs Department, Zionist Organization of America, *Zionist Organization of America*.

[31] From "Zionism and discrimination," by Roy Wilkins, 1975, *The Washington Afro-American: Red Star Edition*.

smell out the fact that 'Zionism' in this context is a code word for antisemitism.[32]

As mentioned in chapter four, former Black Panther, Eldridge Cleaver, was a very vocal anti-Zionist until he lived for several years in Arab Islamic lands. He returned with a very different outlook and joined the Black American fight against the lies and distortions of Israel's foes. He said:

> Two aspects of the recent UN resolution labeling Zionism as racist both shocked and surprised me. Shocked because, of all the people in the world, the Jews have not only suffered particularly from racist persecution, they have done more than any other people in history to expose and condemn racism. Generations of Jewish social scientists and scholars have labored long and hard in every field of knowledge, from anthropology to psychology, to lay bare and refute all claims of racial inferiority and superiority.
>
> To condemn the Jewish survival doctrine of Zionism as racism is a travesty upon the truth.
>
> Secondly, I am surprised that the Arabs would choose to establish a precedent condemning racism because it can so easily and righteously be turned against them. Having lived intimately for several years among the Arabs, I know them to be among the most racist people on earth.[33]

Israel's enemies used the language of justice and the Black struggle for freedom and inverted it to attack a free and democratic Jewish State. The Arab nations portrayed themselves as victims, using the Palestinian people as pawns and holding them hostage in the process. The scheme was diabolically ingenious and continues to produce much sympathy for their unjust cause. However, as demonstrated by BASIC in the 1970s, many Black American leaders refused to accept anti-Zionism or be silent as others attacked Israel and the Jewish people.

---

[32] See previous footnote.

[33] From Cleaver's article published in the *Boston Herald*, 1976. Retrieved from "Cleaver defends Zionism. Israel; charges Arabs with being most racist people; says Moynihan is too soft," by Jewish Telegraphic Agency, 1976, *Jewish Telegraphic Agency* (https://www.jta.org/1976/01/22/archive/cleaver-defends-zionism-israel-charges-arabs-with-being-most-racist-people-says-moynihan-is-too-s).

Today, antisemitism and anti-Zionism within the Black community has a very loud and increasingly influential voice in Minister Louis Farrakhan, leader of the Nation of Islam since 1978. Farrakhan's mentor was Elijah Muhammad, Nation of Islam leader from 1934 to 1975. According to Anti-Defamation League CEO Jonathan Greenblatt, Louis Farrakhan is "quite possibly the most popular anti-Semite in America." The growing influence that Farrakhan has on some of the most powerful Black leaders in America is an ominous sign. Consider Farrakhan in his own words:

> I want to disabuse the Jews today of the false claim that you are "The Chosen of God," and that Israel, or Palestine, belongs to you; I want to disabuse you of that ... And I'm going to tell you about your future: You, that think you have power to frighten and dominate the peoples of the world. I am here to announce the end of your time.[34]

> The Jews talk about 'never again.' ... You cannot say 'Never again' to God because when he puts you in the oven, you're in one indeed! ... 'Never again' don't mean a damn thing when God get ready for you![35]

> So when they talk about Farrakhan, call me a hater, you [know] what they do, call me an antisemite. Stop it, I'm anti-termite.[36]

> Those who call themselves "Jews," who are not really Jews, but are in fact Satan: You should learn to call them by their real name, "Satan;" you are coming face-to-face with Satan, the Arch Deceiver, the enemy of God and the enemy of the Righteous.[37]

The following is the conclusion of Louis Farrakhan's sermon in Chicago's Mosque Maryam on Sunday, July 3, 2012:

---

[34] From "Farrakhan Speaks: Saviours' Day," [Address] by L. Farrakhan, 2017, *Saviours' Day 2017 Convention*.

[35] From Farrakhan's address at the People Organized and Working for Economic Rebirth (POWER) Los Angeles Forum, 1985.

[36] From Farrakhan's address at the 23rd anniversary of the Million Man March, 2018.

[37] From "Have no fear for the future: The future is ours!" by L. Farrakhan, 2017, *Saviours' Day Convention*.

Farrakhan: How many of you are lawyers? Only have one in the house? No wonder we go to jail so much, brother! But at the top of the law profession, who are the top in law?

Audience: Jews.

Farrakhan: Sorry I didn't hear you.

Audience: Jews!

Farrakhan: Any doctors in the house? Ain't got no doctors? Oh there's one way in the back. At the top of the medical profession, the top in that are members of the Jewish community. Anybody in media? Who's the top in that field?

Audience: Jews.

Farrakhan: Anybody a rapper in the house? There's rappers. You can rap, ain't nothing wrong with that, but at the top of that are those that control the industry. Any of you have Hollywood ambitions, Broadway ambitions? Who's the top of that?

Audience: Jews.

Farrakhan: Same people! They're masters in business. Well I'm not a businessman I'm a banker. Well who's the master of the bankers?

Audience: Jews.

Farrakhan: TALK TO ME!

Audience: Jews!

Farrakhan: You don't discredit them because they're masters, you discredit them by the way they use their mastery.

Audience: [applause][38]

Louis Farrakhan delivers these Jew-hating speeches in rooms with thousands of loyal followers and has done so for decades. Again, some of his followers, admirers, and associates are among the most prominent Black men and women in America. These men and women include entertainers and rappers, politicians, congressional lawmakers, professional athletes, and well-funded activists. In his 2018 Commentary article, *The Rise of Black Anti-Semitism*, author Jamie Kirchick illustrates the point of Farrakhan's prominence among the Black American elite.

> In January, a long-hidden photograph was published showing Barack Obama smiling with Farrakhan at a 2005 Congressional Black Caucus reception. A member of the CBC, Andre Carson, later admitted to holding a meeting with the Nation of Islam leader in 2015. Farrakhan claimed that Keith Ellison—current deputy chairman of the Democratic National Committee [now Minnesota Attorney General]—was also present at the meeting, a claim Ellison denies. But given Ellison's record of misleading statements on his relationship with Farrakhan and the NOI, there is no reason to trust him on this question.[39]

Again, Louis Farrakhan enjoys the company and praise of very powerful Black leaders. At 87 years old, he has never been more formidable. What's more, Black criticism of Farrakhan's hate-filled rhetoric for Jews is sparse and dwindling. Though he does not speak for the majority of Black Americans, Farrakhan's open Jew-hatred goes virtually unopposed in the Black community—this must change. In a May 2008 article, Dr. King's attorney and friend, Dr. Clarence Jones, stated:

> Martin was disheartened that so many blacks could be swayed by Elijah Muhammad's Nation of Islam and other black separatists, rejecting his message of nonviolence and grumbling about "Jew landlords" and "Jew interlopers" – even "Jew slave traders."

The resentment and anger displayed toward people who offered so much

---

[38] From "Farrakhan rants about Jewish control during Sunday sermon," by Algemeiner Staff, 2012, *The Algemeiner* (https://www.algemeiner.com/2012/07/03/farrakhan-rants-about-jewish-control-during-sunday-sermon-video/).

[39] From "The rise of black anti-semitism," by C. Gershman, 2018, *The Commentary*.

support for civil rights was then nascent. But it has only festered and grown over four decades [since Dr. King's death]. Today, black-Jewish relations have arguably grown worse, not better.

For that, Martin would place fault principally on the shoulders of black leaders such as Louis Farrakhan, Al Sharpton and Jesse Jackson – either for making anti-Semitic statements, inciting anti-Semitism (including violence), or failing to condemn overt anti-Semitism within the black community.[40]

In 1968, Dr. King candidly addressed the issue of Black-Jewish tension as the source material for those who want to cause division and hatred. Here is the full context of his statement:

> I think we also have to say that the anti-Semitism which we find in the black community is almost completely an urban Northern ghetto phenomenon, virtually non-existent in the South. I think this comes into being because the Negro in the ghetto confronts the Jew in two dissimilar roles. On the one hand, he confronts the Jew in the role of being his most consistent and trusted ally in the struggle for justice in the civil rights movement. Probably more than any other ethnic group, the Jewish community has been sympathetic and has stood as an ally to the Negro in his struggle for justice.
>
> On the other hand, the Negro confronts the Jew in the ghetto as his landlord in many instances. He confronts the Jew as the owner of the store around the corner where he pays more for what he gets. In Atlanta, for instance, I live in the heart of the ghetto, and it is an actual fact that my wife in doing her shopping has to pay more for food than whites have to pay out in Buckhead and Lennox. We've tested it. We have to pay five cents and sometimes ten cents a pound more for almost anything that we get than they have to pay out in Buckhead and Lennox Square where the rich people of Atlanta live.
>
> The fact is that the Jewish storekeeper or landlord is not operating on the

---
[40] From "Martin Luther King would be repulsed by black anti-Semitism," by C. B. Jones and J. Engel, 2008, *Jewish Press*.

basis of Jewish ethics; he is operating simply as a marginal businessman. Consequently the conflicts come into being.

I remember when we were working in Chicago two years ago, we had numerous rent strikes on the West Side. And it was unfortunately true that the persons whom we had to conduct these strikes against were in most instances Jewish landlords. Now sociologically that came into being because there was a time when the West Side of Chicago was almost a Jewish community. It was a Jewish ghetto, so to speak, and when the Jewish community started moving out into other areas, they still owned the property there, and all of the problems of the landlord came into being.

We were living in a slum apartment owned by a Jew in Chicago along with a number of others, and we had to have a rent strike. We were paying $94 for four run-down, shabby rooms, and we would go out on our open housing marches in Gage Park and other places and we discovered that whites with five sanitary, nice, new rooms, apartments with five rooms out in those areas, were paying only $78 a month. We were paying twenty percent tax.

It so often happens that the Negro ends up paying a color tax, and this has happened in instances where Negroes have actually confronted Jews as the landlord or the storekeeper, or what-have-you. And I submit again that the tensions of the irrational statements that have been made are a result of these confrontations.

I think the only answer to this is for all people to condemn injustice wherever it exists. We found injustices in the black community. We find that some black people, when they get into business, if you don't set them straight, can be rascals. And we condemn them. I think when we find examples of exploitation, it must be admitted. That must be done in the Jewish community too.[41]

---

[41] From "Conversation with Martin Luther King," by M. L. King, E. Gendel, and A. J. Heschel, 1968, *Conservative Judaism*, 22(3). Rabbinical Assembly. Copyright 1968 by the Rabbinical Assembly. https://www.rabbinicalassembly.org/sites/default/files/public/resources-ideas/cj/classics/1-4-12-civil-rights/conversation-with-martin-luther-king.pdf.

According to Dr. King, attacking Jews for the negative actions of someone Jewish is akin to attacking Black people for the negative actions of someone Black. One who desires to cause strife and animosity between two groups would intentionally stoke the fires of mistrust. That is what Louis Farrakhan has done between the Black and Jewish communities for decades.

As Black pastors and leaders, we demand that our White counterparts speak up and condemn anti-Black racism, and rightly so. When those White leaders fail or hesitate to speak, we are bitterly disappointed and feel betrayed. If we consider those White leaders friends, we are forced to reevaluate that friendship. Any Black pastor or leader who considers himself a friend of Israel and the Jewish people but is unwilling to speak up and condemn the blatant Jew-hatred of Louis Farrakhan and his surrogates is no friend of Israel or the Jewish people.

If Louis Farrakhan is the most influential antisemite in America, Black Lives Matter has become the most influential antisemitic organization in America. Leaders of Black Lives Matter also support Louis Farrakhan.[42]

#BlackLivesMatter (BLM) was founded in 2013 after the acquittal of the man who killed Trayvon Martin in Orlando, Florida. The movement began to emerge as a global presence in 2014 during the Ferguson protests after the killing of Michael Brown by a White police officer. According to its website, Black Lives Matter Foundation, Inc., is a global organization in the US, UK, and Canada. In the closely associated Movement for Black Lives (M4BL) manifesto, BLM falsely accuses Israel of being an "apartheid state" and of committing "genocide against the Palestinian people." As of the printing of this book, these false accusations against the Jewish State were still on the M4BL website though it is not easily accessible. These are the steps to locate the webpage:

1. Go to www.m4bl.org
2. Click on *Vision for Black Lives* www.m4bl.org/policy-platforms
3. Click on *Invest-Divest* www.m4bl.org/policy-platforms/invest-divest
4. Click on *Cut Military Expenditures Brief*, which is a downloadable file.

BLM has chapters across the country and an untold number of members. Many

---

[42] See "Al Sharpton's group and Black Lives Matter team up for pro-Farrakhan protest," by P. Hasson, 2018, *Daily Caller* for more information.

> **A VISION FOR BLACK LIVES:**
> **POLICY DEMANDS FOR BLACK POWER, FREEDOM, & JUSTICE**
>
> - The US justifies and advances the global war on terror via its alliance with Israel and is complicit in the genocide taking place against the Palestinian people. The US requires Israel to use 75 percent of all the military aid it receives to buy US-made arms. Consequently, every year billions of dollars are funneled from US taxpayers to hundreds of arms corporations, who then wage lobbying campaigns pushing for even more foreign military aid. The results of this policy are twofold: it not only diverts much needed funding from domestic education and social programs, but it makes US citizens complicit in the abuses committed by the Israeli government. Israel is an apartheid state with over 50 laws on the books that sanction discrimination against the Palestinian people. Palestinian homes and land are routinely bulldozed to make way for illegal Israeli settlements. Israeli soldiers also regularly arrest and detain Palestinians as young as 4 years old without due process. Everyday, Palestinians are forced to walk through military checkpoints along the US-funded apartheid wall.

of those members, if not most are unaware of the organization's anti-Zionist ideology and activism. I repeat many, if not most, BLM members are unaware of the organization's demonization of Israel.

BLM's anti-Israel predecessor and partner is a group called Dream Defenders, founded in 2012. One of Dream Defenders' more prominent leaders is anti-Israel activist Marc Lamont Hill. In 2015, members of BLM and Dream Defenders traveled to Israel in what both groups called a "solidarity trip" to "Palestine."[43] Standing in the city of Nazareth, which is in Israel and not the Palestinian territories, the group declared they had "come to land that had been stolen by greed and destroyed by hate."[44] They were learning "laws that had been co-signed in ink but written in the blood of the innocent."[45] In the long tradition of exploiting Black Americans initiated by Yasser Arafat of the PLO, BLM and Dream Defenders also declared, "from Ferguson to Palestine, the struggle for freedom continues."[46]

---

[43] See "How the Black Lives Matter and Palestinian movements converged," by A. Isaacs, 2016, *Moment*. https://momentmag.com/22800-2/.

[44] See "Solidarity demonstration in Nazareth : Ferguson to Palestine," by Dream Defenders, 2015.

[45] See previous footnote.

[46] See previous footnote.

BLM co-founder Patrisse Cullors said of their trip to Israel:

> It was important for the Black Lives Matter movement to show up to Palestine. There was also this sort of kindredness that we felt with Palestinians as black people—the constant sort of battering and terrorizing by military and for us by police is eerily similar, and we thought it was important, even though we knew that it might be a huge risk for a lot of us, to show up and let Palestinians know that we are in deep solidarity with them. And, frankly, we believe that Palestine is the new South Africa.[47]

As we addressed earlier in this chapter, equating the free and democratic state of Israel to apartheid South Africa is a long-practiced anti-Zionist lie. There is not a separate Israel for Jews and Arabs or any other ethnicity or religious faith. There are free and fair elections for all Israelis, Jewish and non-Jewish. All Israelis, Jewish and non-Jewish, are represented in the Knesset, Israel's parliament. Israel is a free, multiethnic, multi-religious society.

Ms. Cullors' statement of Israel's security measures as "battering and terrorizing [Palestinians] by military" is also an established deception and an attempt to link Israel to police brutality against Black people in America. Since the terrorist attacks in America on September 11, 2001, Israel—the world's leading expert in counterterrorism—has helped train police from all over the world. Anti-Zionists cite this fact to blame Israel when a U.S. police officer shoots or otherwise harms and kills a Black man. Israel has not trained police to racially profile or use excessive force. Those are decisions made by individual officers or the policies of a racist police department. Ignoring this fact, BLM launched a nationwide campaign for U.S. police to end their relationship with Israel. In 2016, Atlanta Mayor, Kasim Reed, told of his encounter with BLM and its anti-Israel crusade.

> There was a demand that I stop allowing the Atlanta Police Department to train with the Israeli police department.
>
> I'm not going to do that; I happen to believe that the Israeli police department has some of the best counterterrorism techniques in the

---

[47] From "How the Black Lives Matter and Palestinian movements converged," by A. Isaacs, 2016, *Moment*. https://momentmag.com/22800-2/.

world, and it benefits our police department from that long standing relationship.[48]

In April 2018, the City Council of Durham, North Carolina, voted to bar its police officers from training with Israeli police. It was a unanimous, 6-0 decision. The measure was put forth by the Durham2Palestine Coalition. This is yet another front on the battlefield of Boycott, Divestment, Sanction (BDS) against Israel, placing already vulnerable, high-crime inner-city neighborhoods in even more danger. Barring American law enforcement from the best training available only makes everyone less safe, the residents and the police. In short, this anti-Israel, antisemitic campaign will cost lives—disproportionately, poor Black lives.

Black Lives Matter and their associates are leading a national effort to defund the police.[49] This is another Marxist, destructive movement that 81% of Black Americans oppose.[50]

In a December 2019 interview with the media outlet, Al Jazeera, Patrisse Cullors stated that BLM's solidarity trips to "Palestine" have been "laying the foundation for the more public face in solidarity," which has been "incredibly powerful for our movement."[51] With the 2020 tragic deaths of George Floyd in Minneapolis, Minnesota, Breonna Taylor in Louisville, Kentucky, Ahmad Abery in Glynn County, Georgia, and other Black victims of White police officers, there is no group presumably fighting for justice more visible than Black Lives Matter. Sadly, BLM's activism is grossly tainted with a fixation on demonizing Israel, which has absolutely nothing to do with justice for Black people in America. Conflating the two disparate issues manipulates Black pain and suffering, calling BLM's motives into serious question. If the Black Lives Matter organization is legitimately concerned about improving the quality of Black lives, why is it a mouthpiece for Palestinian terrorism against Israel? How does BLM's anti-Zionist ideology help Black people? For that matter, how does it help the Palestinians?

---

[48] From "Atlanta mayor shuts down Israel boycotters," by A. Soffer, 2016, *Arutz Sheva* (https://www.israelnationalnews.com/News/News.aspx/215205).

[49] See "#DefundThePolice," by Black Lives Matter, 2020, *Black Lives Matter*.

[50] See "81% of black Americans don't want less police presence despite protests—some want more cops: poll," by J. Grzeszczak, 2020, *Newseek*.

[51] See "Studio B, unscripted: With Patrisse Cullors and Lowkey," by Studio B: Unscripted, 2019, *Al Jazeera*.

BLM's anti-Zionism manifests as open Jew-hatred on U.S. streets. This began as "pro-Palestinian" expressions during the Ferguson demonstrations (2014-2015) and grew during the BLM protests that became riots after the death of George Floyd.

Melina Abdullah, the lead organizer of Black Lives Matter in Los Angeles and a professor of Pan-African Studies at Cal State, helped lead what residents described as a *pogrom* (a violent riot or attack) in a Jewish neighborhood.

An article in the Jewish Press stated:

> The looting not only devastated countless small businesses in the area, but graffiti, some of it explicitly anti-Semitic, was scrawled across at least 5 Orthodox Jewish synagogues and 3 religious schools.

> "It's no coincidence that the riots here escalated in Fairfax, the icon of the Jewish community. I saw the Watts and the Rodney King riots [1960's, 1990's]. They never touched a synagogue or house of prayer. The graffiti showed blatant antisemitism. It's Kristallnacht[52] all over again," Rabbi Shimon Raichik, a Chabad Rabbi in Los Angeles wrote.[53]

I received calls from Jewish friends in New York and Chicago who witnessed antisemitic language and actions related to BLM. They were older Jewish people who had seen much hatred directed at their community, but they had never personally witnessed such hatred coming from Black Americans. It was a completely foreign experience. It shook them.

Having observed this rising antisemitism instigated by some in the Black community for years, I am of the earnest opinion that it is the most dangerous form of Jew-hatred since the heyday of the Ku Klux Klan. Unwittingly, the Black community is being used—exploited to usher this hatred into being. This reality is a pain deep within my soul. I am grieved to see what is happening in the midst of my people. After all we have endured in this nation, I can hardly believe we

---

[52] Translates to "night of crystal," and often referred to as the Night of Broken Glass. Refers to the wave of violent anti-Jewish pogroms which took place in Germany on November 9-10, 1938.

[53] From, "The LA Black Lives Matter rally that became a pogrom," by D. Greenfield, 2020, *Jewish Press*.

are at this moment in time. Hatred for Israel and the Jewish people is not only condemned by the word of God; it attacks the one ethnic group that has been the most helpful to us in our struggle for justice. I am committed to fighting this scourge with everything in me, both for he Black community and on behalf of the Jewish people. As Nehemiah prayed multiple times while rebuilding the walls of Jerusalem, "Remember me, O my God, for good!" (Nehemiah 5.19)

The official international BDS movement against Israel began in 2001 at the U.N. World Conference against Racism in Durban, South Africa. It was a fraudulent attempt by Israel's enemies—like Iran and the Palestinian leaders—to portray the Jewish State as a racist, apartheid regime like South Africa of 1948-1990s. In 2005, the organization known as BDS South Africa was formed and is now the largest nonprofit in the country. In March 2020, BDS South Africa announced that it would be "rebranding and broadening our mandate" and would "henceforth function under the name Africa for Palestine (AFP)." As mentioned earlier in this chapter, there are many South Africans who strongly oppose the term *apartheid* being applied to the free and democratic state of Israel. It is a slap in the face to all the Black South Africans who suffered at the hands of the racist National Party.

In the same year that Israel's enemies were doubling-down on the apartheid lie, Arab and Muslim states were making peace with Israel. In August 2020, the United Arab Emirates (UAE) announced that it would normalize ties with Israel. Shortly after normalization with Israel, the UAE announced it was abolishing its 1972 boycott mandate against Israel. Less than two weeks later, the first official commercial flight departed Tel Aviv and landed in Dubai. Saudi Arabia gave permission for the Israeli plane to fly over its airspace. The governments of Lebanon, Morocco, and Sudan also stated their desire to end decades-long enmity with Israel. Through their actions, the Arabs are proving that hatred for Israel has neither brought peace to the region nor helped the plight of the Palestinians. Because oppressive Palestinian leadership is made wealthy and powerful by stealing international aid, the Palestinian people are suffering now more than ever. By the grace of God, there is a growing desire for real peace in the Middle East. As Christians, we know this peace will ultimately come when Jesus, the Prince of Peace, returns. Still, we are told to "pray for the peace of Jerusalem" and are promised that those who love Jerusalem "will prosper." (Psalm 122).

Unlike the Arab states, which have warred against the Jewish State since its independence in 1948, Africa has generally been a friend. However, the Africa-Israel friendship is not nearly as strong or as reciprocal as it should be. For all of the Israeli technology and innovation that continues to improve the lives of countless Africans, Africa has not consistently responded in kind. This is particularly true in the United Nations, where African states have sided with the Arab states against Israel. As we mentioned in chapter one, 3,000 years ago, the Queen of Ethiopia showed how a foreign nation was to relate to Israel. After visiting King Solomon in Jerusalem, the eternal, undivided capital of Israel, she made this declaration:

> 1 Kings 10.6-9
> 6 ...It was a true report that I heard in my country of your deeds and of your wisdom.
> 7 However, I did not believe the words until I came and saw with my own eyes, and I have beheld that not even a half had been told to me. You have wisdom and goodness in excess of that which I have heard.
> 8 Fortunate are your men; fortunate are these your servants who always stand before you and listen to your profound wisdom.
> 9 Blessed be the Lord Your God, who preferred to place you on the throne of Israel; because of the Lord's love for Israel forever, He appointed you as king to do justice and righteousness.

ו וַתֹּאמֶר אֶל־הַמֶּלֶךְ אֱמֶת הָיָה הַדָּבָר אֲשֶׁר שָׁמַעְתִּי בְּאַרְצִי עַל־דְּבָרֶיךָ וְעַל־חָכְמָתֶךָ:
ז וְלֹא־הֶאֱמַנְתִּי לַדְּבָרִים עַד אֲשֶׁר־בָּאתִי וַתִּרְאֶינָה עֵינַי וְהִנֵּה לֹא־הֻגַּד־לִי הַחֵצִי הוֹסַפְתְּ חָכְמָה וָטוֹב אֶל־הַשְּׁמוּעָה אֲשֶׁר שָׁמָעְתִּי:
ח אַשְׁרֵי אֲנָשֶׁיךָ אַשְׁרֵי עֲבָדֶיךָ אֵלֶּה הָעֹמְדִים לְפָנֶיךָ תָּמִיד הַשֹּׁמְעִים אֶת־חָכְמָתֶךָ:
ט יְהִי יְהֹוָה אֱלֹהֶיךָ בָּרוּךְ אֲשֶׁר חָפֵץ בְּךָ לְתִתְּךָ עַל־כִּסֵּא יִשְׂרָאֵל בְּאַהֲבַת יְהֹוָה אֶת־יִשְׂרָאֵל לְעֹלָם וַיְשִׂימְךָ לְמֶלֶךְ לַעֲשׂוֹת מִשְׁפָּט וּצְדָקָה:

(The Complete Jewish Bible with Rashi Commentary, 1 Kings 10.6-9)

Observe how the Ethiopian Queen commends Solomon for his wisdom but then gives glory to the God of Israel for making him king. "Because of the Lord's love for Israel forever, He appointed you as king to do justice and righteousness." The Bible then states:

> 1 Kings 10.10
> *And she gave the king one hundred and twenty talents of gold and very many spices and precious stones; there had never arrived such an abundance of spices as those which the Queen of Sheba gave to king Solomon.*

> י וַתִּתֵּן לַמֶּלֶךְ מֵאָה וְעֶשְׂרִים | כִּכַּר זָהָב וּבְשָׂמִים הַרְבֵּה מְאֹד וְאֶבֶן יְקָרָה לֹא־בָא כַבֹּשֶׂם הַהוּא עוֹד לָרֹב אֲשֶׁר־נָתְנָה מַלְכַּת־שְׁבָא לַמֶּלֶךְ שְׁלֹמֹה:
> (The Complete Jewish Bible with Rashi Commentary, 1 Kings 10.10)

The account of the African queen's visit to Israel was unprecedented. Nowhere in scripture do we find a foreign ruler who visited Jerusalem, honored the Israelite king, blessed the God of Israel, declared God's love for the Jewish people, and brought precious stones, costly spices, and 120 talents of gold (an estimated four tons). The visit was such a significant moment in Jewish history that Jesus made reference to it in His sermon 1,000 years later.

> Matthew 12.42
> *The queen of the South will rise up at the judgment with this generation and condemn it, for she came from the ends of the earth to hear the wisdom of Solomon, and behold, something greater than Solomon is here.*
> (English Standard Version, Matthew 12.42)

Jesus infers that, just as the Ethiopian Queen recognized the importance of visiting the king in Jerusalem, so Africa will come to the King of kings when He reigns in Jerusalem. For those who refuse to come, the Queen will "rise up" and condemn.

It is through Africa that God shows the world how to *enter His gates with thanksgiving* (Psalm 100.4), blessing Him and His people. This is Africa's prophetic call—to lead the nations to Jerusalem. It is time for Africa and her people to reclaim their God-given legacy.

> Psalm 68.31 (verse 32 in Jewish *Tanakh* or Christian Old Testament)
> *Gifts will be brought from Egypt; Cush will cause his hands to run to God.*

> לב יֶאֱתָיוּ חַשְׁמַנִּים מִנִּי מִצְרָיִם כּוּשׁ תָּרִיץ יָדָיו לֵאלֹהִים:
> (The Complete Jewish Bible with Rashi Commentary, Psalm 68.32)

African solidarity with Israel is not only a divine mandate; it is a wise decision. Strong Africa-Israel relations that increase economic opportunity and reduce global terrorism benefit the region and the world.

CHALLENGE TO DEFENDERS OF PALESTINIAN RIGHTS

Within each of the many *Black for Palestine* efforts that existed since the 1960s, there has been one constant, glaring omission—the Arab Palestinian leaders' abuse and exploitation of their own people. By abuse and exploitation, I mean the leaders of the Palestinian people:

- Use minor children as soldiers or enemy combatants and intentionally place them in harm's way.[54] This is one of the most heinous parts of Yasser Arafat's legacy.
- Use school textbooks, summer camps, and children's television programs to indoctrinate children to hate or kill Israelis.[55] [56] [57]
- Commit war crimes, including the murder of their women and children.[58]
- Embezzle billions in international aid money while the Palestinian people remain in poverty. Hamas and PLO leaders have personal net

---

[54] From "Hamas's new army of children," by K. A. Toameh, 2015, *Gatestone Institute* (https://www.gatestoneinstitute.org/5230/hamas-army-children).

[55] See "Palestinian textbooks teach war not peace," by E. Cox, 2018, *The Jerusalem Post* for more information.

[56] See "Hamas's child abuse camps," by K. A. Toameh, 2015, *Gatestone Institute* for more information.

[57] See "Hamas recruits children to terror squads via TV programs," by E. Halevi, 2007, *Arutz Sheva* for more information.

[58] See "Hamas, Islamic Jihad war crimes against children and women," by B. Tawil, 2019, *Gatestone Institute* for more information.

- worths of millions, and some are worth billions.[59][60][61][62][63]
- Block Palestinians from receiving needed medical services in Israel, but access Israeli doctors and hospitals for themselves and their families.[64][65][66][67][68]
- Store missiles in or near active hospitals, schools, and mosques, then launch into Israel from these locations.[69]
- Ban freedom of speech and freedom of the press. Palestinian journalists are routinely harassed, imprisoned, or tortured.[70][71][72] (Hamas arrested a young peace activist from Gaza for having a Zoom conversation with Israelis.).[73]
- Ban free and fair elections. (Palestinian Authority President, Mahmoud Abbas, is in the seventeenth year of his *four-year* term.) Hamas took

---

[59] See "Palestinians: 'The mafia of destruction'," by K. A. Toameh, 2016, *Gatestone Institute* for more information.

[60] See "EU accuses Palestinians of wasting €2 billion in aid," by E. Millar, 2013, *Times of Israel* for more information.

[61] See "Gaza's millionaires and billionaires — how Hamas's leaders got rich quick," by D. Danan, 2014, *The Algemeiner* for more information.

[62] See "The richest terror organizations: #3 – Hamas," by I. Zehorai, 2018, *Forbes* for more information.

[63] See "How many millionaires live in the 'impoverished' Gaza Strip?" by K. A. Toameh, 2012, *Gatestone Institute* for more information.

[64] See "Palestinian leaders use Coronavirus to attack Israel," by K. A. Toameh, 2020, *Gatestone Institute* for more information.

[65] See "Hamas turns away truckloads of Israeli humanitarian aid destined for Gaza," by E. Halon, 2018, *The Jerusalem Post* for more information.

[66] See "Abbas' wife hospitalized in Israel," by E. Senyor, 2014, *Ynet News* for more information.

[67] See "Hamas leader's daughter receives medical care in Israel," by M. Newman and AP, 2014, *Times of Israel* for more information.

[68] See "Palestinian Authority prevents Gazans from leaving strip for urgent medical treatment in Israel," by J. Khoury, 2017, *Haaretz* for more information.

[69] See "Why Hamas stores its weapons inside hospitals, mosques and schools," by T. McCoy, 2014, *The Washington Post* for more information.

[70] See "Palestinians: Arresting, torturing journalists," by K. A. Toameh, 2019, *Gatestone Institute* for more information.

[71] See "Palestinian security forces routinely torture critics, rights group says," by O. Holmes, 2018, *The Guardian* for more information.

[72] See "Palestinian journalist: Car arson won't stop me from criticizing PA," by K. A. Toameh, 2020, *The Jerusalem Post* for more information.

[73] See "Gaza peace activists face prison for holding video call with Israelis," by A. Rasgon, 2020, *The New York Times* for more information.

total control of Gaza in 2007.[74] [75]
- Persecute religious minorities, especially Christians.[76] [77] [78]
- Torture and kill prisoners.[79] [80]
- Allow the honor killing of women.[81] [82] (There have been recent attempts by the Palestinian Authority to end the practice of honor killing, but it persists).[83]
- Torture and kill gay men.[84]

Life for the ordinary person within the Palestinian territories is oppressive and Israel is not the one doing the oppressing. In his article entitled, *Why Palestinians Want Israeli Citizenship*, Arab Israeli journalist, Khaled Abu Toameh writes:

> Many of those who have applied for Israeli citizenship are Christians from Jerusalem who are . . . afraid of ending up under the jurisdiction of the Palestinian Authority or Hamas.
>
> Ironically, obtaining Israeli citizenship has become a way for Palestinians to ensure their social, economic, health and education rights in the country.

---

[74] See "President Mahmoud Abbas: The Palestinian 'untouchable'," by K. A. Toameh, 2016, *Gatestone Institute* for more information.

[75] See "Can Palestinians in Gaza revolt against Hamas?" by K. A. Toameh, 2019, *Gatestone Institute* for more information.

[76] See "Who will save the Christians in the Gaza Strip?" by K. A. Toameh, 2012, *Gatestone Institute* for more information.

[77] See "The beleaguered Christians in Bethlehem," by K. A. Toameh, 2009, *Gatestone Institute* for more information.

[78] See "Get them out: It's time to evacuate Christians from the Gaza Strip," by D. van Zile, 2019, *The Jerusalem Post* for more information.

[79] See "Palestinians speak out about torture in PA prison," by J. Burns, 2017, *Al Jazeera* for more information.

[80] See "Why are Palestinians dying in Hamas prisons?" by B. Taeil, 2020, *Gatestone Institute* for more information.

[81] See "Palestinian woman murdered in honor killing after posting Instagram video with fiancé," by N. Ghoneim, 2019, *Egyptian Streets* for more information.

[82] See "As so-called 'honor killers' get away with murder, Palestinians say law, judges outdated," by D. Lieber, 2017, *Times of Israel* for more information.

[83] See footnote #80.

[84] See "Palestinians: No place for gays," by K. A. Toameh, 2018, *Gatestone Institute* for more information.

There is no denying that applying for Israeli citizenship, in defiance of PLO and Hamas warnings, is also a political statement on the part of the applicants. They are actually making clear that they would prefer to live under Israel than any Arab rule.[85]

The Black Church must also bring light to the actual suffering of the Palestinian people. Just as Dr. King spoke to the issues caused by poverty in the Arab Palestinian Territories, so must the Black Church be concerned about our Palestinian brothers and sisters—Muslim and Christian. However, we must not fall victim to the disinformation and anti-Zionist rhetoric the way so many goodhearted people have done. Just because the State of Israel is no longer the fledgling nation rising from the dust of the Holocaust does not mean that her enemies are any fewer or less vicious. On the contrary, Israel's enemies are more resolute than ever to remove the Jewish State from the map. The battle for Israel's right to live in peace is more crucial now than ever. As in the past, the Black Church's role is paramount in this spiritual and political battle.

Since 2013, I have actively sought a Black pro-Palestinian person or group who defends Palestinian human rights—those who are willing to rebuke the Palestinians' real oppressors. I have found none. For those reading this book who consider themselves *pro-Palestinian* and see Israel or Zionism as the problem, I simply ask, where is the support for the Palestinian struggle against Hamas? Where is the protest against the abuse of the Palestinian Authority? Do you realize that terrorists are using you as cover for their violence and theft? There are brave men and women living under crushing Palestinian rule. When will you be their voice?

THE BLACK HEBREW ISRAELITES

We must address another growing antisemitic threat within the Black community—members of the Black Hebrew Israelites (BHI). As we mentioned in chapter two, there are three distinct BHI groups, two in the U.S. and one based in Dimona, Israel. The BHI in Israel are fully integrated into Israeli society and are known as *Shomrei Hashalom* (Guardians of Peace). The first group in the U.S. is led by very capable, knowledgeable people like Rabbi Capers Funnye of Beth

---

[85] From "Why Palestinians want Israeli citizenship," by K. A. Toameh, 2012, *Gatestone Institute*.

Shalom B'nai Zaken Ethiopian Hebrew Congregation of Chicago. Rabbi Funnye is also a member of the Chicago Board of Rabbis and the chief rabbi of the International Israelite Board of Rabbis.

The second group of BHI in the U.S. and the U.K. is a militant sect that preaches a divisive, race-driven dogma, which states that only Black people in the West are the true Israelites; all others are fake Jews who have stolen Black peoples' heritage. Members of this BHI group are very present on social media, preaching this false doctrine on street corners. Over the past few years, there have also been many incidents of violence against religious Jews in the New York City area perpetrated by some who claimed association with BHI. The most infamous case was December 2019 in Jersey City, where two Black people associated with BHI entered a kosher deli intending to kill Jews. The two shooters were killed by Jersey City police, who also recovered their van in which was a pipe bomb capable of destroying everything within a 500-yard radius. This was a Black terrorist attack against Jews, the first of its kind in this nation.

What makes the Jersey City shooting even more disturbing is the antisemitic rhetoric that preceded it. Six days before the shooting, Jeffrey Dye, President of the NAACP Passaic, N.J. Branch allegedly posted several antisemitic items, including a misleading article about U.S. aid to Israel on one of their official social media sites. The caption read, "The Very Bullshit We Are Talking About Blacks Dying So Jews Can Live." In the posts' comments section, the person continued to demonize Jews and Israel, praising antisemitic statements by Louis Farrakhan. The posts remained on their social media for weeks after the shootings.

I am in no way suggesting that the NAACP—the world's oldest civil rights organization founded by Black and Jewish Americans—is antisemitic. In fact, the NAACP headquarters issued a letter on August 30, 2019 rebuking Jeffrey Dye for his actions, suspending his membership, and removing from office.[86] Sadly, his behavior continued for months afterwards. What I am underscoring is that antisemitism has become dangerously accepted in portions of the Black community. If a horrific incident like this is not a wake-up call for Black leaders, I fear what a wake-up call would be.

---

[86] See "Letter from Derrick Johnson to Jeffrey Dye," by D. Johnson, 2019, for more information.

THE IRANIAN THREAT

The Iranian regime moves closer to nuclear weapons capability daily and is very open about using those weapons against the Jewish State. The Iranian genocidal threat looms so large that officials in Rwanda have expressed grave concerns. According to Dr. Charles Asher Small, Director and Founder of The Institute for the Study of Global Antisemitism and Policy, Rwandan officials approached him after his speech at the United Nations in 2009.

> The Rwandan diplomats and scholars were very much concerned about the future of Israel and the dehumanization by radical Islamists and the Iranian Regime against the Jewish people, and wanted to know why the American Jewish community was not as alarmed as they were.
>
> The Rwandan group implored me to tell the Jewish community, its leaders, intellectuals, professionals, and policy makers that the Iranians were using the same tactics against Jews, as the Tutsis had suffered in Rwanda, which was similar to the Jews during the Holocaust. There is a deep bond between the Rwandan people and the Jewish people, born in the shared experience of tragedy.[87]

The fight for Israel's peace and security is very evident on college campuses globally. Sadly, many faculty members and academic departments have presented an institutionalized version of the anti-Israel ideology fringe in the 1960s and 1970s. Jewish and pro-Israel students are facing systematic harassment and targeting by groups that claim to be pro-Palestinian. Among the most prominent of these groups in the U.S. are the Muslim Student Association (MSA) and National Students for Justice in Palestine (SJP).

The National Students for Justice in Palestine (SJP) gets support and direction from American Muslims for Palestine and Al-Awda: The Palestine Right to Return Coalition;[88] [89] two organizations that oppose Israel's right to exist, condone armed violence and support terrorist groups responsible for the

---

[87] From "Rwandan genocide scholars urge Jews to recognize Iran threat as similar to Nazi regime (INTERVIEW)," by J. Levitt, 2014, *The Algemeiner*.

[88] See "American Muslims for Palestine," by Anti-Defamation League, n.d., *ADL*.

[89] See Tammi Rossman-Benjamin's letter to the 19th president of UCLA Mark G. Yudof, 2013, for more information.

genocidal murder of Jews. SJP National has built alliances with Black Student Unions, African Student Unions, Latino students, and other diverse campus groups with a deceptive message of justice for the Palestinian people. Having seen the group in action across the country, I can tell you that they have yet to publicize the long list of Hamas' and Fatah's abuses of the Palestinian people. Their singular focus is Israel and the alleged "illegal occupation of Palestinian land." The playbook has been the same for the past 50 years. Just as the Arab states appropriated the Black struggle for freedom and coerced the African states to endorse its anti-Zionist agenda, so are anti-Israel college students targeting young people of color. Without students of color in their ranks, groups like SJP have little credibility. As Black pastors and community leaders, we must understand this very crucial point.

In the spring of 2014, I gave a series of lectures as part of a tour for the Institute for Black Solidarity with Israel (IBSI). During the tour, I had the opportunity to speak with several SJP members. It was always a pleasure engaging the young people, some of whom were committed to peace, but had been severely misled by their organization and other sources of anti-Israel rhetoric.

In one college, I had a lengthy conversation with a leader of the campus SJP. (I will call him "Amir" to protect his identity). Amir challenged me with many questions during my *Dr. King's Pro-Israel Legacy* presentation. The debate was lively and sometimes loud, but never dismissive or disrespectful.

After much back-and-forth with Amir and the other students, the meeting was adjourned. I stayed in the room for questions or further dialogue with anyone who wished to engage. Amir and a few students did tarry. One by one, the others students left for their destinations. After a while, only Amir and I remained.

Amir, an East African, extremely intelligent and compassionate young man, seemed genuinely concerned for others. But, like the Ammonite king, he had a false narrative. He was now being encouraged by a person he could identify with to go beyond SJP's talking points and accusations. The following is a portion of our conversation:

> Me: Let's just say that somehow Israel meets every demand given by its enemies. What then? Will Israel's enemies finally stop attacking her?

Will there be peace?

Amir (staring at me for about three seconds): No. It won't stop the violence. They will continue to attack Israel.

Me: Then what is the incentive for Israel to agree to something so suicidal?

Amir (soberly): There is no incentive. There won't be peace.

Our discussion ended. Amir and I shook hands, gave a *bro-hug*, he thanked me for my time, and we parted company. It was at that moment that the need for Black advocacy for Israel on campus became abundantly clear to me.

Black Church leaders must understand our young people are being told lies, half-truths, and blatant false narratives about Israel and the Jewish people. The anti-Israel onslaught is more formidable now than ever. We must not be silent. Defending the Jewish State does not mean Israel is without flaws or a society without challenges. Which nation is without flaws? Which nation has Israel's challenges?

What other country is actively returning its people from all over the world after 2,000 years of exile? How many other countries have some 90 different nationalities—Jewish and non-Jewish—within its borders living in peace? What other country is surrounded by enemy nations wholly committed to its annihilation while being globally delegitimized in the process? Again, which nation is facing these challenges?

INDOCTRINATION OF OUR CHILDREN

In the Black American community and our nation, the single greatest challenge in building solidarity with Israel and the Jewish people is wrong or misleading information—again, a false narrative. Often, this false narrative, which bolsters anti-Zionism, comes from wrong or incomplete reporting on network and cable news and social media. The false narrative is also driven by international organizations like the U.N. Human Rights Council (UNHRC) and its consistent focus on slandering Israel.

The 47-nation (UNHRC) has condemned Israel in 80% of its country censures, in 20 of 25 resolutions. The other 5 texts criticized North Korea once, and Myanmar four times. The Council has ignored the UN's other 189 countries, including the world's worst abusers (i.e. China, Cuba, Russia, Iran, and Saudi Arabia). While Darfur was addressed several times, these resolutions were non-condemnatory, often praising Sudan for "cooperation."[90]

Though this level of international Israel-bias may sound conspiratorial, it is quite easily explained. For decades, mostly Arab or Islamic countries have partnered with the former Soviet Union to wage an ideological war on Israel and its chief ally, the United States. In doing so, they often conspire to manipulate the U.N. to focus negative attention on Israel and the U.S. while giving a pass to human rights atrocities worldwide. Thus, much of the world is oblivious to the estimated one million African slaves in Libya but is aware of the phrase "free Palestine!"

As concerning as this multinational Israel-hatred is, there is something even more lethal and closer to home with which we must contend: The emerging anti-Zionist, antisemitic education in our public schools.

I was raised in California and attended public schools for grades K-8. As a product of California's public schools and one whose wife taught Language Arts and Social Studies for five years, I can attest that the history curriculum is sorely lacking. Not only is there virtually nothing taught on the contributions of *all* Americans to the building of this great nation, what *is* taught often lacks substance and depth. Every American should know something about abolitionist Frederick Douglass, educator Booker T. Washington, and the era of Black Wall Street—people and events that helped shape this country.

In far too many public schools across the U.S., students are not receiving the type of authentic education necessary to make them critical thinkers or informed citizens. What's more, some school districts are beginning to adopt a curriculum that is blatantly antisemitic. Starting with the college level, I cite my former home state for nearly all of my life. In August 2020, Governor Gavin Newsom signed into law the Critical Ethnic Studies program for the California State University

---

[90] From "UN human rights council: History & overview," by Jewish Virtual Library, n.d., *Jewish Virtual Library*.

(CSU) system. This curriculum is part of bill AB-1460.

Spearheaded by the AMCHA Initiative, 90 education, civil-rights and religious groups had called on Newsom to veto the bill, AB-1460.

The groups noted that vetoing AB-1460 was necessary because anti-Zionist advocacy and the promotion of BDS are an intrinsic part of critical ethnic studies; critical ethnic-studies faculty have repeatedly demonstrated a willingness to promote BDS and anti-Zionist advocacy in their academic programming and classrooms; and faculty support and promotion of BDS are linked to the harassment of Jewish students.[91]

Note that leaders of Black Lives Matter strongly support CSU's anti-Israel Critical Ethnic Studies. Earlier in this chapter, we introduced Cal State professor Melina Abdullah, leader of BLM in Los Angeles. As a reminder, during the nationwide protests and riots following the killing of George Floyd, BLM LA targeted the Jewish neighborhood of Fairfax in which five synagogues were vandalized. Ms. Abdullah is campaigning to become the dean of CSU's ethnic studies faculty.

My son, Joshua, is now the Executive Director of the Institute for Black Solidarity with Israel (IBSI). He spoke at multiple hearings on California Critical Ethnic Studies bills AB-1460 (college) and AB-331 (high school). Joshua made this observation of BLM's influence on antisemitic curriculum:

> By ignoring or excusing Black Lives Matter's antisemitism, we helped enable the new push for the new Ethnic Studies course to be a requirement for graduating high school (AB-331). This is especially evident in the fact that at the hearings, BLM (among many other social justice groups) was represented to voice support, and the M4BL anti-Israel literature was included in the curriculum. The cultural fight is connected to the political and biblical. The 87 year-old Jew-hater Louis Farrakhan is more culturally relevant now than ever before, and many BLM leaders follow and admire him. The material in this curriculum concerning the Jewish people is in lock step with many of Farrakhan's writings and sermons. If we thought

---

[91] From "Gov. Newsom signs California ethnic-studies bill into law," by J. Richman, 2020, *Jewish News Syndicate*.

witnessing black celebrities, influencers, and NAACP chapter presidents defame the Jews with Nation of Islam/Nazi anti-Jewish talking points was bad, we are not ready for the fruit this curriculum will bear.[92]

Versions of CSU's now legally mandated Critical Ethnic Studies are being introduced to public schools across the state. In Oakland, a rabbi friend requested support from his friends in the Black and Latino communities to speak against the over-simplistic, anti-Zionist curriculum being considered for the children. Sadly, their efforts to block or amend the ethnic studies curriculum failed, and Oakland Public Schools is moving forward with its plans to implement it. There have been hearings throughout the state to allow the public to weigh in on this crucial issue. This is a battle for the minds of California's youth and, as such, is exponentially more important than combating BDS legislation on a university campus or even in the state legislature. At nearly 40 million people, California is the most populous, ethnically diverse state in the union and the world's fifth-largest economy. California's global influence in the fields of education, technology, arts, and culture is unmatched. Much of the world follows California's lead—for better or worse.

Shortly before this book was published, California's Governor Newsom vetoed high school ethnic studies bill AB-331. While this is a welcomed sign, the fight against anti-Zionist indoctrination in our public schools is by no means over.

According to California's Department of Education's 2017 statistics, 75% of Black boys cannot read at grade level.[93] They are functionally illiterate. This level of illiteracy is a scale not seen since the end of the Civil War and the evidence of the most pressing yet most neglected civil rights issue of our day. This problem of epic proportions must be addressed at home and in the school. Not only are three out of four Black boys in California's public schools unable to read and write proficiently, soon they may be taught anti-Zionist propaganda so they can blame Israel and the Jews for their lot in life. This is something a colleague of mine calls the *Palestinization* of the Black community. Just as Palestinian children in Gaza are taught to hate Jews, so will be the effect of California's Critical Ethnic Studies

---

[92] From "Why CA ethnic studies curriculum should alarm you," by J. Washington, 2020, *Times of Israel*.

[93] See "75% of black California boys don't meet state reading standards," by M. Levin, 2017, *Mercury News* for more information.

on California's students.

The prophet, Hosea, exclaimed, "My people are destroyed for lack of knowledge."

Especially in the Black community, we are at a moment in history where one of our greatest challenges is also fueling a rise in and acceptance of antisemitism: A lack of authentic education. Dr. Carter Woodson called it *Miseducation*, which is worse than a lack of education. Nearly 100 years ago, Dr. Woodson, the father of Black History, explained the goal of proper education by citing the Jewish people as an example.

> The mere imparting of information is not education. Above all things, the effort must result in making a man think and do for himself just as the Jews have done in spite of universal persecution.[94]

Dr. Woodson also explained what happens when a person is not truly educated but rather programmed to think and be exploited.

> If you can control a man's thinking you don't have to worry about his action. When you determine what a man shall think you do not have to concern yourself about what he will do. If you make a man feel inferior, you do not have to compel him to accept an inferior status, for he will seek it himself. If you make a man think that he is justly an outcast, you do not have to order him to the back door. He will go without being told; and if there is no back door, his very nature will demand one.

Among the countless examples of the miseducation that would cause a Black child to choose an inferior status is the oft-abused topic of Tulsa's Black Wall Street. Generally speaking, Black young men and women know one of two things about the historic Greenwood District of Tulsa, Oklahoma. They either know:

1. Nothing, or
2. That White racists destroyed it in 1921.

Tulsa's Black Wall Street (from the name Negro Wall Street given by Booker T.

---

[94] From "Preface," by C. G. Woodson, 2000, *The Miseducation of the Negro*, p. xvi. Original work published 1933. Copyright 2000 by African American Images.

Greenwood District Attorneys B.C. Franklin (right) and I. H. Spears (left), with Secretary Effie Thompson (center)
Received from Greenwood Cultural Center, Tulsa, Oklahoma

Washington) was one of many Black communities throughout Oklahoma and various parts of the nation. It was an economic powerhouse established wholly by Black families, business leaders, and entrepreneurs less than fifty years after slavery ended. According to the Black Wall Street's official website:

> The Greenwood District was home to dozens of prominent African-American businessmen. Greenwood boasted a variety of thriving businesses that were very successful up until the events known as the 1921 Tulsa Race Riot. In fact, the district was so successful that a dollar would stay within the district an estimated nineteen months before being spent elsewhere. Not only did black Americans want to contribute to the success of their own shops, but there were also racial segregation laws that prevented them from shopping anywhere other than Greenwood.

> Following the events known as the 1921 Tulsa Race Riot, the area was rebuilt and thrived (with more than 100 MORE African-American businesses in place than there were before the riot itself) until the 1960s when desegregation allowed blacks to shop in areas from which they were previously restricted.[95]

After the devastation visited on the Greenwood District, the residents also fought a two-year legal battle in which the state of Oklahoma attempted to take their land under the guise of public safety. Oklahoma County declared that all buildings must be built according to new fire codes, increasing the rebuilding cost beyond the residents' reach.[96] [97]Represented by Black Wall Street attorneys B. C. Franklin, along with I. H. Spears, the residents fought the measure all the way to the state Supreme Court and won. In barely two years after the 1921 Massacre, every house and structure was rebuilt. By the third year, there were even more families and businesses. The era of Black Wall Street lasted from the 1910s until the 1960s, a victim of several factors including, ironically, integration.

There is film footage of Tulsa's Black Wall Street and other thriving Black communities of the early 20th century recorded by Baptist minister, Rev. Solomon Sir Jones. By typing *Black Wall Street* or *Greenwood District* in an Internet video search, one can view Black families (fathers, mothers, children), beautiful houses, expensive cars, factories, stores, and their owners, oil barons, teachers, ministers (faith in God was preeminent), World War I veterans, police officers—thriving, successful, happy people.

It is crucial to know the whole story of Tulsa's Greenwood District, like it is crucial to learn authentic history. . Knowing that White racists destroyed it, killing an untold number of innocent Black men, women, and children, is heart-wrenching. It's the stuff that fuels hatred and a desire for revenge. Knowing that the residents rebuilt Greenwood and made it more prosperous than ever and thrived until the 1960s infuses one with great pride. It speaks to the greatness of a

---

[95] From "Black Wall Street," by Greenwood Cultural Center, n.d., *Greenwood Cultural Center*. https://greenwoodculturalcenter.com/black-wall-street.

[96] See "The Tulsa Race Massacre," by Oklahoma Historical Society, n.d., *Oklahoma Historical Society* for more information.

[97] See "Unsung heroes and secret villains: The war between good and evil in Tulsa," by E. A. Grant, 2020, *Medium*.

people who, after centuries of slavery and while facing Jim Crow segregation and violence, accomplished the impossible—twice. Taught manipulatively, the story of Tulsa's Black Wall Street is yet another example of White hatred and Black helplessness in America. Taught honestly, the story of Tulsa's Black Wall Street is a powerful, albeit painful saga of resilience and strength.

A history of tragedy and triumph is one of the many ties that bind the Black American and Jewish people.

Anti-Zionism is based on a lack of authentic education. Anti-Zionism is antisemitism. Anti-Zionism is the hatred of Jewish people and a denial of Israel's right to exist. People who identify as such are today's Amalekites and Philistines. For 72 years, the modern state of Israel has survived and prospered against all odds. This fact has only further enraged Israel's enemies, emboldening them to slander and attack her. God will always protect and defend Israel, doing so, in part, through the Church. There is a divine mandate on the Black American and African Church to lead this effort. This is part of the reason for the spiritual warfare we are experiencing all over the world, as Africa and her diaspora take a sort of center stage. We must seize this moment to do our part in building upon the foundation laid by the Queen of Ethiopia. We must stand with Israel and the Jewish people, now more than ever. The blessing of the God of Abraham, Isaac, and Jacob rests on those who bless His people.

In the final chapter of this book, *What We Must Do Now*, we will discuss how authentic education is the key to moving forward with Black-Jewish solidarity. Just as miseducation is being used to promote antisemitism and Israel-hatred, authentic education can strengthen the ties between the Black and Jewish communities—between Africa and Israel.

CHAPTER 6
WHAT WE MUST DO NOW

> Romans 8.31
> *What then shall we say to these things? If God is for us, who can be against us?*
> (English Standard Version, Romans 8.31)

We ended the previous chapter outlining a viable, sustainable path to Black solidarity with Israel and the Jewish people in the 21st Century—Education. We will divide this chapter into two parts. The first will detail a three-tiered approach to producing effective advocates for the Black-Jewish, Africa-Israel alliance. The second will speak specifically to pastors and church or community leaders.

The three steps in producing effective advocates for the Black-Jewish, Africa-Israel alliance are:

1. Authentic history, Black American and Africa-Israel.
2. Visiting the Land of Israel.
3. Community engagement.

AUTHENTIC HISTORY

There were three essential elements to the rise of the Black American family after centuries of slavery: Faith in God, Education, and Entrepreneurialism.

Faith in God kept enslaved Black families focused on the ultimate source of

WHAT WE MUST DO NOW

their liberation, the power, and grace of Almighty God. Abolitionists, Black and White, were almost always devout Christians whose opposition to slavery was based on their spiritual convictions. They knew that slavery was America's original sin—what Dr. Robert Woodson of the Woodson Center calls, "America's birth defect." And they knew slavery must end lest the wrath of God visited the nation. As we observed in the *Negro Spirituals* of chapter one, Black slaves sang songs of freedom based on the Bible. Black families knew that one day they would be free and that their deliverance would come from the same God who brought the Hebrews out of the bondage of Egypt.

The Juneteenth celebration of freedom from slavery, which should be a national holiday, is marked by songs of thanksgiving and praise to the Lord who brought us out of bondage, "with a mighty outstretched hand." The key was not to forget what God had done for us. Again, as James Weldon Johnson wrote in *Lift Ev'ry Voice and Sing*:

> *God of our weary years, God of our silent tears,*
> *Thou who has brought us thus far on the way;*
> *Thou who hast by Thy might, led us into the light,*
> *Keep us forever in the path, we pray.*

> *Lest our feet stray from the places, our God, where we met Thee,*
> *Lest our hearts, drunk with the wine of the world, we forget Thee.*

Faith to believe God for deliverance from slavery was not a call to inaction. As the Apostle James said, "faith without works is dead." No one knew this like Harriet Tubman and Frederick Douglass, who relied on God for help as they worked to free themselves and their people. It was Harriet Tubman's faith in God that caused her to conduct the Underground Railroad, leading escaped slaves from the south to freedom in Canada over and over again. She stated, "I said to the Lord, I'm going to hold steady on to you, and I know you will see me through."[1] Harriet Tubman, again, known as Black Moses, was never caught.

Frederick Douglass' faith in God caused him to urge President Lincoln to allow the slaves to fight for their freedom as soldiers in the Union Army. The courage of the all-Black 54th Massachusetts Infantry Regiment helped turn the tide of the

---

[1] See *Scenes in the Life of Harriet Tubman* by S. H. Bradford, 1869, p. 20. W. J. Moses, printer.

Civil War. *Glory* was the 1989 motion picture based on the 54th Massachusetts Infantry Regiment. It is also the film in which Denzel Washington won his first Academy Award—Best Supporting Actor. Black slaves *prayed* for freedom and *sang* of freedom. Through those prayers and songs, God gave them the strength to *fight* for freedom. As Frederick Douglass said in his 1852 speech to the National Free Soil Convention at Pittsburgh, "The man who is right is a majority. He who has God and conscience on his side has a majority against the universe."[2] Frederick Douglass also said, "I prayed for freedom for twenty years, but received no answer until I prayed with my legs."[3]

Throughout the history of the Black Church in America, recalling the goodness of God and how He "brought us from a mighty long way" was a mainstay in singing and preaching. This sentiment was never one of ignoring the realities of our hardship and struggle as a people. Instead, it sought to keep life in perspective, remembering both the battles fought and the victories won. This is a spiritual theme based on the Bible and God's relationship with Israel. One of the more beloved songs, *If it Had Not Been for the Lord on My Side*, is based on David's Psalm 124.

> Psalm 124
> 1 *A song of ascents. Of David. Had it not been for the Lord Who was with us, let Israel declare now.*
> 2 *Had it not been for the Lord Who was with us when men rose up against us,*
> 3 *Then they would have swallowed us raw when their anger was kindled against us.*
> 4 *Then the waters would have washed us away; illness would have passed over our soul.*
> 5 *Then the wicked waters would have passed over our soul.*
> 6 *Blessed is the Lord, Who did not give us as prey for their teeth.*
> 7 *Our soul escaped like a bird from the hunters' snare; the snare broke, and we escaped.*
> 8 *Our help is in the name of the Lord, Who made heaven and earth.*

---

[2] See "Speech to the national free soil convention on the fugitive slave law," by F. Douglass, 1852, *Frederick Douglass' Paper*. Retrieved from University of Rochester Frederick Douglass Project. https://rbscp.lib.rochester.edu/4385.

[3] Famous quote by Frederick Douglass, 19th c.

WHAT WE MUST DO NOW

א שִׁיר הַמַּעֲלוֹת לְדָוִד לוּלֵי יְהוָה שֶׁהָיָה לָנוּ יֹאמַר־נָא יִשְׂרָאֵל׃
ב לוּלֵי יְהוָה שֶׁהָיָה לָנוּ בְּקוּם עָלֵינוּ אָדָם׃
ג אֲזַי חַיִּים בְּלָעוּנוּ בַּחֲרוֹת אַפָּם בָּנוּ׃
ד אֲזַי הַמַּיִם שְׁטָפוּנוּ נַחְלָה עָבַר עַל־נַפְשֵׁנוּ׃
ה אֲזַי עָבַר עַל־נַפְשֵׁנוּ הַמַּיִם הַזֵּידוֹנִים׃
ו בָּרוּךְ יְהוָה שֶׁלֹּא נְתָנָנוּ טֶרֶף לְשִׁנֵּיהֶם׃
ז נַפְשֵׁנוּ כְּצִפּוֹר נִמְלְטָה מִפַּח יוֹקְשִׁים הַפַּח נִשְׁבָּר וַאֲנַחְנוּ נִמְלָטְנוּ׃
ח עֶזְרֵנוּ בְּשֵׁם יְהוָה עֹשֵׂה שָׁמַיִם וָאָרֶץ׃

(The Complete Jewish Bible with Rashi Commentary, Psalm 124)

If it Had Not Been for the Lord on My Side was written in 1980 by gospel music great Dr. Margaret Pleasant Douroux, founder and CEO of the Heritage Musical Foundation. I had the honor and privilege of meeting Dr. Douroux in the mid-1980s when I served as Music Coordinator for the San Francisco Christian Center led by Bishop Donald E. Green. Dr. Douroux is as inspirational as she is talented and shared much Godly wisdom with our congregation as she conducted a music seminar. In a 2005 interview with *BlackGospel.com*, Dr. Douroux gave this synopsis of the history of Black gospel music:

> One of the most interesting facts I often discuss in my seminars is that the chronology of Gospel Music matches the events occurring in society. The music of Black America changed according to the landmark changes in the culture. When we were slaves, we sang a slave song that originated mostly from the pain of slavery. The song expressed the pain of slavery but also the faith that God would deliver. *Nobody Knows the Trouble I Seen* to *Over My Head I Hear Music in the Air*. When we learned to read and write, we sang an educated song from the hymnbook. First, we sang the hymn imitating the European style. Then, we added our own Black music flavor. When Black America marched for freedom, we sang freedom songs based on songs from the Black Church . . . *We Shall Over Come*, *Precious Lord Take My Hand* [Thomas A. Dorsey, 1938], *Move On Up A Little Higher* [W. Herbert Brewster, c. 1946]. The contemporary song includes Traditional Gospel to Hip-Hop. From Traditional songs like, *If It Had Not Been For The Lord On My Side* [1980] to Contemporary *Why I Sing* [Kirk Franklin, c. 1993]. Black church sacred music always sings according to what is happening in the culture. We sing according to where we are.[4]

---
[4] Douroux during an interview with Black Gospel (2005).

As both a pastor and music minister, I submit that the Black Church must continue to sing songs of tragedies and triumphs. We must sing of the battles and the victories, always giving thanks to God in Jesus' name. If the focus is only on the battles, bitterness and hatred will take control. Thus, we become vulnerable to dangerous, self-destructive ideologies. If the focus is only on the victories, pride and arrogance will take root, and we will be unable to discern what battles we need to fight today.

Especially to the young people reading this, I encourage you always to give God the praise, no matter what is happening around you. Never let anyone or anything steal your joy. Never let anyone or anything make you stop worshipping the Lord. It is one of the ways the Black community survived and thrived against every imaginable obstacle. There is a great responsibility for your generation to restore the Black family. You can only do this by God's grace. The children of Israel cried out in anguish as they heard the words of the Torah read in Jerusalem after seventy years of exile in Babylon and Persia. Nehemiah told them that it was not the season to cry but to rejoice, not because he wanted them to be in denial, but because there was much work to be done. They had to be strong, and Nehemiah reminded them that "the joy of the Lord is your strength."

We are living in unprecedented times for Israel and the world. Arab states are beginning to normalize relations and even make peace with Israel, which has not happened in this fashion since Israeli independence in 1948. According to the African-based Israel Allies Foundation, Uganda, Ghana, South Africa, Malawi, Kenya, Liberia, Sierra Leone, Zambia, Madagascar, Nigeria, the Democratic Republic of the Congo, and the Republic of the Congo have all initiated pro-Israel caucuses. Malawi and Chad are discussing the opening of diplomatic offices in Jerusalem, Israel's capital, a move that remains controversial as the Palestinians claim East Jerusalem as the capital of their future state. And there are renewed attempts at strengthening the relationship between Black and Jewish Americans. However, we must address the miseducation and disinformation directed at our community, or those attempts at solidarity will be short-lived. Doing so begins with knowledge of genuine history, authentic education.

Education was how Black families took their place in a society not necessarily established to see them succeed. According to economist Dr. Thomas Sowell:

As Blacks emerged from slavery, a minute percentage could read or write. And yet in half a century, over half of the Black population was literate. Economic historians call that one of the most remarkable things in history.[5]

Once again, the thing that caused economic historians to marvel was what freed slaves recognized as the hand of God. Over fifty percent literacy in a population forbidden to read for two centuries was a miracle. Not only had slaves won their freedom, they were now emerging as an educated class, despite crushing racism still surrounding them. Just as it was the Lord who caused them to survive, so they would need the Lord to thrive. Before the turn of the century, signs of thriving were already evident, and why Black leaders like James Weldon Johnson encouraged us not to forget the Lord. It is why he asked God to "Keep us forever in Thy path . . . lest our feet stray from the place where we met Thee." In less than thirty-eight years after the Emancipation Proclamation, Johnson warned freed slaves about becoming "drunk with the wine of the world" and forgetting God. To a people who had known forced servitude, poverty, and brutal racial oppression for over two centuries, the sages of the community echoed the words of Moses.

> Deuteronomy 6.10-12
>
> *10 And it will be, when the Lord, your God, brings you to the land He swore to your fathers, to Abraham, to Isaac, and to Jacob, to give you, great and good cities that you did not build,*
>
> *11 and houses full of all good things that you did not fill, and hewn cisterns that you did not hew, vineyards and olive trees that you did not plant, and you will eat and be satisfied.*
>
> *12 Beware, lest you forget the Lord, Who brought you out of the land of Egypt, out of the house of bondage.*

> י וְהָיָ֞ה כִּ֣י יְבִיאֲךָ֣ ׀ יְהֹוָ֣ה אֱלֹהֶ֗יךָ אֶל־הָאָ֙רֶץ֙ אֲשֶׁ֨ר נִשְׁבַּ֧ע לַאֲבֹתֶ֛יךָ לְאַבְרָהָ֥ם לְיִצְחָ֖ק וּֽלְיַעֲקֹ֑ב לָ֣תֶת לָ֔ךְ עָרִ֛ים גְּדֹלֹ֥ת וְטֹבֹ֖ת אֲשֶׁ֥ר לֹא־בָנִֽיתָ׃
> יא וּבָ֨תִּ֜ים מְלֵאִ֣ים כׇּל־טוּב֮ אֲשֶׁ֣ר לֹא־מִלֵּ֒אתָ֒ וּבֹרֹ֤ת חֲצוּבִים֙ אֲשֶׁ֣ר לֹא־חָצַ֔בְתָּ כְּרָמִ֥ים וְזֵיתִ֖ים אֲשֶׁ֣ר לֹא־נָטָ֑עְתָּ וְאָכַלְתָּ֖ וְשָׂבָֽעְתָּ׃
> יב הִשָּׁ֣מֶר לְךָ֔ פֶּן־תִּשְׁכַּ֖ח אֶת־יְהֹוָ֑ה אֲשֶׁ֧ר הוֹצִֽיאֲךָ֛ מֵאֶ֥רֶץ מִצְרַ֖יִם מִבֵּ֥ית עֲבָדִֽים׃

---

[5] Sowell on "The economic lot of minorities," *The firing line with William F. Buckley, Jr.*, 1981, season 16, episode 40. Firing line broadcast records (Television Program), Hoover Institution Library & Archives, program S0484. Copyright Stanford University.

>(The Complete Jewish Bible with Rashi Commentary, Deuteronomy 6.10-12)

The same year that Johnson wrote *Lift Ev'ry Voice and Sing* (1899), former Black slaves and otherwise racially marginalized people were already distinguishing themselves. A premier example was Paul Laurence Dunbar High School in Washington, DC. Again, Thomas Sowell:

> For a period of 85 years (1870-1955) Dunbar was an academically elite, all-black public high school in Washington, D.C. As far back as 1899, Dunbar students came in first in citywide tests given in *both* black and white schools. Over the 85-year span, most of Dunbar's graduates went on to college, even though most Americans-white or black-did not. Most Dunbar graduates could afford only to attend the low-cost local colleges: either federally-supported Howard University or tuition-free Miner Teachers College. However, those Dunbar graduates who attended Harvard, Amherst, Oberlin, and other prestigious institutions (usually on scholarships) ran up an impressive record of academic honors. For example, it is known that Amherst admitted 34 Dunbar graduates between 1892 and 1954; of these, 74 per cent graduated, and more than one fourth of these graduates were Phi Beta Kappas.[6]

Today, education is possibly the area in which disenfranchised Black communities are the most lacking. It is systemic, racial oppression of the worst kind. Further, decades of miseducation and disinformation have had disastrous effects. These effects include the acceptance or mainstreaming of antisemitism. We can change this sobering reality, but we must first acknowledge it. We cannot build a renewed solidarity with our Jewish brothers and sisters when some of the loudest voices in our community are spewing hatred for Jews and Israel. Like Nehemiah and the Israelites learned in rebuilding the walls of Jerusalem, we cannot build without first removing the debris of destruction. As my Jewish Torah scholar friend says, "you must first remove the cover of dust before you can reveal the *neshama* (Spirit) inside."

Nehemiah 4.10 (New King James Version)

---

[6] From "Black excellence--the case of Dunbar high school," by T. Sowell, 1974, *The Public Interest*, p. 3-4.

WHAT WE MUST DO NOW

Then Judah said, "The strength of the laborers is failing, and there is so much rubbish that we are not able to build the wall."

Those who say that the Jewish community must also fight anti-Black racism, I say, agreed. In the words of Dr. King, "when we find examples of exploitation, it must be admitted. That must be done in the Jewish community too." However, the focus of this book is *Zionism & the Black Church*. There are plenty of Jewish friends who are having anti-racism discussions in their homes and synagogues. I will leave that to them and address *my* community.

A key component in educating the post-slavery population was the collaborative work of Booker T. Washington and Jewish philanthropist Julius Rosenwald beginning in 1912. Though Washington died just three years later in 1915, the venture he started with Rosenwald ultimately produced over 5,000 schools for Black children throughout the Jim Crow South—Rosenwald Schools. Julius Rosenwald also provided fellowship grants for Black students to further their education beyond high school. Rosenwald Fellows included some of the most iconic Black figures in American history. Writer, Langston Hughes; opera singer Marion Anderson; author and activist, James Baldwin; artist Lawrence Jacobs; photographer Gordon Parks Jr.; Dr. Charles Drew—Dunbar High School graduate physician who revolutionized ways to process and store blood plasma; and poet Maya Angelou were all Rosenwald Fellows. Julius Rosenwald's rabbi, Emil G. Hirsch was one of the Jewish founders of the NAACP and encouraged Rosenwald's efforts on behalf of the Black community. As Rosenwald stated, "Whether it is because I belong to a people who have known centuries of persecution, or whether it is because I am naturally inclined to sympathize with the oppressed, I have always felt keenly for the colored race."[7] It is amazing that Rosenwald's words supporting Black people echoed those of Zionist founding father, Theodor Herzl.

Real education efforts must be holistic and teach young Black Americans authentic Black history, including the Black Church's deep identification with Israel and spiritual Zionism. From King Solomon and the Queen of Sheba to

---

[7] Rosenwald introducing Booker T. Washington at a luncheon at the Blackstone Hotel in Chicago, 1911. Quote retrieved from "A historic meeting," by Julius Rosenwald Legacy, n.d., *Julius Rosenwald Legacy*. Originally printed in "Lunch at the Blackstone," by S. Deutsch, 2011, *You need a schoolhouse: Booker T. Washington, Julius Rosenwald, and the building of schools for the segregated south*, p. 96. Copyright 2011 by Stephanie Deutsch.

Golda Meir and African leaders, young Black men and women must learn of the rich, long-standing history of the Africa-Israel relationship. From Washington and Rosenwald to Dr. King and Rabbi Heschel, our youth must know of the deep ties that bind the Black American and Jewish communities. They must understand why those ties hold even more spiritual and political significance today. This type of thorough training will produce young people that not only understand why Black-Jewish, Africa-Israel solidarity is so important, they will protect it. The most influential ambassadors of the Black-Jewish, Africa-Israel alliance, must first know *their* history and love *their* community. They must desire to learn about and love Africa, both the continent and the diverse people.

My first trips to the Motherland were South Africa in 2016 and Ethiopia in 2017, two beautiful countries filled with amazing people. Not only was my life changed being on the continent of my ancestors, but I also saw love for Israel and the Jewish people. In South Africa, I had the privilege of leading Africa-Israel solidarity events while spending time with many gifted, engaging Black South African youth. Their love for God, their families, and the nation of Israel was remarkable. Their knowledge of and respect for their tribal history was impressive and further underscored the necessity of identity. Whether Tswana, Xhosa, Sotho, or Zulu, the children knew who they were and, therefore, could not be defined by someone attempting to redefine them.

At an Israel event in Awasa, Ethiopia, one of the pastors felt the Spirit of God instruct the several hundred in attendance to repent for how the nation historically mistreated the Ethiopian Jews. For nearly an hour, the attendees laid prostrate throughout the church. They cried out to God for forgiveness in Amharic and English. I will never forget that day. And I will never forget the love for Israel and the Jewish people I saw while in Africa. It is a love that is growing in strength and demonstrable action.

The year 2016 was also the fortieth anniversary of the Raid on Entebbe Airport when 100 Israeli commandos rescued nearly all of the 100 Israeli hostages taken to Uganda by German and Palestinian terrorists. The Institute for Black Solidarity with Israel (IBSI) followed the historic visit on social media and witnessed an outpouring of love for the Jewish State and the Jewish people by Africans online. The comments section on posted videos and pictures were expressions like, "We love Israel!" "Long live Israel!" "We are praying for the peace of Jerusalem!" Or,

"Bibi (Benjamin Netanyahu), you must come to Togo and Ghana (West Africa) next!" There are millions of African Christians whose love for Israel is firmly rooted in the Bible, wholeheartedly believing that whoever blesses Israel will be blessed.

As we discussed in chapter five, Ugandan President Idi Amin once enjoyed a close relationship with Israel. Amin severed ties with Israel when the Israelis refused to sell him helicopters and other weapons to kill his people. I have several Ugandan friends who told me that when their nation participated in the attack on the Jewish people, God cursed them according to Genesis 12.3. They explained the wars and calamities that befell Uganda after Entebbe was God's judgment on the nation. There were several events led by Ugandan pastors and leaders in which the people repented for their actions against Israel. During his 2016 East African tour, Prime Minister Netanyahu's first stop was Uganda. There at Entebbe Airport, Ugandan President Yoweri Kaguta Museveni led a moving ceremony affirming the two nations' close bond. Today, Uganda is a relatively peaceful and prosperous nation with one of Africa's fastest-growing economies.

The Raid on Entebbe, known as Operation Thunderbolt, would not have been possible had Israel not refueled its planes carrying the commandos to East Africa. In 1976, Kenyan President, Jomo Kenyatta, allowed the Israeli Mossad to gather intelligence for the mission and then refuel in Kenya. Kenya's president today, Uhuru Kenyatta, is the son of Jomo Kenyatta. In 2016, after leaving Uganda, Israeli Prime Minister Netanyahu flew to Kenya and continued the commemoration of Operation Thunderbolt, thanking Kenya once again for its help in 1976. The ceremonies in Uganda and Kenya were deeply personal and a clear sign of a significant shift in the long Africa-Israel story. Cooperation and collaboration between the Jewish State and Africa have never been stronger. As Netanyahu said to African leaders after his 2016 visit, "We want to be great partners for you. Africa is a continent on the rise, and it could rise to unbelievable heights. It excites our imagination."

Education and faith in God resulted in the era of Black Wall Street (the 1910s – 1960s), the Tuskegee Institute and Tuskegee Airmen, the Harlem Renaissance, and much more. By the 1920s, Black men and women were entrepreneurs, factory owners, manufactures, architects, inventors, oil barons, bankers, and more. Like their Jewish brothers and sisters often were, Black people were shut out of the broader White society. So, they formed their own social and economic centers, which both rivaled and surpassed their White counterparts.

In 2019, Black billionaire tech investor Robert Smith announced that his family would cover the student loan debt of the entire graduating class of Morehouse College. Smith made the announcement during his keynote address at Morehouse's commencement. As impressive as his gesture was, his speech was just as, if not, even more significant. He gave a history of the disenfranchisement of the Black community from slavery to the modern era, then underscored three crucial things:

1. Primary education (K-12) is foundational to academic and career success.
2. Racism exists, but don't let that be your focus. America is "extraordinary."
3. Black people are enough to care for their community.

Robert Smith's commencement speech, in many ways, echoed the truths that have guided the Black community for centuries. No matter what the obstacle, with education and God's help, there is nothing we cannot accomplish. At the 2020 World Values Network gala at Carnegie Hall in New York City, Smith also spoke of the deep ties that bind Jewish and Black people in America.

> The Jewish people and the African American people share a birthright burden. We are wanderers in search of a place to call home, to plant roots, to build community. We can begin to heal our world when we acknowledge the similarities in the burdens we carry—and work together to liberate them.[8]

VISIT THE HOLY LAND

The land of Israel speaks for itself. Every Christian—every person should visit the Holy Land at least once. It is the Promised Land of the children of Abraham, Isaac, and Jacob. It is the land where Jesus walked, where He taught, where He healed the sick, raised the dead, where He was crucified and rose again. It is the land from where Jesus ascended into heaven and where He will return. It is the land that God personally cares for and the land of His chosen dwelling

---

[8] Smith at the World Values Network's Eighth Annual International Champions of Jewish Values Awards Gala, 2020.

place, Zion.

> Deuteronomy 11.11-12
> *11 But the land, to which you pass to possess, is a land of mountains and valleys and absorbs water from the rains of heaven,*
> *12 a land the Lord, your God, looks after; the eyes of Lord your God are always upon it, from the beginning of the year to the end of the year.*

> יא וְהָאָ֗רֶץ אֲשֶׁ֨ר אַתֶּ֜ם עֹבְרִ֥ים שָׁ֙מָּה֙ לְרִשְׁתָּ֔הּ אֶ֥רֶץ הָרִ֖ים וּבְקָעֹ֑ת לִמְטַ֥ר הַשָּׁמַ֖יִם תִּשְׁתֶּה־מָּֽיִם:
> יב אֶ֕רֶץ אֲשֶׁר־יְהֹוָ֥ה אֱלֹהֶ֖יךָ דֹּרֵ֣שׁ אֹתָ֑הּ תָּמִ֗יד עֵינֵ֨י יְהֹוָ֤ה אֱלֹהֶ֙יךָ֙ בָּ֔הּ מֵֽרֵשִׁית֙ הַשָּׁנָ֔ה וְעַ֖ד אַחֲרִ֥ית שָׁנָֽה:
> (The Complete Jewish Bible with Rashi Commentary, Deuteronomy 11.11-12)

Israel is the ancestral homeland of the Jewish people. After almost 2,000 years, they have been returning from all over the world.

> Ezekiel 11.17
> *Therefore, say; So said the Lord God: I will gather you from the peoples, and I will assemble you from the lands which you have been scattered therein, and I shall give you the land of Israel.*

> לָכֵ֞ן אֱמֹ֗ר כֹּֽה־אָמַר֮ אֲדֹנָ֣י יֱהֹוִה֒ וְקִבַּצְתִּ֣י אֶתְכֶ֔ם מִן־הָ֣עַמִּ֔ים וְאָסַפְתִּ֣י אֶתְכֶ֔ם מִן־הָ֣אֲרָצ֔וֹת אֲשֶׁ֥ר נְפֹצוֹתֶ֖ם בָּהֶ֑ם וְנָתַתִּ֥י לָכֶ֖ם אֶת־אַדְמַ֥ת יִשְׂרָאֵֽל:
> (The Complete Jewish Bible with Rashi Commentary, Ezekiel 11.17)

Israel is home to Jews and non-Jews from some 90 different nations, by far the most ethnically diverse country in the region. Israel is also tightly surrounded by enemies. The Jewish State is roughly the size of New Jersey. It borders Iran-controlled Lebanon and Syria to the north, and Hamas-ruled Gaza to the south. Despite Israel's geopolitical reality, it is one of the safest, most peaceful places on earth. Peaceful Israel may seem impossible unless you have visited. When you make a pilgrimage to Zion, then you will see.

One Nigerian young man told me about his time in Israel. He wandered away from his tour group, wanting to take in Jerusalem on his own. As the Sabbath approached, a young lady introduced herself and invited him to welcome the Sabbath with her and her family. He welcomed the Sabbath with the Israeli family. They visited another house where they ate, laughed, talked, and fellowshipped, like Psalm 133, "Behold, how good and pleasant it is for brothers to dwell together in unity." For the next several weeks that he remained in Israel, his time continued in this way. He described the Israelis as down to earth, approachable, and genuinely loving. Over the years, I have heard very similar testimonies from many different people. There is something special about the people and the Land.

COMMUNITY ENGAGEMENT

After being empowered with authentic history, and after touching the land of Israel, young Black men and women will be prepared to bring that knowledge and experience to their local community. Adequately funded, organized, and led, these young people will be powerful advocates for Black-Jewish synergy at a grassroots level. Their work will include:

- Building relationships between Black and Jewish religious leaders.
- Organizing after-school tutoring with the help of Black and Jewish teachers.
- Connecting Black and Jewish entrepreneurs.
- Connecting Black and Jewish artists and music performers for joint events and much more.

As residents in their city, these young ambassadors will help foster healthy Black-Jewish, Africa-Israel relations and provide a constant source of accurate information about the Jewish State. Rosenwald Schools stood for decades as a symbol of Black-Jewish cooperation that changed American history. Likewise, these local centers will help set a new course for the future.

Based on authentic education, this holistic, grassroots approach to Zionism in the Black community would succeed where many others have failed. The breach in the relationship between the Black American and Jewish American communities did not occur because there are not enough organizations taking Black people to Israel. It occurred because of decades of a concerted effort by Israel's enemies to force-feed anti-Zionism into the hearts and minds of Black people—especially Black leaders. Sadly, this effort of sabotage was somewhat successful, fostering resentment and distrust. The first step to repairing the breach is a commitment to increase our knowledge of our history in this nation, including how the Jewish people have played a significant and recurring role. Because this is a long-term approach to Black-Jewish solidarity, pro-Israel organizations do not have the time to employ it or simply do not see the relevance. It is not their mandate. First and foremost, Zionism in the Black Church is a Black Church issue. The Africa-Israel alliance—which has been so beneficial to Africa—is an African issue.

As Black Americans and Africans create and demonstrate an education-based model of Israel advocacy, there will be no shortage of partners to join us in the effort. A new paradigm begins with people who have a prophetic vision. God says that without a vision, the people perish (Proverbs 29.18).

PERSONAL ENCOUNTERS AND EXPERIENCES

PASTOR/COMMUNITY LEADER

If you are a pastor or community leader, what tangible things can you do to strengthen Black Jewish relations where you live? If you sense the call to stand with the Jewish people and the State of Israel, there are five steps you can take. These are progressive steps, so you would need to start with number one first. If, or when, you're ready for more, proceed to the next.

1. Pray for the peace of Jerusalem.
   Our Biblical mandate to stand with Israel begins as all things do in the Church—with prayer. God promises a blessing of prosperity on those who love the Holy City. Pastors and leaders, when leading your congregation in prayer, read Psalm 122 in their hearing. Remind the people that God's covenant with Israel is forever, and we have the honor of praying for the nation at a time of its reestablishment. Pray for the continued Redemption as the Israeli government and other entities actively return the Jewish exiles to their homeland. Read Psalm 147 in your prayer service or Bible study and remind the people that God heals the brokenhearted in Israel and throughout the Body of Christ.

2. Teach Biblical Zionism.
   Pastors and leaders, in your sermons, Sunday school lessons, Bible studies, or

Bible college classes, remind your people what scripture says about Israel and the Jewish people. Remind them that because God's covenant with Israel is forever, the land of Israel is theirs forever. There are great video resources to introduce the principle of Zionism, the modern state of Israel and the return of the Jewish Diaspora including, *The Case for Israel (Alan Dershowitz)* and *Against All Odds Israel Survives Series (American Trademark Pictures)*.

Remind the people that when Jesus returns, He will reign from Jerusalem. While He tarries, the scattered of Israel are returning to their homeland, which is a sign of Jesus' soon return. The Jewish people are awaiting the Messiah, as is the Church. And as one older rabbi said (somewhat in jest), "when He comes, we will ask Him if this is His first or second time."

3. Reach out to your local rabbi or leader in the Jewish community. I recommend that before embarking on number three, you read *Honest to God: Christian Zionists Confront 10 Questions Jews Need Answered* by Victor Styrsky. Jewish people who know the horrific history between their ancestors and the Church may be very skeptical of your motives. Much like the Black community, there is a justifiable reason for caution when dealing with outsiders. Styrsky's book will help you understand how a Jewish person potentially sees Christian Zionism and how you can effectively establish good ties with no ulterior motives.

My first adult interaction with someone Jewish was my freshman year in college. I went to college at a performing arts school, the San Francisco Conservatory of Music. . In 1985 the entire student body was a little over 200. Classes were small and intimate. During the first week of school, I connected with a young man named Ariel. Ariel was about six feet tall. He had a stocky build, baritone voice, deep olive skin, straight black hair with a heavy Middle Eastern accent—and he played the tuba. He was a Jewish Israeli, though I did not know this until later. The day I learned that Ariel was Jewish was the day we stopped being friends. Though it was almost 40 years ago, the story is still painful to tell.

As Ariel and I sat in class talking when we should have been paying attention to the professor, he told me he was from Israel.

"You're Jewish?" I asked.

"Yes," he said, somewhat suspiciously.

"Jesus was Jewish!" I yelled.

"...I know," he hesitated.

Fascinated at this revelation, I promptly brought my Bible to class the next day. While the professor continued to teach without our attention, I opened my Bible to the gospels and began proselytizing Ariel right there. I opened to John 3:16, Matthew 24, Luke 2, and more. I brought both barrels. Ariel sat there and stared at me with what I know now was a pained expression on his face. I had no idea of the almost 2,000-year bloody history between the Church and the Jewish people or how the Church became the instrument of death for countless Jews. I had no idea that the Jewish people consider Christian missionaries worse than Hitler because "Hitler destroyed our bodies, but the missionary wants our souls." My love for Jesus notwithstanding, I had no idea I was offending Ariel beyond words.

Finally, he asked, "Why are you trying to convert me?"

"What do you mean?" I replied. "Jesus was Jewish. You're Jewish," I explained.

"I lived for a semester with 40 Jesuit priests, and none of them ever tried to convert me," Ariel said.

For me, that statement was a testament to my Christian diligence, and I beamed with pride.

The conversation ended. Ariel stopped speaking to me and avoided me for the rest of the semester. In my ignorance and religious piety, I said to myself, "His loss. He needs Jesus." It was not until years later that I realized my lack of understanding drove away a potential friend to whom I truly wanted to show the love of Jesus. I needed to start by respecting Ariel's identity by knowing something about him. Instead of ignorantly, albeit, honestly, forcing Jesus on him, I could have learned something about the Hebrew roots of my faith or Israel.

Little did I know the exchange with my Israeli classmate was a prelude of things to come. I've learned over the years, and by observing people much more spiritually mature than I, Christian relationships with Jewish people must be built on mutual respect. Simply stated, if we cannot come together in what Dr. King called a spirit of brotherhood with our Jewish neighbors, then our Christian witness will be short-circuited. However, if we are willing to build bridges, God will do amazing things as Christians and Jews come together.

4. Plan an event with your Jewish colleague.

After number three is accomplished, talk to your Jewish counterpart about a joint venture. You may have a project in your community with which your local rabbi or Jewish leaders can help. Maybe there is a church celebration, a musical, or a play that your Jewish friends may enjoy. It can be as simple as breakfast, lunch, or dinner together. Perhaps you can attend their Passover Seder or a Rosh Hashanah service.

The result of this type of coming together holds great potential and spiritual worth. Whether a major church program or a simple meal, scripture reveals the power of fellowship.

Psalm 133.1-3

1 A song of ascents of David. Behold how good and how pleasant it is for brothers also to dwell together!
2 As the good oil on the head runs down upon the beard, the beard of Aaron, which runs down on the mouth of his garments.
3 As the dew of Hermon which runs down on the mountains of Zion, for there the Lord commanded the blessing, life forever.

א שִׁיר הַמַּעֲלוֹת לְדָוִד הִנֵּה מַה טּוֹב וּמַה נָּעִים שֶׁבֶת אַחִים גַּם יָחַד:
ב כַּשֶּׁמֶן הַטּוֹב | עַל הָרֹאשׁ יֹרֵד עַל הַזָּקָן זְקַן אַהֲרֹן שֶׁיֹּרֵד עַל פִּי מִדּוֹתָיו:
ג כְּטַל חֶרְמוֹן שֶׁיֹּרֵד עַל הַרְרֵי צִיּוֹן כִּי שָׁם | צִוָּה יְהֹוָה אֶת הַבְּרָכָה חַיִּים עַד הָעוֹלָם:

(The Complete Jewish Bible with Rashi Commentary, Psalm 133.1-3)

The Hebrew for "Behold How Good" is *hineh ma tov*. There is an old Hebrew melody to those lyrics, which, when I hear it, I will forever remember the winter of 2011.

In March 2011, I attended and played keyboard at Christians United for Israel's (CUFI) Night to Honor Israel in Rochester, New York. Over 1200 people filled Bethany Christian Fellowship. Jewish men and women, including an Israeli

Defense Force (IDF) soldier, several Holocaust survivors, and rabbis, sat together with Christians throughout the Greater Rochester area. There were speeches and acknowledgments, readings from the Tanakh (Old Testament), fundraising for charitable organizations, and much music.

As the band began playing celebratory Hebrew songs, the Jewish attendees erupted into dancing, singing, and laughter. Bethany Pastor, Ron Domina, had previously told his members not to dance first. He wanted to honor the cultural expression of the Jewish guests and allow them to lead. The church only had to wait about 7.5 seconds. Five people formed a circle that grew to ten, fifteen, twenty—another circle was started with just the men—another group was led to the platform by one of the rabbis as there was no more "dance floor" left. Within moments, most of the people in the building were dancing before the Lord. A spirit of rejoicing was in the atmosphere every bit as real as a Christian church service with Believers in every aisle. I sensed the anointing just as strong as I had leading worship in any other place. God was in the room. Jews and Christians joined hands and sang, celebrating the God of Israel and His love for His people—the biological and the adopted. People wept and hugged each other. Healing was released. Divine revelation was imparted. When it was over, Rabbi Kilimnick of Congregation Beth Shalom and Pastor Domina gave the benediction together. Rabbi Kilimnick became a dear friend and great encouragement; he passed away in 2020.

I was unsure what I witnessed that night. It defied my Christian theological upbringing. There were "non-Believers" in God's house, and not one evangelizing tract was handed out, no "sinner's prayer"—nothing. But, what happened was prophetic. Without my permission, pre-approval, or understanding, as we say in our culture, God "showed up and showed out."

5. Go to Israel.
   As I stated to the young, aspiring Israel advocates, if you have never been to the Holy Land, you should go. Every Christian should make at least one pilgrimage to the land of the Bible, if at all possible. You should touch the Sea of Galilee. You should pray in the Garden of Gethsemane. You should pray at the Western Wall. Israel is modern and ancient, yesterday and today. The people are warm and gracious. They are vibrant and engaging. I've spoken with several friends and acquaintances who traveled to Israel, and

their stories were strikingly similar. While their experiences in the Land were indeed unique, each commented on the genuineness of the people.

My personal experience at the Kotel in Jerusalem is a large part of why I wrote this book. I received what I can only describe as a divine commission, one I will ponder until my old age—if the Lord says the same.

On my last day of the pilgrimage, I got up before sunrise and took a cab from my hotel to the Western Wall. As I walked toward the Wall to pray, early morning "intercessors" were hurrying in the same direction. Weeping, I placed my face in my hands and leaned on the stones of the Kotel. The Spirit of God truly hovers there and His presence is enveloping.

I customarily walk while praying and noticed a couple of men doing the same. I saw one man whose clothing was little worn carrying a paper cup while asking for alms. I approached him as he was on my way to the Wall, but he didn't ask me anything. He just reached out his hand, shook my hand, smiled, and said, "Welcome. Go—go pray," gesturing to the Wall like an usher. It was as if he was expecting me.

I stood about fifty yards from the Wall and attempted to take it in again before leaving Israel. An elder, who had been observing me for a while, asked if I wanted a Siddur (prayer book) in English. I told him, yes, and he went to a room off to the left. He brought back a Siddur in what looked like Portuguese. I chuckled to myself and resumed praying and walking. I could sense God's presence all around. I felt God continue to talk to me about favor, His timing, a new season, increased authority, divine appointment, and a particular assignment—Africa-Israel. I was overwhelmed. I walked toward the group of men sitting by the partition near the women's section. One man with reddish hair and wire-rimmed glasses walked toward me praying and began speaking as if he were talking to someone else. As we made eye contact, he was in the process of saying, "the right man for the precise moment." I stared at him and was about to ask if he was talking to me when he asked, "Where are you from?"

"California."

"Where?"

"Stockton. Near Sacramento."

"Very good," he said and returned to the section where he and the others were praying and reading. It was as if he was a third party to my conversation with God.

After I finished praying, I returned to the elder who gave me the Siddur. As I thanked him, he shook my hand, smiled broadly, and said, "Good day! Good day to you, my friend!"

I often reflect on that morning at the Western Wall. God ordered my steps in a way that left me forever changed. To this day, whenever I return to Jerusalem, early morning prayer at the Kotel is a priority.

Pastors and leaders, I genuinely believe that in these last days, we are entering a time of great synergy between the Church and the Synagogue. Christians and Jews are uniting in a way not seen since the Church's beginning. As the Jewish sages say, these are the days of *Moshiach* (Messiah).

In these opening years of the 21st Century, Black Americans, Jews, and the African States have an unprecedented opportunity to do great good in the world. With the help of Black pastors and leaders, the bitter debate over Israel's right to exist and defend itself can be replaced with peace, freedom, and prosperity for Israel, Africa, and the world. Some of the decades-long problems in our neglected neighborhoods (crime, poor education, lack of job prospects) can be tackled by the combined ingenuity of the Christians and Jews in the city. With Black and Jewish leaders coming together, international attention can focus on addressing human rights abuses in various parts of the world. With the combined forces of *Tikkun Olam*[9] and Black social activism, people can work to repair breaches that government cannot address.

> Psalm 122.1-9
> *1 A song of ascents of David. I rejoiced when they said to me, "Let us go to the house of the Lord."*

---

[9] Hebrew for "world repair." *Tikkun olam* represents a concept widely taught in Judaism that connotes any activity that brings good to the world and brings it closer to a harmonious state.

2 Our feet were standing within your gates, O Jerusalem.

3 The built-up Jerusalem is like a city that was joined together within itself.

4 There ascended the tribes, the tribes of God, testimony to Israel, to give thanks to the name of the Lord.

5 For there were set thrones for judgment, thrones for the house of David.

6 Request the welfare of Jerusalem; may those who love you enjoy tranquility.

7 May there be peace in your wall, tranquility in your palaces.

8 For the sake of my brethren and my companions, I shall now speak of peace in you.

9 For the sake of the house of the Lord our God, I shall beg for goodness for you.

א שִׁיר הַמַּעֲלוֹת לְדָוִד שָׂמַחְתִּי בְּאֹמְרִים לִי בֵּית יְהֹוָה נֵלֵךְ:
ב עֹמְדוֹת הָיוּ רַגְלֵינוּ בִּשְׁעָרַיִךְ יְרוּשָׁלָ͏ִם:
ג יְרוּשָׁלַ͏ִם הַבְּנוּיָה כְּעִיר שֶׁחֻבְּרָה־לָּהּ יַחְדָּו:
ד שֶׁשָּׁם עָלוּ שְׁבָטִים שִׁבְטֵי־יָהּ עֵדוּת לְיִשְׂרָאֵל לְהֹדוֹת לְשֵׁם יְהֹוָה:
ה כִּי שָׁמָּה | יָשְׁבוּ כִסְאוֹת לְמִשְׁפָּט כִּסְאוֹת לְבֵית דָּוִד:
ו שַׁאֲלוּ שְׁלוֹם יְרוּשָׁלָ͏ִם יִשְׁלָיוּ אֹהֲבָיִךְ:
ז יְהִי־שָׁלוֹם בְּחֵילֵךְ שַׁלְוָה בְּאַרְמְנוֹתָיִךְ:
ח לְמַעַן אַחַי וְרֵעָי אֲדַבְּרָה־נָּא שָׁלוֹם בָּךְ:
ט לְמַעַן בֵּית־יְהֹוָה אֱלֹהֵינוּ אֲבַקְשָׁה טוֹב לָךְ:

(The Complete Jewish Bible with Rashi Commentary, Psalm 122.1-9)

BIBLIOGRAPHY

INTRODUCTION

1. Office of the Chaplains and Religious Life. (n.d.) *Awards and Recognitions*. Brown University. https://www.brown.edu/campus-life/spiritual-life/chaplains/awards-and-recognition.
2. News Staff. (2018, September 23). *Celebrating a rich and profound history of black legacy at Brown*. Brown University. https://www.brown.edu/news/2018-09-23/black-legacy.
3. Encyclopedia of Arkansas. (2010, September 9). Little Rock Nine. *Encyclopedia of Arkansas*. http://www.encyclopediaofarkansas.net/encyclopedia/entry-detail.aspx?entryID=723.
4. Institute for Black Solidarity with Israel (IBSI). (2013, April). *Interview with Yaffa* [Interview].
5. Kirchick, J. (2018, June). *The rise of black anti-Semitism*. Commentary Magazine. https://www.commentarymagazine.com/articles/james-kirchick/rise-black-anti-semitism/.
6. Jewish Virtual Library. (1998, November). *Black-Jewish relations: ADL survey finds anti-Semitism high in black community*. Jewish Virtual Library. https://www.jewishvirtuallibrary.org/adl-survey-finds-anti-semitism-high-in-black-community.
7. King, M. L., Jr., King, C. S., & Harding, V. (2010). *Where Do We Go from Here: Chaos Or Community?* (p. 163). Beacon Press.
8. King, M. L. (1968, April 3). *I've been to the mountaintop* [Address]. Memphis, T. N. Copyright by the Estate of Martin Luther King, Jr. https://kinginstitute.stanford.edu/king-papers/documents/ive-been-mountaintop-address-delivered-bishop-charles-mason-temple.
9. *The Complete Jewish Bible with Rashi Commentary*. Chabad. http://www.chabad.org/library/Bible_cdo/aid/8176.

CHAPTER 1
THE AFRICAN BIBLICAL TIE TO ISRAEL

1. Science Encyclopedia. (n.d.). Origins of the name Africa. In *Idea of Africa*. https://science.jrank.org/pages/8198/Africa-Idea-Origins-Name-Africa.html#ixzz6iAqTdHbV.
2. Felder, C. H. and Peebles, J. W. (Eds.). (1993). The curse of Canaan. *The Original African Heritage Study Bible: King James Version* (p. 15). The James C. Winston Publishing Company. Copyright 1993 by the James C. Winston Publishing Company.
3. Yamauchi, E. M. (2004). The curse of Ham. *Africa & the Bible*. Africa (p. 25). Copyright 2004 by Edwin M. Yamauchi.
4. Diop, C. A. (1991). *Civilization or Barbarism: An authentic anthropology*. (H. J. Salemson & Y. M. Ngemi, Eds.). (M. de Jager. Trans.). Lawrence Hill Books. (Original work published 1981). Copyright 1991 by Lawrence Hill Books.
5. Gearon, E. (2011, June 6). Arab Invasions: The First Islamic Empire. *History Today, 61(6)*. https://www.historytoday.com/archive/arab-invasions-first-islamic-empire.
6. Ullendorff, E. (1968). Introduction. *Ethiopia and the Bible: The Schweich Lectures 1967*. (pp. 2-3). Oxford University Press. Copyright 1968 by the British Academy.
7. Hurston, Z. N. (1991). Author's Introduction. *Moses, man of the mountain*. (pp. xxiii-xiv). HarperPerennial. Copyright 1990 by Henry Louis Gates, Jr.
8. Aubin, H. T. (2002). The Kushites' Self-Interest. *The rescue of Jerusalem*. (p. 77). Doubleday Canada. Copyright 2002 by Henry T. Aubin.
9. Felder, C. H. and Peebles, J. W. (Eds.). (1993). The Africology of church music. *The Original African Heritage Study Bible: King James Version*. (p. 1841). The James C. Winston Publishing Company. Copyright 1993 by the James C. Winston Publishing Company.
10. Johnson, J. W. & Johnson, J. R. (1899). *Lift every voice and sing*.
11. *The Complete Jewish Bible with Rashi Commentary*. Chabad. https://www.chabad.org/library/Bible_cdo/aid/9863.
12. *The Complete Jewish Bible with Rashi Commentary*. Chabad. https://www.chabad.org/library/Bible_cdo/aid/16289.
13. *The Complete Jewish Bible with Rashi Commentary*. Chabad. https://www.chabad.org/library/Bible_cdo/aid/16326.
14. *The Complete Jewish Bible with Rashi Commentary*. Chabad. https://www.

BIBLIOGRAPHY

chabad.org/library/Bible_cdo/aid/15951.
15. *The Complete Jewish Bible with Rashi Commentary*. Chabad. https://www.chabad.org/library/Bible_cdo/aid/8174.
16. *The Complete Jewish Bible with Rashi Commentary*. Chabad. https://www.chabad.org/library/Bible_cdo/aid/8174.
17. *The Complete Jewish Bible with Rashi Commentary*. Chabad. https://www.chabad.org/library/Bible_cdo/aid/8174.
18. *The Complete Jewish Bible with Rashi Commentary*. Chabad. https://www.chabad.org/library/Bible_cdo/aid/8175.
19. *The Complete Jewish Bible with Rashi Commentary*. Chabad. https://www.chabad.org/library/Bible_cdo/aid/8174.
20. *The Complete Jewish Bible with Rashi Commentary*. Chabad. https://www.chabad.org/library/Bible_cdo/aid/8173.
21. *The Complete Jewish Bible with Rashi Commentary*. Chabad. https://www.chabad.org/library/Bible_cdo/aid/9940. (Original work published 1517).
22. *The Complete Jewish Bible with Rashi Commentary*. Chabad. https://www.chabad.org/library/Bible_cdo/aid/15790.
23. The Holy Bible. *English Standard Version*. (Original work published 1517).
24. *The Complete Jewish Bible with Rashi Commentary*. Chabad. https://www.chabad.org/library/Bible_cdo/aid/9873. (Original work published 1517).
25. *The Complete Jewish Bible with Rashi Commentary*. Chabad. https://www.chabad.org/library/Bible_cdo/aid/16514. (Original work published 1517).
26. *The Complete Jewish Bible with Rashi Commentary*. Chabad. https://www.chabad.org/library/Bible_cdo/aid/9879. (Original work published 1517).
27. *The Complete Jewish Bible with Rashi Commentary*. Chabad. https://www.chabad.org/library/Bible_cdo/aid/15949. (Original work published 1517).
28. *The Complete Jewish Bible with Rashi Commentary*. Chabad. https://www.chabad.org/library/Bible_cdo/aid/9868. (Original work published 1517).
29. *The Complete Jewish Bible with Rashi Commentary*. Chabad. https://www.chabad.org/library/Bible_cdo/aid/16358.

CHAPTER 2
THE JEWISH DIASPORA AND PROPHETIC RETURN TO ISRAEL

1. Moseley, R. & Wilson, M. (1996). Introduction. *Yeshua: A guide to the real Jesus and the original church.* (p. 4). Messianic Jewish Publishers.
2. *Ancient Jewish History: The Diaspora.* The Jewish Virtual Library. http://www.jewishvirtuallibrary.org/jsource/History/Diaspora.html.
3. *Ancient Jewish History: The Bar-Kokhba Revolt 132-135 CE.* Jewish Virtual Library. http://www.jewishvirtuallibrary.org/jsource/Judaism/revolt1.html.
4. Boas, F., & Bunzel, R. (1987). *Anthropology and Modern Life.* Mineola: Dover Publications, Inc.
5. Sondberg, S. (n.d.). *Greece Virtual Jewish History Tour.* Jewish Virtual Library. https://www.jewishvirtuallibrary.org/greece-virtual-jewish-history-tour.
6. Barnavi, E. (Ed.). (1992). *A historical atlas of the Jewish people: From the time of the patriarchs to the present.* Knopf.
7. Adichie, C. N. (2009, July 23). *The danger of a single story* [Address]. TEDGlobal, Oxford, U. K. http://www.ted.com/talks/chimamanda_adichie_the_danger_of_a_single_story.
8. Sharon, I & Staff, T. (2014, March 22). Missing Iranian Jews were mistaken for rebels, killed by authorities." *The Times of Israel.* http://www.timesofisrael.com/missing-iranian-jews-were-mistaken-for-rebels-killed-by-authorities/.
9. Jewish Virtual Library. (n.d.). *Spain Virtual Jewish History Tour.* Jewish Virtual Library. http://www.jewishvirtuallibrary.org/jsource/vjw/spain1.html.
10. Jewish Virtual Library. (n.d.). *Spain Virtual Jewish History Tour.* Jewish Virtual Library. http://www.jewishvirtuallibrary.org/jsource/vjw/spain1.html.
11. Shavei Israel. (n.d.). *Bnei Menashe.* Shavei Israel. http://www.shavei.org/category/communities/bnei_menashe/?lang=en.
12. Jewish Virtual Library. (n.d.). *India Virtual Jewish History Tour.* Jewish Virtual Library. http://www.jewishvirtuallibrary.org/jsource/vjw/India.html.
13. Shavei Israel. (n.d.). *The Kaifeng Jews.* Shavei Israel. https://shavei.org/communities/kaifeng-jews/.
14. Romero, S. (2009, June 21). Adopting forebears' faith and leaving Peru for Israel. *The New York Times.* http://www.nytimes.com/2009/06/22/world/americas/22peru.html?pagewanted=all&_r=1&.
15. Shavei Israel. (n.d.). *Jamaica.* Shavei Israel. http://www.shavei.org/category/communities/other_communities/caribbean/jamaica/?lang=en.
16. Lattin, D. (2008). *Choosing to be Chosen: Religious leaders gather to challenge*

notions of "Who is a Jew?" California Magazine. https://alumni.berkeley.edu/california-magazine/july-august-2008-summer-sports-issue/choosing-be-chosen.
17. Washington, D. (2013, August 25). *Interview with Pnina Tamano-Shata* [Video]. YouTube. https://www.youtube.com/watch?v=vjfdhFPanFw.
18. Jewish Virtual Library. (n.d.). *Lemba*. The Jewish Virtual Library. http://www.jewishvirtuallibrary.org/jsource/judaica/ejud_0002_0012_0_12113.html.
19. Diop, C. A. (1991) Critical Review of the Most Recent Theses of the Origin of Humanity. *Civilization or barbarism: An authentic anthropology*. (p. 65). In H. J. Salemson & Y. M. Ngemi (Eds.). (M. de Jager, Trans.). Lawrence Hill Books. (Original work published 1981).
20. Israel Ministry of Foreign Affairs. (2006, September 29). *The Hebrew Israelite Community*. Israel Ministry of Foreign Affairs. https://mfa.gov.il/MFA/AboutIsrael/People/Pages/The%20Black%20Hebrews.aspx.
21. Ogbonnaya, V. (2013). *[Israel] is a country that went to great lengths to bring Jews of diverse ethnicities into its borders* [Status update]. Facebook.
22. *The Complete Jewish Bible with Rashi Commentary*. Chabad. https://www.chabad.org/library/Bible_cdo/aid/16135.
23. *The Complete Jewish Bible with Rashi Commentary*. Chabad. https://www.chabad.org/library/Bible_cdo/aid/16135.
24. *The Complete Jewish Bible with Rashi Commentary*. Chabad. https://www.chabad.org/library/Bible_cdo/aid/16135.
25. *The Complete Jewish Bible with Rashi Commentary*. Chabad. https://www.chabad.org/library/Bible_cdo/aid/15896.
26. *The Complete Jewish Bible with Rashi Commentary*. Chabad. https://www.chabad.org/library/Bible_cdo/aid/9994.
27. *The Complete Jewish Bible with Rashi Commentary*. Chabad. https://www.chabad.org/library/Bible_cdo/aid/16368.
28. *The Complete Jewish Bible with Rashi Commentary*. Chabad. https://www.chabad.org/library/Bible_cdo/aid/16028.
29. *The Complete Jewish Bible with Rashi Commentary*. Chabad. https://www.chabad.org/library/Bible_cdo/aid/15942.
30. *The Complete Jewish Bible with Rashi Commentary*. Chabad. https://www.chabad.org/library/Bible_cdo/aid/16202.
31. *The Complete Jewish Bible with Rashi Commentary*. Chabad. https://www.chabad.org/library/Bible_cdo/aid/8174.

32. *The Complete Jewish Bible with Rashi Commentary.* Chabad. https://www.chabad.org/library/Bible_cdo/aid/8174.
33. *The Complete Jewish Bible with Rashi Commentary.* Chabad. https://www.chabad.org/library/Bible_cdo/aid/15961.
34. *The Complete Jewish Bible with Rashi Commentary.* Chabad. https://www.chabad.org/library/Bible_cdo/aid/16514.
35. 35. The Holy Bible. *English Standard Version.* (Original work published 1517).

CHAPTER 3
ZIONISM AND THE HISTORIC BLACK STRUGGLE FOR FREEDOM

1. Dorsey, T. A. (1950). Old Ship of Zion [Recorded by the Roberta Martin Singers].
2. Watts, I. & Lowry, R. (1707). Marching to Zion [Song].
3. Hill, L. (1998). To Zion [Song]. On *The miseducation of Lauryn Hill*. Ruffhouse Records.
4. King, M. K. (1968, April 3). *I've been to the mountaintop* [Address]. Memphis, Tennessee. Copyright 1968 by the Estate of Dr. Martin Luther King, Jr.
5. Netanyahu, B. (2012). "Foreword to the English edition." *The founding fathers of Zionism*. (location 48 in Kindle edition). Balfour Books. Copyright 2012 by Balfour Books.
6. Meir, G. (1975). "We are alone." *My Life.* (p. 371). G. P. Putnam & Sons. Copyright 1975 by Golda Meir.
7. Herzl, T. (2007). *Old New Land (Altneuland)* (1st ed.). Filiquarian Publishing.
8. Brackman, H. (2010). Jews African Americans and Israel: The ties that bind. *Simon Wiesenthal Center/Museum of Tolerance January–February, 2010*, 1. https://docplayer.net/21380720-Jews-african-americans-and-israel-the-ties-that-bind-dr-harold-brackman-for-simon-wiesenthal-center-museum-of-tolerance-january-february-2010.html.
9. Neuberger, B. (1996). Black nationalism, Jews, and Zionism. *AVAR veATID: A Journal of Jewish Education, Culture and Discourse*, 18-22. https://www.bjpa.org/search-results/publication/12840.
10. Garvey, M. (1921). *If you believe the Negro has a soul* [Address]. http://historymatters.gmu.edu/d/5124/.

BIBLIOGRAPHY

11. JIMENA. (n.d.). FAQ on Jews From Arab Countries. https://www.jimena.org/faq/.
12. Ferris State University. (2000). What was Jim Crow? In *Jim Crow Museum of Racist Memorabilia*. http://www.ferris.edu/jimcrow/what.htm.
13. Pogrom or "violent dispossession" enacted against the Jewish population of Baghdad, Iraq from June 1-2, 1941.
14. *The Complete Jewish Bible with Rashi Commentary*. Chabad. https://www.chabad.org/library/Bible_cdo/aid/8176.
15. *The Complete Jewish Bible with Rashi Commentary*. Chabad. https://www.chabad.org/library/Bible_cdo/aid/15865.
16. *The Complete Jewish Bible with Rashi Commentary*. Chabad. https://www.chabad.org/library/Bible_cdo/aid/16535.
17. *The Complete Jewish Bible with Rashi Commentary*. Chabad. https://www.chabad.org/library/Bible_cdo/aid/16349.
18. *The Complete Jewish Bible with Rashi Commentary*. Chabad. https://www.chabad.org/library/Bible_cdo/aid/16353.
19. *The Complete Jewish Bible with Rashi Commentary*. Chabad. https://www.chabad.org/library/Bible_cdo/aid/16172.
20. *The Complete Jewish Bible with Rashi Commentary*. Chabad. https://www.chabad.org/library/Bible_cdo/aid/16318
21. *The Complete Jewish Bible with Rashi Commentary*. Chabad. https://www.chabad.org/library/Bible_cdo/aid/15983.
22. *The Complete Jewish Bible with Rashi Commentary*. Chabad. https://www.chabad.org/library/Bible_cdo/aid/16447.
23. *The Complete Jewish Bible with Rashi Commentary*. Chabad. https://www.chabad.org/library/Bible_cdo/aid/16290.
24. *The Complete Jewish Bible with Rashi Commentary*. Chabad. https://www.chabad.org/library/Bible_cdo/aid/8210.
25. *The Complete Jewish Bible with Rashi Commentary*. Chabad. https://www.chabad.org/library/Bible_cdo/aid/9864.
26. *The Complete Jewish Bible with Rashi Commentary*. Chabad. https://www.chabad.org/library/Bible_cdo/aid/15785.
27. *The Complete Jewish Bible with Rashi Commentary*. Chabad. https://www.chabad.org/library/Bible_cdo/aid/15933.
28. *The Complete Jewish Bible with Rashi Commentary*. Chabad. https://www.chabad.org/library/Bible_cdo/aid/15933.
29. *The Complete Jewish Bible with Rashi Commentary*. Chabad. https://www.

chabad.org/library/Bible_cdo/aid/16353.
30. *The Complete Jewish Bible with Rashi Commentary*. Chabad. https://www.chabad.org/library/Bible_cdo/aid/16269.
31. *The Complete Jewish Bible with Rashi Commentary*. Chabad. https://www.chabad.org/library/Bible_cdo/aid/16498.
32. *The Complete Jewish Bible with Rashi Commentary*. Chabad. https://www.chabad.org/library/Bible_cdo/aid/16509.
33. *The Complete Jewish Bible with Rashi Commentary*. Chabad. https://www.chabad.org/library/Bible_cdo/aid/16498.
34. *The Complete Jewish Bible with Rashi Commentary*. Chabad. https://www.chabad.org/library/Bible_cdo/aid/16509.
35. *The Complete Jewish Bible with Rashi Commentary*. Chabad. https://www.chabad.org/library/Bible_cdo/aid/16510.
36. *The Complete Jewish Bible with Rashi Commentary*. Chabad. https://www.chabad.org/library/Bible_cdo/aid/16511.
37. *The Complete Jewish Bible with Rashi Commentary*. Chabad. https://www.chabad.org/library/Bible_cdo/aid/16513.
38. *The Complete Jewish Bible with Rashi Commentary*. Chabad. https://www.chabad.org/library/Bible_cdo/aid/16172.
39. *The Complete Jewish Bible with Rashi Commentary*. Chabad. https://www.chabad.org/library/Bible_cdo/aid/16342.
40. *The Complete Jewish Bible with Rashi Commentary*. Chabad. https://www.chabad.org/library/Bible_cdo/aid/16569.
41. The Holy Bible. *English Standard Version*. (Original work published 1517).

CHAPTER 4
THE PRO-ISRAEL LEGACY OF THE REVEREND DR. MARTIN LUTHER KING, JR.

1. Jones, C. (2008, April 30). King and the Jews. *Wall Street Journal*. https://www.wsj.com/articles/SB120951797764154811.
2. King, M. L., Gendel, E., & Heschel, A. J. (1968, March 25). Conversation with Martin Luther King [Conference session], *Conservative Judaism 22* (3). 68th Annual of the Convention of the Rabbinical Assembly for Conservative Judaism, New York. Copyright 1968 by the Rabbinical Assembly. https://www.rabbinicalassembly.org/sites/default/files/public/resources-ideas/cj/classics/1-4-12-civil-rights/conversation-with-martin-lu-

ther-king.pdf.
3. Gilbert, M. Jewish and Arab Nationalism: The First World War and after. *In Ishmael's House: A History of Jews in Muslim Lands* (p. 157). Yale University Press. Copyright 2010 by Martin Gilbert.
4. Jewish Virtual Library. (n.d.). Black-Jewish relations: Martin Luther King & Israel. *Jewish Virtual Library*. https://www.jewishvirtuallibrary.org/martin-luther-king-and-israel.
5. Jewish Virtual Library. (n.d.). The Six-Day War: Background & Overview. *Jewish Virtual Library*. https://www.jewishvirtuallibrary.org/background-and-overview-six-day-war.
6. Forman, J. (1972). The Arab-Israel dispute. *The making of black revolutionaries* (pp. 496-497). University of Washington Press. Copyright 1985 by James Forman.
7. King, M. L. (1967). *Letter to Dr. Maurice N. Eisendrath*. Copyright by the Estate of Dr. Martin Luther King, Jr.
8. Kramer, M. (2016). In the words of Martin Luther King. *The war on error: Israel, Islam, and the Middle East* (p. 259). Transaction Publishers. Copyright 2016 by Transaction Publishers. https://scholar.harvard.edu/files/martinkramer/files/words_of_martin_luther_king.pdf.
9. Jewish Telegraphic Agency. (1970, February 17). Aj committee charges Black Panther's anti-zionist statements close to antisemitism. *Jewish Telegraphic Agency*. https://www.jta.org/1970/02/17/archive/aj-committee-charges-black-panthers-anti-zionist-statements-close-to-anti-semitism.
10. (1976, May 8). He chose to switch than fight. *The Free-Lance Star*. https://news.google.com/newspapers?id=Pv1NAAAAIBAJ&sjid=iYsDAAAAIBAJ&pg=5966%2C1289716.
11. De Witt, K. (1996, April 14). Conversations/Kwame Ture; formerly Stokely Carmichael and still ready for the revolution. *The New York Times*. https://www.nytimes.com/1996/04/14/weekinreview/conversations-kwame-ture-formerly-stokely-carmichael-still-ready-for-revolution.html.
12. See #2.
13. See previous footnote.
14. See previous footnote.
15. See previous footnote.
16. See previous footnote.
17. Quackenbush, C. (2017, December 1). The Libyan slave trade has

shocked the world. Here's what you should know. *TIME*. https://time.com/5042560/libya-slave-trade/.
18. See #2.
19. See previous footnote.
20. See previous footnote.
21. Pontz, Z. (2013, October 3). Report: Billions of dollars of aid to Palestinian Authority lost to corruption. *The Algemeiner*. http://www.algemeiner.com/2013/10/13/report-billions-of-dollars-of-aid-to-palestinian-authority-lost-to-corruption/.
22. Dias, T. (2013, September 17). The UNRWA Dilemma. *The Gatestone Institute*. https://www.gatestoneinstitute.org/3979/unrwa-dilemma.
23. The Martin Luther King, Jr. Research and Education Institute. (1955). Montgomery Improvement Association (MIA). In *the Martin Luther King, Jr. Encyclopedia*. Stanford University. https://kinginstitute.stanford.edu/encyclopedia/montgomery-improvement-association-mia.
24. Toameh, K. A. (2013, August 30). How many millionaires live in the "impoverished" Gaza Strip? *The Gatestone Institute*. https://www.gatestoneinstitute.org/3308/gaza-millionaires.
25. Reuters. (2014, February 2). Hamas considers economic reforms as Gaza's economic activity plummets. *Haaretz*. https://www.haaretz.com/hamas-considers-economic-reforms-1.5325293.
26. King, M. L. (1963, April 16). *Letter from a Birmingham Jail [King, Jr.]*. In A. B. Ali-Dinar (Ed.), *African Studies Center*. University of Pennsylvania. http://www.africa.upenn.edu/Articles_Gen/Letter_Birmingham.html.
27. Osborne, P. and Beezer, A. (1993). *Interview with Edward Said* [Interview]. Radical Philosophy Archive; Radical Philosophy. https://www.radicalphilosophyarchive.com/interview/edward-said.
28. 28. Abukhater, M. (2014, May 8). Human rights complaints rise in Palestinian territories, group says. *Los Angeles Times*. http://www.latimes.com/world/middleeast/la-fg-un-human-rights-palestinian-20140508-story.html.
29. Winer, S. (2014, June 15). Mahmoud Abbas's wife undergoes surgery in Israel. *The Times of Israel*. http://www.timesofisrael.com/mahmoud-abbass-wife-undergoes-surgery-in-israel/.
30. Toameh, K. A. (2013, November 18). Hamas PM Haniyeh's granddaughter transferred to Israeli hospital for treatment. *The Jerusalem Post*. http://www.jpost.com/Breaking-News/Hamas-PM-Haniyehs-granddaughter-transferred-to-Israeli-hospital-for-treatment-332153.

31. Video Manager. (2014, March 25). Hamas PM Ismail Haniyeh calls for Israel's destruction. *Israel365 News*. http://www.breakingisraelnews.com/12738/hamas-pm-ismail-haniyeh-calls-israels-destruction/#4SuSw5jqfrWZDDQB.97.
32. A. P. (2014, June 3). Haniyeh's mother-in-law treated in Israel. *The Times of Israel*. http://www.timesofisrael.com/haniyehs-mother-in-law-treated-in-israel/.
33. TIME. (n.d.). Palestinian Fatah fighters rehabilitate in Israel. *TIME*. http://content.time.com/time/video/player/0%2C32068%2C85555888001_1991530%2C00.html.
34. San Diego Jewish World. (2014, February 28). Israel, Harlem Baptists celebrate MLK's legacy. *San Diego Jewish World*. http://www.sdjewishworld.com/2014/02/28/israel-harlem-baptists-celebrate-mlks-legacy/.
35. Schneier, M. (1998, January 16). Remembering MLKs ties to Israel, Promised Land vision. *The Jewish News of Northern California*. https://www.jweekly.com/1998/01/16/remembering-mlk-s-ties-to-israel-promised-land-vision/.
36. *The Complete Jewish Bible with Rashi Commentary*. Chabad. https://www.chabad.org/library/Bible_cdo/aid/15993.
37. *The Complete Jewish Bible with Rashi Commentary*. Chabad. https://www.chabad.org/library/Bible_cdo/aid/15932.
38. *The Complete Jewish Bible with Rashi Commentary*. Chabad. https://www.chabad.org/library/Bible_cdo/aid/16211.
39. *The Complete Jewish Bible with Rashi Commentary*. Chabad. https://www.chabad.org/library/Bible_cdo/aid/16346.

CHAPTER 5
ANTI-ZIONISM: HATRED FOR ISRAEL

1. The United States Holocaust Memorial Museum. (n.d.). Afro-Germans during the Holocaust. *In the Holocaust Encyclopedia*. https://encyclopedia.ushmm.org/content/en/article/afro-germans-during-the-holocaust.
2. Abdulateef, A. (2014, May 14). May 15: Nakba or defeat? *Arab News*. http://www.arabnews.com/news/570476.
3. Wilkinson, P. (2011, August). *Christian Palestinianism* [Conference session]. The Berean Call 2011 Conference, The Berean Call, Bend, OR, United States. https://www.youtube.com/watch?v=osIx3tmvioY.

4. Baron, K. H. (2011, June). *Interview with Reverend Dr. Stephen Sizer and Professor Achin Vanaik* [Interview]. Astro Awani, Kuala Lampur, Maylasia. https://www.youtube.com/watch?v=IicvHC8wgyQ.
5. Rozenbaum, K. (2013, September 29). "Israeli apartheid? I know what apartheid is." *Arutz Sheva*. https://www.israelnationalnews.com/News/News.aspx/172282.
6. Jewish Telegraph Agency. (1962, November 15). Daily news bulletin. *Jewish Telegraphic Agency*. http://pdfs.jta.org/1962/1962-11-15_220.pdf?_ga=2.181740071.102291247.1601802119-383428676.1601802119
7. Anti-Defamation League. (n.d.). *Yom Kippur War 1973*. ADL. https://www.adl.org/resources/glossary-terms/yom-kippur-war-1973.
8. Troy, G. (2013). Introduction: Just a matter of decency. *Moynihan's moment: America's fight against Zionism as racism*. (p. 4). Oxford University Press. Copyright 2013 by Gil Troy.
9. Troy, G. (2013). Moynihan on the move, October 1975. *Moynihan's moment: America's fight against Zionism as racism*. (page 100). Oxford University Press. Copyright 2013 by Gil Troy.
10. Barak, A. (2018, June 8). Israel should be Zambia's closest ally. *Mida*. https://en.mida.org.il/2018/08/06/israel-should-be-zambias-closest-ally/.
11. Rychlak, R. J. & I. M. Pacepa. (2013). Global war on religion. *Disinformation: Former spy chief reveals secret strategy for undermining freedom, attacking religion, and promoting terrorism* (p. 94). WND Books. Copyright 2013 by Ion Ion Mihai Pacepa and Ronald J. Rychlak.
12. Rychlak, R. J. & I. M. Pacepa. (2013). Liberation theology. *Disinformation: Former spy chief reveals secret strategy for undermining freedom, attacking religion, and promoting terrorism* (p. 106). WND Books. Copyright 2013 by Ion Mihai Pacepa and Ronald J. Rychlak.
13. Baker, A. (2018, May 9). Did the Palestinians ever really recognize Israel? *The Algemeiner*. https://www.algemeiner.com/2018/05/09/did-the-palestinians-ever-really-recognize-israel/.
14. Pileggi, T. (2016, September 7). Soviet documents 'show Abbas was KGB agent'; Fatah decries 'smear campaign.' *The Times of Israel*. https://www.timesofisrael.com/soviet-documents-said-to-reveal-abbas-was-kgb-agent-in-syria/.
15. Rychlak, R. J. & I. M. Pacepa. (2013). Liberation theology. *Disinformation: Former spy chief reveals secret strategy for undermining freedom, attacking religion, and promoting terrorism* (pp. 108-109). WND Books. Copyright 2013

by Ion Mihai Pacepa and Ronald J. Rychlak.
16. Richardson, B. (2015, October 10). Jeremiah Wright: 'Jesus was a Palestinian.' *The Hill.* https://thehill.com/blogs/blog-briefing-room/256592-jeremiah-wright-jesus-was-a-palestinian.
17. Gates, H. L. (1992, July 20). Black demagogues and pseudo-scholars. *The New York Times.* https://www.nytimes.com/1992/07/20/opinion/black-demagogues-and-pseudo-scholars.html.
18. United Nations, General Assembly, Agenda item 108: Question of Palestine (*continued*)*, A/29/2282 (13 November 1974), available from undocs.org/en/a/pv.2282.
19. Gilbert, M. (2008). The fourth postwar era. *Israel: A history* (p. 467). HarperPerennial. Copyright 2008 by Martin Gilbert.
20. TOI Staff. (2017, October 20). Quoting Arafat, Palestinian mission in Colombia calls for Israel's destruction. *The Times of Israel.* https://www.timesofisrael.com/quoting-arafat-palestinian-mission-in-colombia-calls-for-israels-destruction/.
21. Sama'an Ashrawi. (2015, February 16). *Method Man Talks "P.L.O. Style" | @SamaanAshrawi* [Video]. YouTube. https://www.youtube.com/watch?v=n-hOQ19IQxeA.
22. Heins, S. (2015). Method Man speaks out on "P.L.O. Style" & Black-Palestinian solidarity in a new interview. *Okayplayer.* https://www.okayplayer.com/news/method-man-plo-style-interview.html.
23. United Nations, General Assembly, Agenda item 9: General debate (*continued*), A/30/2370 (1 October 1975), available from undocs.org/en/a/pv.2370.
24. Gershman, C. (1979, November). The Andrew Young Affair. *Commentary Magazine.* https://www.commentarymagazine.com/articles/carl-gershman-2/the-andrew-young-affair/.
25. See previous footnote.
26. See previous footnote.
27. Rustin, B. (1975, January 8). The PLO: Terrorists or freedom fighters. *The Chicago Defender.* https://www.ibsi-now.org/s/BAYARD-RUSTIN-Jan-18-1975-Freedom-fighters-or-terrorists.pdf.
28. See previous footnote.
29. BASIC. (1975, November 23). Black Americans to support Israel committee. *The New York Times.*
30. Zionist Organization of America. (date unknown). *Excerpts from a major*

address by Barbara Jordan: Congress of the United States, Texas. Public Affairs Department, Zionist Organization of America.
31. Wilkins, R. (1975, November 11). Zionism and discrimination. *The Washington Afro-American: Red Star Edition*. https://news.google.com/newspapers?id=DpglAAAAIBAJ&sjid=JPUFAAAAIBAJ&pg=1212%2C2206279.
32. Troy, G. (2013). Backlash. *Moynihan's moment: America's fight against Zionism as racism*. (p. 174). Oxford University Press.
33. Jewish Telegraphic Agency. (1976, January 22). Cleaver defends Zionism: Israel; charges Arabs with being most racist people; says Moynihan is too soft. *Jewish Telegraphic Agency*. https://www.jta.org/1976/01/22/archive/cleaver-defends-zionism-israel-charges-arabs-with-being-most-racist-people-says-moynihan-is-too-s.
34. Farrakhan, L. (2017, February 19). *Farrakhan Speaks: Saviours' Day* [Address]. Saviours' Day 2017 Convention, Detroit, MI, United States. Retrieved from Saviours Helper on YouTube. https://www.youtube.com/watch?v=yuO9Jeg5lC8.
35. Farrakhan, L. (1985, September 14). *POWER Speech at the Forum in Los Angeles* [Address]. Los Angeles, CA, United States. Retrieved from [reelblack] on YouTube. https://www.youtube.com/watch?v=AUXB17Si9FY.
36. Farrakhan, L. (2018, October). *Speech at the 23rd anniversary of the Million Man March* [Address]. Million Man March, Detroit, MI, United States. Retrieved from [Brother King Cam] on YouTube. https://www.youtube.com/watch?v=xZcIqQvs1iA.
37. Farrakhan, L. (2017, February 26). *Have no fear for the future: The future is here!* [Address]. Saviours' Day 2017 Convention, Detroit, MI, United States. Retrieved from Saviours Helper on YouTube. https://www.youtube.com/watch?v=oXOb2nH04M0.
38. Algemeiner Staff. (2012, July 3). Farrakhan rants about Jewish control during Sunday sermon. *The Algemeiner*. https://www.algemeiner.com/2012/07/03/farrakhan-rants-about-jewish-control-during-sunday-sermon-video/.
39. Kirchik, J. (2018 June). The rise of black anti-Semitism. *The Commentary*. https://www.commentarymagazine.com/articles/james-kirchick/rise-black-anti-semitism/.
40. Jones, C. B. & Engel, J. (2008, May 7). Martin Luther King would be repulsed by black anti-Semitism. *Jewish Press*. https://www.jewishpress.com/

indepth/opinions/martin-luther-king-would-be-repulsed-by-black-anti-semitism/2008/05/07/.
41. King, M. L., Gendel, E., & Heschel, A. J. (1968, March 25). Conversation with Martin Luther King [Conference session], *Conservative Judaism 22*(3). 68th Annual of the Convention of the Rabbinical Assembly for Conservative Judaism, New York. Copyright 1968 by the Rabbinical Assembly. https://www.rabbinicalassembly.org/sites/default/files/public/resources-ideas/cj/classics/1-4-12-civil-rights/conversation-with-martin-luther-king.pdf.
42. Hasson, P. (2018, March 18). Al Sharpton's group and Black Lives Matter team up for pro-Farrakhan protest. *Daily Caller*. https://dailycaller.com/2018/03/18/al-sharpton-black-lives-matter-farrakhan-protest/.
43. Isaacs, A. (2016). How the Black Lives Matter and Palestinian movements converged. *Moment*. https://momentmag.com/22800-2/.
44. Dream Defenders. (2015). *Solidarity demonstration in Nazareth : Ferguson to Palestine* [Video]. Vimeo. https://vimeo.com/116675694.
45. See previous footnote.
46. See previous footnote.
47. See footnote #42.
48. Soffer, A. (2016, July 19). Atlanta mayor shuts down Israel boycotters. *Arutz Sheva*. https://www.israelnationalnews.com/News/News.aspx/215205.
49. Black Lives Matter. (2020, May 30). #DefundThePolice. *Black Lives Matter*. https://blacklivesmatter.com/defundthepolice/.
50. Grzeszczak, J. (2020, August 5). 81% of black Americans don't want less police presence despite protests—some want more Cops: Poll. https://www.newsweek.com/81-black-americans-dont-want-less-police-presence-despite-protestssome-want-more-cops-poll-1523093?fbclid=IwAR0uQ_6Xa_Cg-CYAbsEPSJMTiSRsZw2BgytDDqM7SGv3hgNbXgMr4L3NHyOA.
51. Studio B: Unscripted. (2019, December 11). Studio B, unscripted: With Patrisse Cullors and Lowkey. *Al Jazeera*. https://www.aljazeera.com/program/episode/2019/12/11/studio-b-unscripted-with-patrisse-cullors-and-lowkey/.
52. Translates "night of crystal," and often referred to as the Night of Broken Glass. *Kristallnacht* refers to the Nazi-orchestrated wave of violent anti-Jewish pogroms which took place in Germany on November 9-10, 1938.
53. Greenfield, D. (2020, June 22). The LA Black Lives Matter rally that became a pogrom. *Jewish Press*. https://www.jewishpress.com/indepth/

54. Toameh, K. A. (2015, February 18). Hamas's new army of children. *Gatestone Institute*. https://www.gatestoneinstitute.org/5230/hamas-army-children.
55. Cox, E. (2018, March 13). Palestinian textbooks teach war not peace. *The Jerusalem Post*. https://www.jpost.com/Opinion/Palestinian-textbooks-teach-war-not-peace-545015.
56. Toameh, K. A. (2015, July 30). Hamas's child abuse camps. *Gatestone Institute*. https://www.gatestoneinstitute.org/6259/hamas-camps-child-abuse.
57. Halevi, E. (2007, April 1). Hamas recruits children to terror squads via TV programs. *Arutz Sheva*. https://www.israelnationalnews.com/News/News.aspx/122026.
58. Tawil, B. (2019, February 12). Hamas, Islamic Jihad war crimes against children and women. *Gatestone Institute*. https://www.gatestoneinstitute.org/13710/hamas-war-crimes-children.
59. Toameh, K. A. (2016, September 21). Palestinians: "The mafia of destruction." *Gatestone Institute*. https://www.gatestoneinstitute.org/8989/palestinians-medical-corruption.
60. Millar, E. (2013, October 13). EU accuses Palestinians of wasting €2 billion in aid. *The Times of Israel*. https://www.timesofisrael.com/eu-accuses-palestinians-of-wasting-e2-billion-in-aid/.
61. Danan, D. (2014, July 28). Gaza's millionaires and billionaires — how Hamas's leaders got rich quick. *The Algemeiner*. https://www.algemeiner.com/2014/07/28/gazas-millionaires-and-billionaires-how-hamass-leaders-got-rich-quick/.
62. Zehorai, I. (2018, January 1). The richest terror organizations: #3 – Hamas. *Forbes*. https://forbes.co.il/e/3-hamas/.
63. Toameh, K. A. (2012, August 30). How many millionaires live in the "impoverished" Gaza Strip? *Gatestone Institute*. https://www.gatestoneinstitute.org/3308/gaza-millionaires.
64. Toameh, K. A. (2020, March 20). Palestinian leaders use Coronavirus to attack Israel. *Gatestone Institute*. https://www.gatestoneinstitute.org/15773/palestinian-leaders-coronavirus-israel.
65. Halon, E. (2018, May 16). Hamas turns away truckloads of Israeli humanitarian aid destined for Gaza. *The Jerusalem Post*. https://www.jpost.com/

BIBLIOGRAPHY

Arab-Israeli-Conflict/Hamas-turns-away-truckloads-of-Israeli-humanitarian-aid-destined-for-Gaza-556565.
66. Abbas' wife hospitalized in Israel https://www.ynetnews.com/articles/0,7340,L-4530637,00.html
67. Seynor, E. (2014, June 15). Hamas leader's daughter receives medical care in Israel. *YNet News*. https://www.timesofisrael.com/hamas-leaders-daughter-said-to-receive-medical-care-in-israel/.
68. Khoury, J. (2017, June 25). Palestinian Authority prevents Gazans from leaving Strip for urgent medical treatment in Israel. *Haaretz*. https://www.haaretz.com/middle-east-news/.premium-pa-keeping-gazans-from-medical-treatment-in-israel-1.5488669.
69. McCoy, T. (2014, July 31). Why Hamas stores its weapons inside hospitals, mosques and schools. *The Washington Post*. https://www.washingtonpost.com/news/morning-mix/wp/2014/07/31/why-hamas-stores-its-weapons-inside-hospitals-mosques-and-schools/.
70. Toameh, K. A. (2019, March 7). Palestinians: Arresting, torturing journalists. *Gatestone Institute*. https://www.gatestoneinstitute.org/13842/palestinians-arrest-torture-journalists.
71. Holmes, O. (2018, October 23). Palestinian security forces routinely torture critics, rights group says. *The Guardian*. https://www.theguardian.com/world/2018/oct/23/palestinian-authority-hamas-torture-peaceful-critics-rights-group-says.
72. Toameh, K. A. (2020, July 18) Palestinian journalist: Car arson won't stop me from criticizing PA. *The Jerusalem Post*. https://www.jpost.com/middle-east/palestinian-journalist-car-arson-wont-stop-me-from-criticizing-pa-635502.
73. Rasgon, A. (2020, September 24). Gaza peace activists face prison for holding video call with Israelis. *The New York Times*. https://www.nytimes.com/2020/09/24/world/middleeast/gaza-zoom-activists-palestinian.html.
74. Toameh, K. A. (2016, June 23). President Mahmoud Abbas: The Palestinian "untouchable." *Gatestone Institute*. https://www.gatestoneinstitute.org/8320/mahmoud-abbas-untouchable.
75. Toameh, K. A. (2019, August 13). Can Palestinians in Gaza revolt against Hamas? *Gatestone Institute*. https://www.gatestoneinstitute.org/14713/palestinians-gaza-hamas-revolt.
76. Toameh, K. A. (2012, July 20). Who will save the Christians in the Gaza Strip? *Gatestone Institute*. https://www.gatestoneinstitute.org/3181/ga-

za-christians.
77. Toameh, K. A. (2009, May 12). The beleaguered Christians in Bethlehem. *Gatestone Institute*. https://www.gatestoneinstitute.org/501/the-beleaguered-christians-in-bethlehem.
78. Van Zile, D. (2019, January 3). Get them out: It's time to evacuate Christians from the Gaza Strip. *The Jerusalem Post*. https://www.jpost.com/Opinion/Get-them-out-Its-time-to-evacuate-Christians-from-the-Gaza-Strip-576294.
79. Burns, J. (2017, September 27). Palestinians speak out about torture in PA prison. *Al Jazeera*. https://www.aljazeera.com/features/2017/09/27/palestinians-speak-out-about-torture-in-pa-prison/.
80. Tawil, B. (2020, March 2). Why are Palestinians dying in Hamas prisons? *Gatestone Institute*. https://www.gatestoneinstitute.org/15664/palestinians-hamas-prisons.
81. Ghoneim, N. (2019, August 31). Palestinian woman murdered in honor killing after posting Instagram video with fiancé. *Egyptian Streets*. https://egyptianstreets.com/2019/08/31/palestinian-woman-murdered-in-honor-killing-after-posting-instagram-video-with-fiance/.
82. Lieber, D. (2017, May 18). As so-called 'honor killers' get away with murder, Palestinians say law, judges outdated. *The Times of Israel*. https://www.timesofisrael.com/as-so-called-honor-killers-get-away-with-murder-palestinians-say-law-judges-outdated/.
83. See footnote #80.
84. Toameh, K. A. (2018, June 12). Palestinians: No place for gays. *Gatestone Institute*. https://www.gatestoneinstitute.org/12496/palestinians-gays.
85. Toameh, K. A. (2012, October 23). Why Palestinians want Israeli citizenship. *Gatestone Institute*. https://www.gatestoneinstitute.org/3407/palestinians-israeli-citizenship.
86. Johnson, D. (2019, August 30). *Letter from Derrick Johnson to Jeffrey Dye*. NAACP. https://naacp.org/wp-content/uploads/2020/01/Letter-from-Derrick-Johnson-to-Jeffrey-Dye.pdf.
87. Levitt, J. (2014, April 1). Rwandan genocide scholars urge Jews to recognize Iran threat as similar to Nazi regime (INTERVIEW). *The Algemeiner*. https://www.algemeiner.com/2014/04/01/rwandan-genocide-scholars-urge-jews-to-recognize-iran-threat-as-similar-to-nazi-regime-interview/.
88. Anti-Defamation League (n.d.). *American Muslims for Palestine*. ADL. https://www.adl.org/resources/profiles/american-muslims-for-palestine.
89. Rossman-Benjamin, T. (2013, May 8). *Dear President Yudof*. https://

BIBLIOGRAPHY

www.amchainitiative.org/wp-content/uploads/2013/05/Letter-to-Yudof-with-appendix8final_updated2.pdf.

90. Jewish Virtual Library. (n.d.). UN human rights council: History & overview. *Jewish Virtual Library*. https://www.jewishvirtuallibrary.org/history-and-overview-of-the-un-human-rights-council.
91. Richman, J. (2020, August 18). Gov. Newsom signs California ethnic-studies bill into law. *Jewish News Syndicate*. https://www.jns.org/gov-newsom-signs-california-ethnic-studies-bill-into-law/.
92. Washington, J. (2020, August 29). Why CA ethnic studies curriculum should alarm you. *The Times of Israel*. https://blogs.timesofisrael.com/why-ca-ethnic-studies-curriculum-should-alarm-you/.
93. Levin, M. (2017, June 5). 75% of black California boys don't meet state reading standards. *Mercury News*. https://www.mercurynews.com/2017/06/05/75-of-black-california-boys-dont-meet-state-reading-standards/.
94. Woodson, C. G. & Kunjufu, J. (2000). Preface. *The Miseducation of the Negro* (p. xvi). African American Images. (Original work published 1933). Copyright 2000 by African American Images.
95. Greenwood Cultural Center. (n.d.). Black Wall Street. *Greenwood Cultural Center*. https://greenwoodculturalcenter.com/black-wall-street.
96. Oklahoma Historical Society. (n.d.). The Aftermath. *In the Tulsa Race Massacre*. https://www.okhistory.org/learn/trm5.
97. Grant, E. A. (2020, June 20). Unsung heroes and secret villains: The war between good and evil in Tulsa. *Medium*. https://medium.com/@elaineagrant/unsung-heroes-and-secret-villains-the-war-between-good-and-evil-in-tulsa-915ace99b94d.
98. *The Complete Jewish Bible with Rashi Commentary*. Chabad. https://www.chabad.org/library/Bible_cdo/aid/16224.
99. *The Complete Jewish Bible with Rashi Commentary*. Chabad. https://www.chabad.org/library/Bible_cdo/aid/15819.
100. *The Complete Jewish Bible with Rashi Commentary*. Chabad. https://www.chabad.org/library/Bible_cdo/aid/16569.
101. *The Complete Jewish Bible with Rashi Commentary*. Chabad. https://www.chabad.org/library/Bible_cdo/aid/15894.
102. *The Complete Jewish Bible with Rashi Commentary*. Chabad. https://www.chabad.org/library/Bible_cdo/aid/15894.
103. *The Complete Jewish Bible with Rashi Commentary*. Chabad. https://www.

chabad.org/library/Bible_cdo/aid/16289.
104. The Holy Bible. *English Standard Version*. (Original work published 1517).

CHAPTER 6
WHAT WE SHOULD DO NOW

1. Bradford, S. H. (1869). *Scenes in the life of Harriet Tubman*. (p. 20). W. J. Moses, printer.
2. Douglass, F. (1852). *Speech to the national free soil convention on the fugitive slave law* [Address]. National Free Soil Convention, Pittsburgh, PA. https://rbscp.lib.rochester.edu/4385.
3. Quote by famous abolitionist and writer Frederick Douglass.
4. Douroux, M. (2005, October). *Interview with Margaret Douroux* [Interview]. Black Gospel. https://www.umcdiscipleship.org/resources/history-of-hymns-if-it-had-not-been-for-the-lord.
5. Hoover Institution Library & Archives. (1981, November 12). The economic lot of minorities. (Season 16, Episode 40) [TV series episode]. *Firing Line with William F. Buckley, Jr.* Firing line (Television Program) broadcast records, program S0484. Copyright Stanford University. https://digitalcollections.hoover.org/objects/6660
6. Sowell, T. (1974). Black excellence—the case of Dunbar high school. *The Public Interest* (35), 3-4. https://nationalaffairs.com/storage/app/uploads/public/58e/1a4/ba6/58e1a4ba616e4230354245.pdf.
7. Deutsch, S. (2011). Lunch at the Blackstone. *You need a schoolhouse: Booker T. Washington, Julius Rosenwald, and the building of schools for the segregated south* (p. 96). Northwestern University Press. Copyright 2011 by Stephanie Deutsch.
8. Smith, R. F. (2020, March 3). *Robert F. Smith honored at World's Values Network's Eighth Annual International Champions of Jewish Values Awards Gala on March 3, 2020 at Carnegie Hall* [Address]. Eighth Annual International Champions of Jewish Values Awards Gala, New York City, N.Y. https://robertfsmith.org/post/617937614626029568/robert-f-smith-honored-at-world-values-networks.
9. *Tikkun olam* translates to "world repair." It represents a concept widely taught in Judaism that connotes any activity that brings good to the world and brings it closer to a harmonious state.

BIOGRAPHY

Dumisani Washington is the Founder, former Director, and now Board President of the Institute for Black Solidarity with Israel (IBSI). He is also a Regional Field Coordinator and the Diversity Outreach Coordinator for the over 10 million member Christians United for Israel (CUFI). Dumisani is a pastor, author, husband, and father. He and his wife, Valerie, have been married 32 years and have six children and two grandchildren.

Printed in Great Britain
by Amazon